T0138857

Applied Evolutionary Algorithms for Engineers Using Python

Leonardo Azevedo Scardua

Federal Institute of Technology of Espírito Santo
Vitoria, Brazil

CRC Press
Taylor & Francis Group
Boca Raton London New York

CRC Press is an imprint of the
Taylor & Francis Group, an **informa** business

A SCIENCE PUBLISHERS BOOK

First edition published 2021
by CRC Press
6000 Broken Sound Parkway NW, Suite 300, Boca Raton, FL 33487-2742

and by CRC Press
2 Park Square, Milton Park, Abingdon, Oxon, OX14 4RN

© 2021 Taylor & Francis Group, LLC

CRC Press is an imprint of Taylor & Francis Group, LLC

ISBN: 978-0-367-26313-3 (hbk)
ISBN: 978-0-367-71136-8 (pbk)
ISBN: 978-0-429-29802-8 (ebk)

Typeset in Times New Roman
by Radiant Productions

Preface

This book has been written for those who seek to apply evolutionary algorithms to problems in engineering and science. To this end, it provides the theoretical background necessary for the understanding of the presented evolutionary algorithms and their shortcomings, while also discussing themes that are pivotal to the successful application of evolutionary algorithms to real-world problems.

The theoretical descriptions are illustrated with Python implementations of the algorithms, which not only allow readers to consolidate their understanding but also provide a sound starting point for those intending to apply evolutionary algorithms to optimization problems in their fields of work. Python has been chosen due to its widespread adoption in the Artificial Intelligence community. Those familiar with high level languages such as MATLAB™ would find no difficulty in reading the provided Python implementations of the evolutionary algorithms.

Instead of attempting to encompass most of the existing evolutionary algorithms, this book focuses on those algorithms that researchers have recently applied to difficult engineering optimization problems, such as control problems with continuous action spaces and the training of high-dimensional convolutional neural networks. The basic characteristics of real-world optimization problems are presented, together with advice on how to properly apply evolutionary algorithms to them. The applied nature of this book is enforced by the presentation of cases of successful application of evolutionary algorithms to optimization problems which are closely related to real-world problems. The presentation is complemented by Python source code, allowing the user to gain insight into the idiosyncrasies of the practical application of evolutionary algorithms.

All source code presented in this book was developed in Python 3.7.6. The implementations are meant to be didactic instead of computationally efficient. For this reason, vectorization and other Python implementation tricks which specifically aim at reducing execution times, but add extra complexity to the source code, have been avoided.

This book is organized as follows. Chapter 1 provides an introduction to what makes an optimization problem harder to solve and why evolutionary algorithms are a suitable approach to the solution of those problems. Chapter 2 presents an introduction to the field of optimization. Those familiar with the core concepts of this field can safely skip the chapter. Chapter 3 presents an introduction to evolutionary algorithms, providing the theoretical basis necessary for understanding of the remainder of the book. Chapters 4, 5, 6 and 7 describe evolutionary algorithms designed to deal with single-objective optimization problems. Evolutionary algorithms designed to handle multi-objective optimization problems are presented in Chapters 8 and 9. Chapter 10 describes how to apply evolutionary algorithms to difficult optimization problems, while Chapter 11 describes how to assess the solutions produced by evolutionary algorithms. Chapters 12 and 13 provide detailed descriptions of the application of evolutionary algorithms to two difficult optimization problems.

Contents

SECTION II: SINGLE-OBJECTIVE EVOLUTIONARY ALGORITHMS

SECTION III: MULTI-OBJECTIVE EVOLUTIONARY ALGORITHMS

SECTION IV: APPLYING EVOLUTIONARY ALGORITHMS

Glossary

ACO	Ant Colony Optimization
Adam	Adaptive Moment Estimation
AI	Artificial Intelligence
AS	Ant System
CMAES	Covariance Matrix Adaptation Evolution Strategies
COP	Constrained Optimization Problem
CSP	Chebyshev Scalarization Problem
DE	Differential Evolution
EA	Evolutionary Algorithm
Elitist AS	Elitist Ant System
EMO	Evolutionary Multi-Objective Optimization
ES	Evolution Strategies
FFNN	Feed-Forward Neural Network
GA	Genetic Algorithm
IGD	Inverted Generational Distance
MOEA	Multi-Objective Evolutionary Algorithm
MOEA/D	Multi-Objective Evolutionary Algorithm Based on Decomposition
MOP	Multi-Objective Optimization Problem
NES	Natural Evolution Strategies
NFL	No Free Lunch
NN	Neural Network
NSGA	Non-dominated Sorting Genetic Algorithm
NSGA-II	Non-dominated Sorting Genetic Algorithm II
PSO	Particle Swarm Optimization
RMSE	Root Mean Squared Error
SBX	Simulated Binary Crossover
SGD	Stochastic Gradient Descent
SUS	Stochastic Universal Sampling
TSP	Traveling Salesman Problem

INTRODUCTION I

Chapter 1

Evolutionary Algorithms and Difficult Optimization Problems

The best starting point to solve an optimization problem is seeking to understand the problem as much as possible. A better understanding of the problem's characteristics offers two essential benefits. The first benefit is that it allows the selection of the most suitable tools for tackling the problem. The second benefit is that it allows better assessment of candidate solutions, which is of paramount importance when there are multiple solutions and there isn't one that is clearly superior to the others. All this seems to be true for all kinds of problems, but it is certainly true for difficult optimization problems. Before diving into the theory and practice of evolutionary algorithms, it is important to first discuss what makes an optimization problem more difficult to solve, since it will help understand why evolutionary algorithms are a sound approach for solving them.

Take for instance a common problem in engineering and science, which is to find the real roots of a given polynomial function, such as $f(x) = x^3 + 2x - 1$, shown in Figure 1.1. If the search space is limited to $-2 \leq x \leq 2$, as depicted in plot (a) of Figure 1.1, even a random search algorithm would be able to rapidly find a very good approximate solution, because any point in the search space would be already close to the true solution.

Nonetheless, simply increasing the search space to $[-100, 100]$, as depicted in plot (b) of Figure 1.1, makes the root finding problem harder, entailing that the random search algorithm would likely need many more evaluations of $f(x)$ to find the root than were needed when the search space was smaller. It is thus not difficult to guess that a big search space is one of the characteristics that make an optimiza-

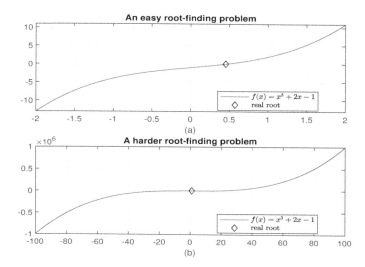

Figure 1.1: A root-finding problem.

tion problem harder to solve, and that for problems with bigger search spaces more sophisticated optimization algorithms should be used.

The size of the search space and other characteristics that contribute to making an optimization problem harder to solve, as seen in [9], [16] and [59], are described in what follows. Before proceeding, it is important to note that the characteristics below may not be all present in a given optimization problem. Nonetheless, when one or more of them are present, they make the optimization problem harder to solve.

1.1 What Makes an Optimization Problem Harder to Solve

The first characteristic is the *presence of noise*. One way noise enters the optimization process is when there is noise in the measurements of $f(\mathbf{x})$. When this is true, instead of having access to perfect information about the value of the objective function $f(\mathbf{x})$ at a given search point $\mathbf{x}$, the optimization algorithm receives $y(\mathbf{x}) = f(\mathbf{x}) + \varepsilon(\mathbf{x})$, where ε is the term corresponding to the noise.

Noise can also be injected in the optimization process as a result of Monte Carlo simulations. When the optimization is being carried out via Monte Carlo simulations, the evaluation of the objective function at a given search point is not straightforward, because Monte Carlo simulations are inherently random. The final effect of the noise injected by Monte Carlo simulation is that the optimization algorithm receives $y(\mathbf{x}) = f(\mathbf{x}) + \varepsilon(\mathbf{x})$ instead of $f(\mathbf{x})$.

As seen in Figure 1.2, noise gives the optimization algorithm misleading information about the objective function, precluding the adoption of optimization solution

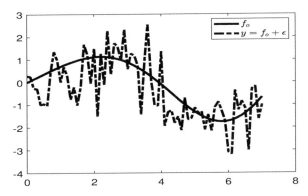

Figure 1.2: Noise can mislead the optimization algorithm. f_o is the objective function and $y = f_o + \varepsilon$ is the information received by the optimization algorithm.

methods that need perfect information about the loss function (and/or also about its derivatives) to deterministically find the search direction.

The second characteristic is the *size of the problem*. Suppose an optimization problem with two discrete variables, where each variable can assume only 4 different values. The search space of this two-dimensional optimization problem is comprised of $4^2 = 16$ different points. If another discrete variable with 4 different possible values is added to the problem, the search space of the resulting three-dimensional optimization problem will be comprised of $4^3 = 64$ different points. Adding a fourth dimension would yield a search space of $4^4 = 256$ points. For each dimension added, the number of search points is multiplied by 4. Figure 1.3 depicts the relation between the number of dimensions and the number of search points in this toy problem. Appropriately, the explosive growth in the number of search points (volume of the search space) that results from increases in the number of dimensions of the search space in optimization problems in general was called *the curse of dimensionality* according to [7].

The third characteristic is the *existence of constraints*. Hardly a real-world problem will place no constraints on the possible values of its variables. A car engine, for instance, has an upper limit on the number of rotations per minute it can deliver under the penalty of sustaining structural damage. Any optimization problem that involves a particular car engine will have to restrict the number of rotations per minute according to the engine's maximum capacity. The immediate effect of the existence of constraints is to invalidate all search points that violate the constraints as possible solutions, thus making the job of the optimization algorithm much harder.

The fourth characteristic of a difficult optimization problem is the existence of *multiple and possibly conflicting objectives*. Real-world problems usually involve smaller subproblems that interact with each other. Unfortunately, these subproblems are usually non-separable. This means that one cannot try to tackle each subproblem individually, since optimizing one of the subproblems may have a negative impact on the other subproblems. Solutions to multi-objective optimization problems are a fam-

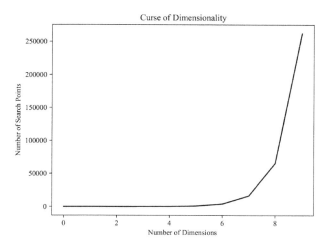

Figure 1.3: Growth in the number of search points as a function of the number of dimensions.

ily of search points known as Pareto-optimal solutions. Each Pareto-optimal solution is a compromise solution in the sense that attempts to change it in order to improve its performance in one of the subproblems inevitably degrades its performance in other subproblems. Due to the multiplicity of solutions, population-based methods such as evolutionary algorithms are a proper approach to solving multi-objective optimization problems. The so-called evolutionary multi-objective optimization algorithms form an established field of research [24], and will be seen later in this book.

The fifth characteristic is that many problems involve *environments that are dynamic*, meaning that they can change over time. This poses a serious challenge to optimization algorithms in general, since solutions to a given optimization problem must be found before the environment changes significantly. Rapidly changing environments are a characteristic of financial markets, for instance.

The sixth characteristic of difficult optimization problems is the presence of strong nonlinearities and/or discontinuities. Such characteristics usually prevent the application of deterministic optimization methods, such as gradient-based methods. Fortunately, evolutionary algorithms can handle both strong nonlinearities and/or discontinuities [59].

The seventh characteristic is *lack of knowledge about the problem structure*. Many real-world optimization problems are so complex that for all practical purposes their internal structure can be considered to be unknown. This means that one cannot devise a mathematical function that properly describes the objective function, thus preventing the adoption of optimization algorithms that, for instance, need to calculate gradients.

1.2 Why Evolutionary Algorithms

Evolutionary Algorithms (EAs) are problem-independent optimization techniques that share a number of characteristics that make them particularly suitable for dealing with difficult optimization problems.

EAs are problem-independent because they *do not require knowledge about the problem structure*. They see objective functions as black boxes, obtaining knowledge about the problem structure by proposing candidate solutions and using the objective function to evaluate them. The information they gather is then used to propose better solutions, in an iterative process that ends when the budget of evaluations of the objective function has been achieved or when a satisfactory solution has been found.

As Evolutionary Algorithm (EA)s don't need information about the problem's structure, they can handle both linear and *nonlinear* objective functions. The fact that they do not need to calculate precise gradients to find search directions allows them to solve problems with *discontinuities*, and their stochastic nature allows them to explore *huge search spaces*.

Another characteristic that makes EAs suitable to solving difficult optimization problems is the fact that EAs are population-based algorithms. This feature allows them to *deal with noise*, as will be seen latter. It also allows them to deal with multi-objective optimization problems, since each member of the population can be seen as being a candidate Pareto solution. Last but not least, EAs also allow the implementation of *constraints*.

Chapter 2

Introduction to Optimization

Real-world optimization problems may involve may variables and tradeoffs. Take for instance the manager of an auto repair shop that is trying to minimize its operational costs. One way to decrease those costs is by reducing the quantity and the types of parts that are kept in inventory. Reducing the size and diversity of the inventory may indeed reduce operational costs and thus maximize profits, but only if it is done in a way that does not significantly increase the average time taken to repair the costumers' cars.

If the average time taken to repair the costumers' cars increases beyond a certain level, the repair shop will probably lose clients to other repair shops, and the profits will start decreasing. To find the proper tradeoff between the inventory size/diversity and the time taken to repair the costumers' cars, the manager of the repair shop would probably need to formulate the quest for cost minimization as an optimization problem.

2.1   What is Optimization

Optimization is the process of seeking the values of a vector $\mathbf{x}$ that minimize or maximize a function $f(\mathbf{x})$, called *objective function*. The objective function is a mathematical representation of the *performance measure* that we seek to maximize or minimize. When the optimization is framed as a minimization problem $f(\mathbf{x})$ is called a *cost function* and when it is framed as a maximization problem $f(\mathbf{x})$ is called a *fitness function*.

Vector $\mathbf{x} \in \mathbf{X}$ is the vector of *independent* or *decision* variables, which are the variables that can be adjusted by the optimization algorithm in order to satisfy the performance criterion. Vector $\mathbf{x}$ is the *decision vector* of the problem.

2.2 Solutions of an Optimization Problem

The values of the decision vector **x** that maximize/minimize the objective function are the *solutions* to the optimization problem. The dimensionality of **x** determines the *dimensionality* or *size* of the optimization problem. If there is only one decision variable, the optimization problem is said to be *one-dimensional*. If there are N decision variables, the optimization problem is said to be *N-dimensional*.

2.3 Maximization or Minimization

Given a function $f(\mathbf{x})$, the value of **x** that minimizes $f(\mathbf{x})$ is the same value that maximizes $g(\mathbf{x}) = -f(\mathbf{x})$, as can be seen in Figure 2.1. It is thus possible to convert a maximization problem into a minimization problem by simply changing the sign of the objective function. This possibility implies that any algorithm that is designed for maximizing/minimizing a function can also be used for minimizing/maximizing it. Hence, to simplify notation, optimization problems in this book are considered to be minimization problems, unless stated otherwise.

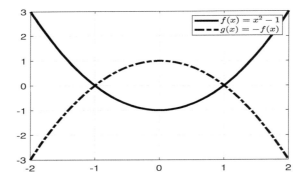

Figure 2.1: The minimum of **f(x)** and the maximum **g(x)** both occur at **x** = **0**.

2.4 Basic Mathematical Formulation

An unconstrained single-objective optimization problem can be mathematically written as

$$\underset{\mathbf{x}}{\text{minimize}} \quad f_o(\mathbf{x}) \tag{2.1}$$

where $f_o : \mathbb{R}^n \to \mathbb{R}$ is the objective function, and $\mathbf{x} = (x_1, \ldots, x_n)$ is the decision vector of the problem. An example of an unconstrained optimization problem would be finding the minimum of the bidimensional sphere function

$$\underset{x_1, x_2}{\text{minimize}} \quad x_1^2 + x_2^2. \tag{2.2}$$

2.5   Constraints and Feasible Regions

One important aspect of an optimization problem is the existence of constraints on the values that the independent variables **x** can assume. Constraints can make the optimization problem much harder to solve, because combinations of the values of the independent variables that violate any of the constraints are not *feasible solutions* of the problem. Constraints thus establish a set S of allowed values for **x** (feasible solutions) that is different from the unconstrained domain X of the objective function $f(\mathbf{x})$. The region formed by the feasible solutions is called the *feasible region*.

Feasible Regions

The feasible region of a hypothetical constrained optimization problem is shown in Figure 2.2. By definition, the feasible region of an optimization problem is comprised of the points that satisfy all constraints.

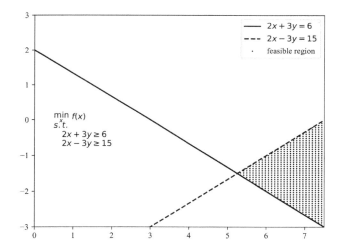

Figure 2.2: The feasible region of a constrained optimization problem.

The effect of adding another constraint to the optimization problem is shown Figure 2.3. Note that the new constraint reduces the area of the feasible region, making the problem harder to solve.

Hard and Soft Constraints

A noteworthy distinction is between *hard* constraints and *soft* constraints. When a constraint is hard, the optimization algorithm cannot take values of **x** that are not in S, not even during the search for a solution. A constraint is soft when the optimization algorithm is allowed to take values of **x** that are not in S during the search for a solution. For both types of constraints, the final solution must always be in S. Hard constraints make the search process more difficult, since they do not allow the opti-

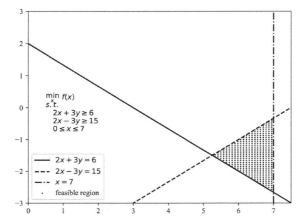

Figure 2.3: Adding another constraint reduces the area of the feasible region.

mization algorithm to search regions of the domain X that could end up leading to a better solution.

Constrained Optimization Problem

An optimization problem is said to be *constrained* when there are constraints on the values that the decision variables can assume. Constraints can be mathematically expressed as *equality constraints*, such as $h(\mathbf{x}) = 0$; *inequality constraints*, such as $g(\mathbf{x}) \leq 0$; and *bound constraints*, such as $a \leq \mathbf{x} \leq b$, where a and b are constants.

The mathematical formulation of a Constrained Optimization Problem (COP) just adds to Equation (2.1) the equations that define the constraints. The formulation of a COP is thus:

$$
\begin{aligned}
\underset{\mathbf{X}}{\text{minimize}} \quad & f_o(\mathbf{x}) \\
\text{subject to} \quad & g_k(\mathbf{x}) \leq 0, \quad k = 1, \ldots, m, \\
& h_k(\mathbf{x}) = 0, \quad k = 1, \ldots, p, \\
& x_i^{(lb)} \leq x_i \leq x_i^{(ub)}, i = 1, \ldots, n
\end{aligned}
\tag{2.3}
$$

where

- g_k are the inequality constraints,

- h_k are the equality constraints,

- $x_i^{(lb)} \leq x_i \leq x_i^{(ub)}$ are the bound constraints,

- $x_i^{(lb)}$ and $x_i^{(ub)}$ are respectively the scalar lower bound and the scalar upper bound on the values of x_i, which is the ith component of vector $\mathbf{x}$.

One example of constrained optimization problem is the G6 benchmark function [51]:

$$\underset{x_1,x_2}{\text{minimize}} \quad f_o(\mathbf{x}) = (x_1 - 10)^3 + (x_2 - 20)^3$$

$$\text{subject to} \quad g_1(\mathbf{x}) = -(x_1 - 5)^2 - (x_2 - 5)^2 + 100 \leq 0,$$

$$g_2(\mathbf{x}) = (x_1 - 6)^2 + (x_2 - 5)^2 - 82.81 \leq 0, \tag{2.4}$$

$$13 \leq x_1 \leq 100,$$

$$0 \leq x_2 \leq 100.$$

where the optimal solution is $f(\mathbf{x}^\star) = -6961.81387558015$ at $\mathbf{x}^\star = (14.095, 0.84296)$.

2.6   Local Solutions and Global Solutions

A feasible $\mathbf{x}^\star$ is a *global* optimal solution if the value of the objective function at $\mathbf{x}^\star$ is smaller than or equal to the value of the objective function at any other feasible solution $\mathbf{x}_c$, that is:

$$f(\mathbf{x}^\star) \leq f(\mathbf{x}_c), \quad \forall \mathbf{x}_c \neq \mathbf{x}^\star. \tag{2.5}$$

If the value of the objective function at $\mathbf{x}^\star$ is smaller than or equal to the value of the objective function only at the feasible solutions $\mathbf{x}_c$ which are within a given distance of $\mathbf{x}^\star$, then $\mathbf{x}^\star$ is a *locally optimal* or *local* solution, that is:

$$f(\mathbf{x}^\star) \leq f(\mathbf{x}_c), \quad \mathbf{x}^\star - \varepsilon \leq \mathbf{x}_c \leq \mathbf{x}^\star + \varepsilon \tag{2.6}$$

where ε is a constant vector. At first, it may seem natural to think that there will always be a single global solution, but there are cases where the value of the objective function is optimal at different feasible solutions.

2.7   Multimodality

When there is more than one local and/or global solution, the optimization problem is said to be *multimodal*. An example of multimodal function is the n-dimensional Griewank function (2.7), which has many local optima and a single global solution at $\mathbf{0}^n$. The landscape of a multimodal function has peaks and valleys, as seen in the two-dimensional ($n = 2$) render of the Griewank function shown Figure 2.4.

$$f(x_1, ..., x_n) = 1 + \sum_{i=1}^{n} \frac{x_i^2}{4000} - \prod_{i=1}^{n} cos(\frac{x_i}{\sqrt{i}}). \tag{2.7}$$

2.8   Multi-Objective Optimization

So far we have seen examples of optimization problems that contain only one objective function, but in real-world situations, we are usually interested in simultaneously optimizing a number of performance measures for the problem at hand. This

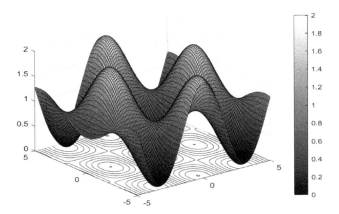

Figure 2.4: Two-dimensional Griewank function.

is tantamount to saying that there is more than one optimization goal for the same optimization problem, characterizing what is called a Multi-Objective Optimization Problem (MOP).

Researchers make a distinction between problems with up to 3 objectives and problems with more than 3 objectives. The first class of problems is called *multi-objective optimization problems* while the second class is called *many-objective optimization problems*. For the sake of simplicity, this book prefers to use the term multi-objective optimization for both classes of problems, making adjustments when necessary.

The general mathematical representation of a multiobjective optimization problem with L different optimization goals is

$$
\begin{aligned}
\underset{\mathbf{x}}{\text{minimize}} \quad & \{f_{o1}(\mathbf{x}), f_{o2}(\mathbf{x}), \dots, f_{oL}(\mathbf{x})\} \\
\text{subject to} \quad & g_k \leq 0, \quad k = 1, \dots, m, \\
& h_k = 0, \quad k = 1, \dots, p, \\
& x_i^{(lb)} \leq x_i \leq x_i^{(ub)}, i = 1, \dots, n.
\end{aligned}
\tag{2.8}
$$

The L objective functions form a L-dimensional space $Z \in \mathbb{R}^L$, called *objective space*. The *objective vector* is the vector $\mathbf{z} = \mathbf{f_o}(\mathbf{x})$, $\mathbf{f_o}(\mathbf{x}) = \{f_{o1}(\mathbf{x}), f_{o2}(\mathbf{x}), \dots, f_{oL}(\mathbf{x})\}$. The image of the feasible region S in the objective space, $Z_S = \mathbf{f}_o(S)$, is called *feasible objective region*. In what follows the term *solution* means in fact *feasible solution*.

Finding Solutions for a Multi-Objective Optimization Problem

In a single-objective optimization problem, the superiority of a solution over other solutions is determined by comparing their objective function values. If $f_o(\mathbf{x}_a) < f_o(\mathbf{x}_b)$, then $\mathbf{x}_a$ is a better solution then $\mathbf{x}_b$. In multi-objective optimization problems, determining wether a solution is superior to another is much more difficult.

The correlation between the optimization goals can be very complex, with all possible combinations of positive, negative and no correlation between goals. In general, at least some of the goals will be conflicting, meaning that if one solution minimizes one goal, it necessarily does not minimize the other. Hence, there is no feasible solution that simultaneously minimizes all L objective functions. In this context a new concept, mentioned by Francis Y. Edgeworth in 1881 and generalized by Italian economist Vilfredo Pareto in 1896, is used.

Pareto noticed that many economic solutions benefited some groups of people at the cost of hurting the interests of other groups. He wanted to find solutions that simultaneously maximized benefits (minimized costs) to everybody, but since different groups of people have different needs, it was hard to assess the global effectiveness of a solution. He then conceived a concept of optimality based on the idea of balancing the tradeoffs represented by conflicting objectives. This idea is embodied in the concept of *domination*.

Pareto Dominance Relation

A solution $\mathbf{x}_a$ is said to *dominate* solution $\mathbf{x}_b$, denoted by $\mathbf{x}_a \prec \mathbf{x}_b$, if for each scalar objective function f_{oi} we have

$$f_{oi}(\mathbf{x}_a) \leq f_{oi}(\mathbf{x}_b) \tag{2.9}$$

and at least for one objective function j we have

$$f_{oj}(\mathbf{x}_a) < f_{oj}(\mathbf{x}_b). \tag{2.10}$$

Non-Dominated Solutions

A solution $\mathbf{x}_a$ is *non-dominated* if there is no other solution $\mathbf{x}_b$ that dominates it. Note however that the statement that $\mathbf{x}_a$ is non-dominated does not necessarily mean that it dominates all other solutions. For a given MOP, there are many solutions that are not dominated by any other solution.

Pareto Optimality

A solution $\mathbf{x}_a$ is *Pareto optimal* if there is no solution $\mathbf{x}_b$ such that $\mathbf{x}_b \prec \mathbf{x}_a$. In other words, a non-dominated solution is a Pareto-optimal solution.

Pareto Optimal Set

The *Pareto optimal set* P_{opt} of a given MOP is defined as the set of all its non-dominated solutions:

$$P_{opt} = \{\mathbf{x}_a \in \mathcal{X} | \nexists \mathbf{x}_b \in \mathcal{X} : \mathbf{x}_b \prec \mathbf{x}_a\}, \tag{2.11}$$

where $\mathcal{X}$ is the set of feasible solutions.

Pareto Front

The Pareto front, PF_{opt}, is the set of points in the objective space that correspond to the Pareto optimal set, P_{opt}:

$$PF_{opt} = \{\mathbf{z} = (f_{o1}(\mathbf{x}), f_{o2}(\mathbf{x}), \ldots, f_{oj}(\mathbf{x}))|\mathbf{x} \in P_{opt}\} \tag{2.12}$$

Example 1 *Consider a two-dimensional optimization problem whose data are given in Table 2.1. Applying conditions (2.9) and (2.10) to the data yields the Pareto set and the Pareto front respectively shown in columns 1 and 2 of Table 2.2.*

Table 2.1: Candidate solutions before Pareto dominance check.

$\mathbf{x}$	$\mathbf{f_o(x)}$
(2, 3)	(1, 3)
(5, 6)	(3, 8)
(1, 4)	(10, 3)
(3, 1)	(6, 15)
(4, 4)	(2, 2)
(5, 3)	(4, 7)
(1, 2)	(9, 2)

Table 2.2: Pareto set and Pareto front.

$\mathbf{x}$	$\mathbf{f_o(x)}$
(2, 3)	(1, 3)
(4, 4)	(2, 2)

Diversity of Non-Dominated Solutions

The Pareto front may be comprised by infinite points, but the best a given optimization algorithm can do is to find a finite set of non-dominated solutions. It is thus important that the solutions found by the optimization algorithm cover the Pareto front as well as possible, in order to better represent the entire range of the Pareto-optimal front.

Example 2 *While Example 1 displayed a very small Pareto set, a more complex multi-objective optimization problem could have a huge number of Pareto solutions. To illustrate this idea, consider the two-dimensional optimization problem:*

$$
\begin{aligned}
\underset{x_1, x_2}{\text{minimize}} \quad & \begin{bmatrix} x_1^4 - 10x_1^2 + x_1x_2 + x_2^4 - x_1^2x_2^2 \\ x_2^4 - x_1^2x_2^2 + x_1^4 + x_1x_2 \end{bmatrix} \\
\text{subject to} \quad & -5 \leq x_1 \leq 5, \\
& -5 \leq x_2 \leq 5.
\end{aligned}
\tag{2.13}
$$

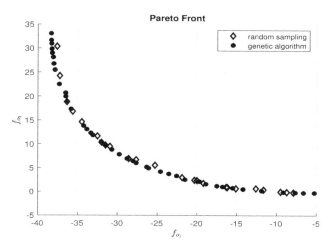

Figure 2.5: The approximate Pareto fronts obtained by random sampling and by a multi-objective genetic algorithm.

Figure 2.5 displays the Pareto fronts obtained by two distinct optimization algorithms. The first is a naive random sampling algorithm and the second is a multi-objective genetic algorithm. Though random sampling performed millions of evaluations of the objective function, it was able to find only a handful of solutions close to the Pareto front, while the genetic algorithm found a well-spread set of solutions, covering almost the entire range of the Pareto front. As will be seen in Chapter 11, the spread of the solutions found by an multi-objective optimization algorithm is one of the criteria used to assess the performance of the algorithm.

Solving a MOP

Solving a MOP means finding the best approximation of its Pareto set and then picking one or more non-dominated solution as the final solutions to the MOP. A finite set of mutually non-dominated solutions, P_{approx}, is said to be good approximation of P_{opt} if both following criteria [13] are satisfied:

■ The Pareto front PF_{approx} corresponding to P_{approx} is close enough to the true Pareto front PF_{opt}.

■ The objective points in PF_{approx} are uniformly spread over PF_{opt}.

2.9 Combinatorial Optimization

It is usual to find problems where the decision variables are continuous. Continuity is a common feature of physical systems and it is thus natural to think in continuous quantities, such as temperature and speed. Nonetheless, there are situations in which the decision variables do not vary continuously, instead, they can only assume discrete values. These are called *discrete* or *combinatorial* optimization problems.

The most commonly found example of combinatorial optimization are shortest-path problems, but many important real-world problems are of combinatorial nature. Examples of such real-world problems include finding the best routing scheme for Internet data packets, optimizing the allocation of people to tasks, etc. In essence, a combinatorial optimization problem is composed of:

■ A finite set of N_c components $C = \{c_1, c_2, \dots, c_{N_c}\}$ that are the building blocks of the solutions.

■ The candidate solutions, which are finite-length sequences $x = (c_i, c_j, \dots, c_h, \dots)$ of the elements of C.

■ A cost function.

■ A set of restrictions.

Example 3 *Probably the most common combinatorial optimization problem found in the literature is the Traveling Salesman Problem (TSP). In one of the versions of TSP, there is a business person who needs to visit a number of cities, starting and ending the travel in its home office. The person is free to visit the cities in any possible order, provided that the order chosen minimizes the total distance travelled and that each city in between is visited exactly once.*

If, for instance, there are four cities to be visited, the components of the problem are cities A, B, C and D, as show in Figure 2.6.

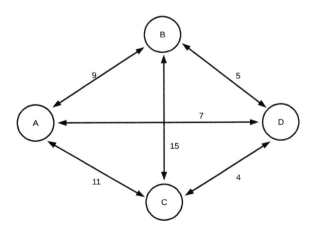

Figure 2.6: The cities that have to be visited by the travelling business person.

The possible solutions are:

$$
\begin{aligned}
S_1 &= (A,B,C,D,A) \\
S_2 &= (A,B,D,C,A) \\
S_3 &= (A,C,B,D,A) \\
S_4 &= (A,C,D,B,A) \\
S_5 &= (A,D,B,C,A) \\
S_6 &= (A,D,C,B,A)
\end{aligned}
$$

The cost function of a given solution is the total distance travelled by the business person to visit all the cities in the solution in the order specified by the solution. The cost for solution S_1 is thus $\mathrm{cost}(S_1) = 9+15+4+7$.

This toy problem can be solved by simply comparing the costs of all candidate solutions, but this approach is not feasible if the number of cities is increased, because of the curse of dimensionality. Evolutionary algorithms for solving combinatorial optimization problems will be seen later in the book.

Chapter 3

Introduction to Evolutionary Algorithms

In broad terms, an EA is a direct stochastic search algorithm that simulates a Darwinian evolutionary system [17], which means that an EA solves optimization problems by numerically simulating organic evolution. As any direct search method, EAs use minimal information about the fitness function. In particular, they do not require computing the gradient of the fitness function nor they need that the fitness function is unimodal or even continuous. These features allow evolutionary algorithms to work with difficult optimization problems, in the sense described in Chapter 1.

There are many different evolutionary algorithms, but they all share a common general structure. They are composed by a population of individuals, a fitness function (or cost function), a selection mechanism and a set of probabilistic genetic operators. These components work together according to Algorithm 3.1.

Algorithm 3.1. Basic Structure of Evolutionary Algorithms

1: $f_s(\cdot) \leftarrow$ parent selection function
2: $f_g(\cdot) \leftarrow$ genetic operator function
3: $f_p(\cdot) \leftarrow$ population update function
4: $f_f(\cdot) \leftarrow$ fitness function
5: $pop \leftarrow$ initial population
6: **while** not termination condition **do**
7:     $F_p \leftarrow f_f(pop)$ ▷ Compute the fitness values of the population
8:     $P \leftarrow f_s(F_p, pop)$ ▷ Select individuals for mating
9:     $C \leftarrow f_g(F_p, P)$ ▷ Produce offspring
10:    $F_c \leftarrow f_f(C)$ ▷ Compute the fitness values of the offspring
11:    $pop \leftarrow f_p(pop, P, F_p, C, F_c)$ ▷ Update the population
12: **end while**

Algorithm 3.1 is performing the following operations:

- In line 5, a population of candidate solutions is created.

- In line 7, the fitness value of each candidate solution is computed.

- In line 8 occurs the selection of the individuals that will father the next generation.

- In line 9, the selected parents mate, generating an offspring by means of a set of genetic operators.

- In line 10, the fitness values of the offspring C are computed.

- In line 11, the new population is created, taking into account the fitness values of the offspring and other heuristics.

[22] emphasizes that though the adoption of a general structure such as Algorithm 3.1 evidences the powerful similarities between evolutionary algorithms, it also hides many differences. For instance, different algorithms may use different data structures to represent chromosomes, different operators to alter the population, reverse the order of some of the operations or even eliminate some of them altogether. Nonetheless, we believe that the pros of viewing evolutionary algorithms as having a general structure outweigh the cons.

The remainder of this chapter describes the main elements of an evolutionary algorithm. The presentation is not exhaustive, but it provides the reader theoretical background on some important topics related to evolutionary algorithms. Sections 3.1 and 3.2 present the most common mathematical representations of candidate solutions. Section 3.3 describes how to use a mathematical function to evaluate the quality of a given individual with respect to the optimization process. Section 3.4 discusses the initialization of the population, while Section 3.5 describes commonly used parent selection mechanisms. Finally, Sections 3.6, 3.7 and 3.8 discuss some regularly used genetic operators.

3.1   Representing Candidate Solutions

Perhaps the first question that must be answered when using an evolutionary algorithm is how to mathematically represent a candidate solution to the problem at hand, in a way that the solution can be stored in a digital computer and manipulated by the algorithm. In a parlance mostly adopted by genetic algorithms, but still valid for evolutionary algorithms in general, a candidate solution to a problem expressed in the form of the decision variables is called *phenotype*, while its mathematical representation used by the evolutionary algorithm is called *chromosome*, which represents the genetic information (*genotype*) of the individual.

To start the optimization process the user has to first devise a way to encode the phenotypes into genotypes. After the optimization has finished, the final solution to the problem is obtained by decoding the best genotype found by the evolutionary algorithm into the corresponding phenotype.

3.1.1 Discrete Representations

The most commonly used discrete representations encode the decision variables of the problem with binary strings. Let us use an example in the area of mechanical design optimization to illustrate the two most common binary representation approaches: *standard binary representation* and *gray code representation*.

Design of a Gear Train System

Consider the problem of designing a double-reduction gear train with four gears, named A, B, C and D, proposed in [73]. The design variables, n_A, n_B, n_C and n_D are the number of teeth in each gear. To simplify the notation we will respectively denominate them x_1, x_2, x_3 and x_4. The design variables are integer numbers constrained to the interval $[12, 60]$. The goal is to obtain values for x_1, x_2, x_3 and x_4 so that the double-reduction gear train is as close as possible to $\frac{1}{6.931}$ and no constraint is violated. This optimization problem is written as

$$
\begin{aligned}
&\underset{x_1, x_2, x_3, x_4}{\text{minimize}} && \left(\frac{1}{6.931} - \frac{x_1 x_2}{x_3 x_4} \right)^2 \\
&\text{subject to} && 12 \le x_i \le 60, \quad i = 1, 2, 3, 4.
\end{aligned}
\tag{3.1}
$$

Standard Binary Encoding

As each gear must have any number of teeth from 12 to 60, each variable x_i, with $i = 1, 2, 3, 4$, can be represented by a string of 6 bits, because $2^6 = 64$. Our chromosome would thus have $4 \times 6 = 24$ bits. An example of a candidate solution to this problem, where $x_1 = 58$, teeth, $x_2 = 30$ teeth, $x_3 = 32$ teeth and $x_4 = 12$ teeth, is shown in Figure 3.1.

phenotype →	$x_1 = 58$	$x_2 = 30$	$x_3 = 32$	$x_4 = 12$
chromosome →	111010	011110	100000	001100

Figure 3.1: Binary representation of a candidate solution to the gear train design problem.

Converting a Decimal Number to its Binary Representation. To convert a decimal number to its binary representation, use the Python code in Listing 3.1.

```
 1 # -------------------------------------------------
 2 #                   dec2bin
 3 # Converts a decimal number in its binary representation
 4 # -------------------------------------------
 5 # Inputs:
 6 #    dec          - decimal number
 7 # Output:
 8 #    bstr         - binary string
 9 # Usage:
10 #    Converting 58 into binary
```

```
11 #    bstr = dec2bin(58)
12 # ---------------------------------------------------------
13 # file: dec2bin.py
14 # ---------------------------------------------------------
15 def dec2bin(dec):
16     return bin(dec).replace("0b", "")
```

Listing 3.1: Converting decimal numbers to standard binary code.

Gray Code Encoding

A gray code [28] is a binary encoding technique where the codes for neighboring numbers differ by only one bit. Table 3.1 shows that binary codes for neighboring numbers can differ by more than one bit (compare binary representations for numbers 3 and 4), but can also produce very close representations for numbers that are very different (compare binary representations for numbers 0 and 4). Gray code representation, on the other hand, always changes exactly by one bit for neighboring numbers.

Table 3.1: Gray vs binary coding.

Decimal	Binary	Gray
0	0000	0000
1	0001	0001
2	0010	0011
3	0011	0010
4	0100	0110

Gray coding is seen as a method of overcoming the representational bias inherent to standard binary encoding, as the Hamming distance between adjacent values is constant. Some researchers suggest that large Hamming distances between adjacent values can render the search process incapable of efficiently locating the global optimum [14].

Converting Standard Binary to Gray code. The pseudocode for converting binary number $b = (b_1, b_2, \ldots, b_m)$ to gray coded number $g = (g_1, g_2, \ldots, g_m)$ is shown in Algorithm 3.2, where the first bit is the most significant bit (MSB). The Python implementation of Algorithm 3.2 is shown in Listing 3.2.

Algorithm 3.2. Converting Binary to Gray Code

1: **procedure** BIN2GRAY
2:    $g_1 = b_1$ ▷ The MSBs are the same
3:    **for** $k = 2$ to m **do**
4:       $g_k = b_{k-1}$ XOR b_k ▷ XOR of previous and current binary bits
5:    **end for**
6: **end procedure**

```
1 # -------------------------------------------------------
2 # Converts a binary coded number into its Gray code
3 # representation
4 # -------------------------------------------------------
5 # Input:
6 #    bstr       - Binary coded bit string
7 # Output:
8 #    gcstr      - Gray coded bit string
9 # Usage:
10 #    gcstr = bin2gray('0011')
11 # -------------------------------------------------------
12 # file: bin2gray.py
13 # -------------------------------------------------------
14 def bin2gray(bstr):
15     nbits = len(bstr)      # number of bits in bstr
16     gcstr = ""             # string containing the binary
17                            # representation
18
19     # The MSBs of the binary and the Gray codes
20     # are the same
21     gcstr = gcstr + str(bstr[0])
22     # The next bit  is computed as the XOR of the
23     # previous  and current  binary bits
24     for i in range(1,nbits):
25         gcstr = gcstr + str(int(bstr[i - 1]) ^ int(bstr[i]))
26
27     return gcstr
```

Listing 3.2: Converting binary to Gray code.

Converting Gray to Standard Binary Code. The conversion from $g = (g_1, g_2, \ldots, g_m)$ to $b = (b_1, b_2, \ldots, b_m)$ is shown in Algorithm 3.3. The Python implementation of Algorithm 3.3 is shown in Listing 3.3.

Algorithm 3.3. Converting Gray Code to Binary

1: **procedure** GRAY2BIN
2:     $b_1 = g_1$ ▷ The MSBs are the same
3:     **for** $k = 2$ to m **do**
4:         **if** $g_k == 0$ **then**
5:             $b_k = b_{k-1}$
6:         **else**
7:             $b_k = \text{flip}(b_{k-1})$
8:         **end if**
9:     **end for**
10: **end procedure**

```
1 # -------------------------------------------------------
2 # Converts a string representing a gray coded number
3 # into a string with the corresponding binary representation
```

```
 4 #  -----------------------------------------------------------
 5 # Input:
 6 #    gcstr      - Gray coded bit string
 7 # Output:
 8 #    bstr       - Binary coded bit string
 9 # Usage:
10 #    bstr = gray2bin('0010')
11 #  -----------------------------------------------------------
12 # file: gray2bin.py
13 #  -----------------------------------------------------------
14 # flip a bit
15 def flip(c):
16     return '1' if(c == '0') else '0'
17 #  -----------------------------------------------------------
18 def gray2bin(gcstr):
19     nbits = len(gcstr)    # number of bits in gcstr
20     bstr = ""             # string containing the binary
21                           # representation
22
23     # The MSBs of the binary and the Gray codes
24     # are the same
25     bstr = bstr + str(gcstr[0])
26     # Remaining bits
27     for i in range(1,nbits):
28         # If current Gray bit is 0,
29         # add the previous binary bit
30         if gcstr[i] == '0':
31             bstr = bstr + str(bstr[i-1])
32         # If current Gray bit is 1, flip the
33         # previous binary bit before adding
34         else:
35             bstr = bstr + str(flip(bstr[i-1]))
36     return bstr
```

Listing 3.3: Converting Gray code to binary code.

Converting Floating Point Decimal to Gray Code. To convert real-valued decision variables into Gray-coded vectors it is necessary to first convert each decision variable to its binary representation then use Algorithm 3.2 to convert the binary numbers to the corresponding Gray code representations.

The gray coding representation for the example candidate solution $x_1 = 58, x_2 = 30, x_3 = 32, x_4 = 12$ is shown in Figure 3.2.

phenotype →	$x_1 = 58$	$x_2 = 30$	$x_3 = 32$	$x_4 = 12$
chromosome →	100111	10001	110000	001010

Figure 3.2: Gray code representation of a candidate solution to the gear train design problem.

3.1.2   Integer Representation

A more natural representation for optimization problems with integer decision variables is to simply represent the candidate solutions as vectors of integer numbers. In the case of the gear train problem, a candidate solution is shown in Figure 3.3.

phenotype →	$x_1 = 58$	$x_2 = 30$	$x_3 = 32$	$x_4 = 12$

chromosome →	$x_1 = 58$	$x_2 = 30$	$x_3 = 32$	$x_4 = 12$

Figure 3.3: Integer representation of a candidate solution to the gear train design problem.

3.1.3   Real-valued Representation

While binary coding variants are still much used, there has been growing interest in integer and real-valued representations. Wright [91] claims that the use of real-valued representation can offer a number of advantages over binary encodings. The main advantages are that there is no loss in precision due to discretization to binary and that a wider range of different genetic operators can be used. In the case of the gear train problem, a candidate solution is shown in Figure 3.4.

phenotype →	$x_1 = 58$	$x_2 = 30$	$x_3 = 32$	$x_4 = 12$

chromosome →	$x_1 = 58.0$	$x_2 = 30.0$	$x_3 = 32.0$	$x_4 = 12.0$

Figure 3.4: Real-valued representation of a candidate solution to the gear train design problem.

3.2   Comparing Representations on a Benchmark Problem

Here, the problem of finding the minimum value of the sphere function is used to compare the standard binary, Gray and real-value representations. The integer representation would not be suitable to this problem.

The sphere function is a widely used benchmark problem for continuous optimization algorithms. The equation that defines the sphere function is

$$f(\mathbf{x}) = \sum_{i=1}^{d} x_i^2 \, , \tag{3.2}$$

where d is the number of dimensions of the problem. The landscape of the 2-dimensional sphere is shown in Figure 3.5. The optimal value of the d-dimensional sphere function is located at the d-dimensional vector $\mathbf{x} = [0, 0, ..., 0]$.

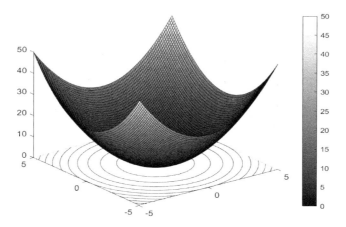

Figure 3.5: The bi-dimensional sphere function.

Three experiments are performed. The only difference between them being the number of dimensions of the sphere function. The first experiment uses a bi-dimensional sphere, the second uses a 10-dimensional sphere, and the third uses a 20-dimensional sphere. In all three experiments, ten Monte Carlo runs were performed by a genetic algorithm using binary, Gray and real-valued representations. All other parameters of the genetic algorithm were the same.

Figures 3.6, 3.7 and 3.8 show the variability of the Root Mean Squared Error (RMSE) of the solutions found by the genetic algorithm using each of the three representation strategies. It is clear that Gray code worked better than the standard binary code in all cases. As expected for a continuous optimization problem, the real-valued representation outperformed both binary representations when the number of dimensions was higher.

The performance degradation of the genetic algorithm when using binary representations is mainly linked to the discretization problem. In all three experiments, the two binary representations used 4 bits per dimension, respectively resulting in chromosomes with 8, 40 and 80 bits. The point is that bigger chromosomes imply bigger search spaces, making it harder for an optimization algorithm to find a good solution. Thus, as the dimensionality increased, the harder it was for the genetic algorithm with binary representations to find a good solution.

3.3   The Fitness Function

The formulation of an optimization problem involves minimizing an objective function $f_o(\cdot)$. This function computes the quality of a given candidate solution $\mathbf{x}$ expressed in terms of the decision variables of the problem. For instance, the mini-

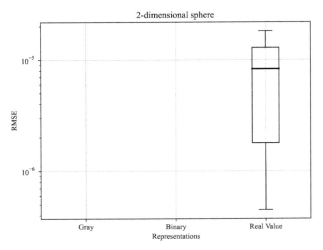

Figure 3.6: Comparing the representation techniques on the bi-dimensional sphere function minimization problem.

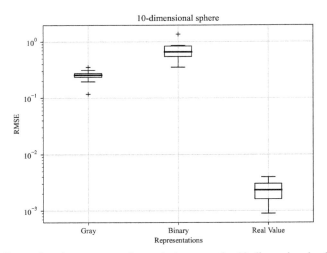

Figure 3.7: Comparing the representation techniques on the 10-dimensional sphere function minimization problem.

mization of the sphere function with $\mathbf{x} \in [-5, 5]$ can be written as

$$\underset{\mathbf{x}}{\text{minimize}} \quad f_o(\mathbf{x}) = \sum_{i=1}^{d} x_i^2$$

$$\text{subject to} \quad -5 \le x_i \le 5 \quad i = 1, \ldots, d \tag{3.3}$$

where $f_o(\mathbf{x}) = \sum_{i=1}^{d} x_i^2$ is the objective function.

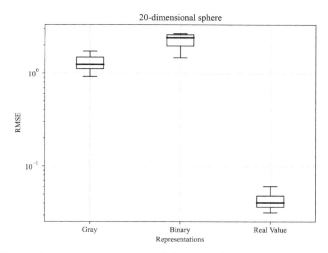

Figure 3.8: Comparing the representation techniques on the 20-dimensional sphere function minimization problem.

To perform the optimization process in the context of an evolutionary algorithm, candidate solutions must be numerically encoded, as seen in Section 3.1. The function that measures the quality of encoded candidate solutions in the context of an evolutionary algorithm is the fitness (or cost) function $f(\cdot)$. In this section the term fitness will be used. The difference between fitness and cost is just a minus signal.

The fitness function receives a chromosome (candidate solution numerically encoded) from the evolutionary algorithm, converts it to its corresponding phenotype (candidate solution expressed in terms of the decision variables of the original optimization problem (3.3)), measures the quality of the phenotype using the objective function $f_o(\cdot)$ and then returns this quality measurement to the evolutionary algorithm. The pseudocode for a general fitness function is

---

Algorithm 3.4. Fitness Function

1: $\mathbf{x}_e \leftarrow$ receive encoded candidate solution
2: $\mathbf{x} = \text{decode}(\mathbf{x}_e)$ ▷ decode $\mathbf{x}_e$
3: $v = f_o(\mathbf{x})$ ▷ Objective function computes the fitness value
4: return v

Let us now present the fitness functions used in the comparison between representations (encodings) of Section 3.2, but first let us see the Python code corresponding to the objective function in Listing 3.4.

```
1 # ------------------------------------------------------------
2 #                    Sphere
3 # Implements the n-dimensional sphere function
4 # ------------------------------------------------------------
```

```
5 # file: sphere.py
6 # ------------------------------------------------------------
7 def sphere(x):
8     d = len(x)
9     y = 0
10    for ii in range(d):
11        y = y + x[ii]**2
12    return y
```

Listing 3.4: Sphere function.

Fitness Function for the Real-Valued Encoding

As the decision variables of optimization problem (3.3) are continuous, the real-valued representation does not imply any encoding. The fitness function in this case just demands changing the signal of the objective function, since Equation (3.3) is a minimization problem and the genetic algorithm used was coded for maximization.

Algorithm 3.5. Fitness Function for Real-Valued Representation

---

1: $\mathbf{x} \leftarrow$ receive candidate solution
2: $v = -f_o(\mathbf{x})$ $\triangleright$ Multiply the objective function by -1
3: return v

The Python code corresponding to Algorithm 3.5 is

```
1 # ------------------------------------------------------------
2 # Fitness for the real-valued sphere function
3 # ------------------------------------------------------------
4 # Input:
5 #    X    - real-valued chromosome
6 # Output:
7 #    F    - f(X)
8 # ------------------------------------------------------------
9 # file: fitness_sphere_rv.py
10 # ------------------------------------------------------------
11 from test_functions_rep.so.sphere import sphere
12 # ------------------------------------------------------------
13 def fitness_sphere_rv(X):
14     fitness = -sphere(X)
15     return fitness
```

Listing 3.5: Real-valued fitness function for the minimization of the sphere function.

Fitness Function for Discrete Encoding

The fitness function for the binary representations is more involved. It demands first converting the binary/Gray encoded search point $\mathbf{x}_e$ to its corresponding representation in the original domain of the fitness function, $\mathbf{x}$, as in Algorithm 3.4.

The pseudocode of the function that decodes a standard binary/Gray coded chromosome $\mathbf{x}_e$ into $\mathbf{x}$ is given in Algorithm 3.6. The corresponding Python code is shown in Listing 3.6.

Algorithm 3.6. Converts binary/Gray code to real-valued

1: $\mathbf{x}_e \leftarrow$ receive encoded candidate solution
2: $f_d \leftarrow$ receive the decoding function
3: $[a,b] \leftarrow$ receive the interval for the decoded $\mathbf{x}$
4: $n_b \leftarrow$ receive the number of bits used to encode a single decision variable
5: $N \leftarrow$ receive the number of decision variables
6: **for** i = 1 to N **do**
7:     $bstr \leftarrow$ extract the n_b bits from $\mathbf{x}_e$ that correspond to the ith decision variable
8:     $x_i = f_d(bstr,a,b)$ ▷ compute the ith real-valued decision variable
9: **end for**
10: Return $\mathbf{x} = [x_1, x_2, \ldots, x_N]$

```
 1 # -------------------------------------------------------------
 2 #    Converts binary coded array X into N decimal decision
 3 #                     variables in [a,b]
 4 # -------------------------------------------------------------
 5 # Inputs:
 6 #    disc2decf  --> bin2decInterval for binary
 7 #                      representation
 8 #               --> gray2decInterval for gray-coded
 9 #                      representation
10 #    X - vector containing the discrete representation of
11 #        the array of decision variables
12 #    N - number of phenotypic decision variables
13 #    a, b - [a, b] interval for the phenotype decision
14 #           variables
15 #    nbits_word - number of bits used in the discrete
16 #                   representation of the vector of decision
17 #                   variables
18 # Output:
19 #    Xdv - array of phenotypic decision variables
20 # -------------------------------------------------------------
21 # file: gen2phen.py
22 # -------------------------------------------------------------
23 import numpy as np
24 def gen2phen(disc2decf,X,N,a,b,nbits_word):
25     # nbits_dv - number of bits for each decision variable
26     nbits_dv = int(nbits_word / N)
27     inii = 0 # initial pointer for slicing X
28     endi = nbits_dv # final pointer for slicing X
29     Xdv = np.zeros(N) # array of decimal decision variables
30     for ii in range(N):
31         # binary representation of the ith decision variable
32         bxdv = X[inii:endi]
33         # convert bxdv to string
34         xstr = np.array2string(bxdv, separator='')
35         # remove the delimiting square brackets from xstr
```

```
36        xstr = xstr[1:nbits_dv + 1]
37        # convert from binary to decimal in the interval [a,b]
38        dnum = disc2decf(xstr, a[ii], b[ii], nbits_dv)
39        # store in the array of decision variables
40        Xdv[ii] = dnum
41        # update the pointers for the next iteration
42        inii = endi
43        endi = endi + nbits_dv
44    return Xdv
```

Listing 3.6: Converting binary encoded into its real-valued representation.

After obtaining the representation of the search point in the domain of the fitness function, all that has to be done is to use the real-valued fitness function multiplied by -1. The final fitness function is seen in Listing 3.7.

```
1 # ------------------------------------------------------------
2 # Calculates the fitness value of search point X for the
3 #     minimization of the sphere function
4 # ------------------------------------------------------------
5 # Inputs:
6 #   X - string containing the binary representation of
7 #       the search point
8 #   N - number of phenotypic decision variables
9 #   a and b - [a, b] interval
10 #   nbits_word - how many bits are used in the
11 #                representation of the vector X = [x1, x2]
12 # Output:
13 #   fitness - fitness value of candidate solution X
14 # ------------------------------------------------------------
15 #   file: fitness_sphere_binary.py
16 # ------------------------------------------------------------
17
18 from encoding_rep.gen2phen import gen2phen
19 from encoding_rep.bin2dec import bin2decInterval
20 from test_functions_rep.so.sphere import sphere
21 def fitness_sphere_bin(X,N,a,b,nbits_word):
22     # Xdv - vector of decision variables in the original
23     # domain of the objective function
24     Xdv = gen2phen(bin2decInterval, X, N, a, b, nbits_word)
25     # Calculate the fitness value of the decision variables
26     fitness_value = -sphere(Xdv)
27     # Return the fitness value
28     return fitness_value
```

Listing 3.7: Binary fitness function for the minimization of the sphere function.

Function bin2decInterval, used by the fitness function in Listing 3.7, performs the conversion of a standard binary number to a decimal number in a given interval. Its is presented in Listing 3.8.

```
1 # ------------------------------------------------------------
2 #                 bin2decInterval
3 # Converts a binary number into a floating-point decimal
4 # in the interval [a,b]. Each decimal number is represented
```

```
5 # by a string of nbits bits.
6 # -----------------------------------------------------------
7 # Inputs:
8 #    bstr - string containing the binary number to be converted
9 #    a and b - [a, b] interval
10 #   nbits - how many bits are used in the representation of a
11 #   decimal number
12 # Output:
13 #   decnum - decimal number in [a,b] interval
14 # Usage:
15 #   Converting the binary string '0001' in a decimal in the
16 #   interval [-4,1].
17 #   The answer is decnum = -3.6875
18 #   decnum = bin2decInterval('0001',-4,1,4)
19 # -----------------------------------------------------------
20 # file: bin2dec.py
21 # -----------------------------------------------------------
22 def bin2decInterval(bstr, a, b, nbits):
23     # Step of the representation in base 10
24     delta = (b - a) / (2 ** nbits)
25     # int(bstr,2) - converts a string representing a number
26     # in given base to decimal.
27     dnum = int(bstr,2)
28     # position dnum in [a,b]
29     decnum = a + delta * dnum
30     return decnum
```

Listing 3.8: Conversion of a standard binary number to a decimal number in a given interval.

Function gray2decInterval, used by the fitness function in Listing 3.7, performs the conversion of a Gray coded number to a decimal number in a given interval. Its is presented in Listing 3.9.

```
1 # -----------------------------------------------------------
2 #               gray2decInterval
3 # Converts a Gray number into a decimal in [a,b].
4 # Each decimal number is represented by a string of
5 # nbits_dv bits.
6 # -----------------------------------------------------------
7 # Inputs:
8 #   gcstr       - string containing the gray coded number
9 #   a and b     - [a, b] decimal interval
10 #  nbits_dv     - how many bits are used in the representation
11 #                 of a decimal number
12 # Output:
13 #   decnum      - decimal number in [a,b] interval
14 # Usage:
15 #   Converting the binary string '0001' in a decimal in
16 #   the interval [-4,1].
17 #   decnum = gray2decInterval('0001',-4,1,4)
18 #   The answer is decnum = -3.6875
19 # -----------------------------------------------------------
20 # file: gray2dec.py
21 # -----------------------------------------------------------
22 from encoding_rep.gray2bin import gray2bin
23 # -----------------------------------------------------------
```

```
24
25 def gray2decInterval(gcstr, a, b, nbits_dv):
26     # Step of the representation in base 10
27     delta = (b - a) / (2 ** nbits_dv)
28     # converts a gray coded string representing a number in given
        base to decimal.
29     dnum =gray2dec(gcstr)
30     # position dnum in [a,b]
31     decnum = a + delta * dnum
32     return decnum
33
34 def gray2dec(gcstr):
35     bstr =  gray2bin(gcstr)
36     dnum = int(bstr, 2)
37     return dnum
```

Listing 3.9: Conversion of a Gray coded number to a decimal number in a given interval.

3.4 Population

Once the representation of candidate solutions has been decided and the fitness function has been formulated, it is time to form a population. A population is a set of genotypes. In other words, it contains the encoded representations of the candidate solutions to the optimization problem. The diversity of a population is directly correlated with the number of different candidate solutions that are present in the population. More diversity indicates that more areas of the search space have representatives in the population. More diversity can thus be an interesting feature, especially in the beginning of the optimization process.

One way to obtain more diversity is by having bigger populations. Bigger populations have more chances to better cover the search space than smaller populations, but the extra coverage comes at the cost of more computational resources. There is thus a tradeoff between the size of the population and the demand for computational resources. Unfortunately there are no formulas that can accurately estimate the right size of the population to a given problem.

3.5 Selecting Parents

For evolution to occur, the individuals in the population have to produce offspring. The concept of natural selection states that individuals that are more adapted to the environment have more chances of surviving and producing offspring than less adapted individuals. An algorithm that emulates the natural selection mechanism must thus implement a proper selection strategy.

A proper selection strategy is one that properly balances exploration and exploitation. Exploration gives more chances of survival and reproduction to the less fit individuals, while exploitation gives more chances to individuals with higher fitness levels. Favoring exploration can increase the likelihood of finding better solutions, but it can also slow down the progress of the optimization process, because it will demand more evaluations of the fitness function. Favoring exploitation can accelerate the convergence of the optimization process, but too much exploitation can lead to premature convergence.

Selective pressure is the name given to the tendency to favor the selection of individuals with higher fitness levels. High selective pressure increases exploitation but may lead to premature convergence. Low selective pressure increases exploration by decreasing the rate of selection of individuals with high fitness levels, but it may slow down the progress of the optimization process. It is hence interesting to have lower selection pressure in the initial stages of the optimization process to improve exploration and avoiding premature convergence, and higher selection pressure in the final stages to improve exploitation.

The full selection process is comprised of two steps [6]. The first step, called *selection*, calculates the selection probability of each individual in the population. The second step, called *sampling*, samples from those selection probabilities and actually picks the winners.

3.5.1 Selection Probabilities

Fitness-Proportionate Selection Probability

The fitness-proportionate selection probability [44] P_i of a candidate solution $\mathbf{x}_i$ is computed according to

$$P_i = \frac{f(\mathbf{x}_i)}{\sum_{i=1}^{N} f(\mathbf{x}_i)}, \tag{3.4}$$

where N is the number of candidate solutions in the population of the evolutionary algorithm and $f(\mathbf{x}_i)$ is the value of the fitness function for the candidate solution $\mathbf{x}_i$.

An important issue with Equation (3.4) is that fails in the presence of negative fitness values. To prevent this issue from happening, linear scaling [36] can be applied to the fitness values, such that

$$f(\mathbf{x}) = af(\mathbf{x}) + b \tag{3.5}$$

where a is a positive scaling factor and b is a scalar value used to ensure that the scaled fitness values are all non-negative numbers. The usual values of those numbers are $a = 1$ and b equal to the module of the worst fitness values in the population. The Python code for Equation (3.5) is given in Listing 3.10.

```
 1 #  ------------------------------------------------------------
 2 #                   Fitness  Linear  Scaling
 3 # Computes  the  normalized  fitness  values  of  the  population
 4 # using  linear  fitness  scaling
 5 #  ------------------------------------------------------------
 6 # Inputs:
 7 #    pop_fit       -  fitness  values  of  the  population  members
 8 # Outputs
 9 #    norm_fitness  -  normalized  fitness  values
10 # Usage:
```

```
11 #    fits = np.array([2,8,20,18,6])
12 #    norm_fits = fitness_linear_scaling(fits)
13 # --------------------------------------------------------
14 # file: fitness_linear_scaling.py
15 # --------------------------------------------------------
16 import numpy as np
17 # --------------------------------------------------------
18 def fitness_linear_scaling(pop_fit):
19     M = np.shape(pop_fit)[0]
20     # Linear scaling
21     # scaled(f) = a * f + b
22     a = 1
23     b = abs( min( pop_fit ))
24     scaled_fitness = a * pop_fit + b
25     # Computes normalized fitness values
26     norm_fitness = scaled_fitness / np.sum(scaled_fitness)
27     # Returns normalized fitness values
28     return norm_fitness
```

Listing 3.10: Fitness linear scaling.

Though the idea of using fitness-proportionate selection probabilities to sample individuals from a population has an almost intuitive appeal, it suffers from scaling problems [38], as show by the following example. Given a population of individuals, simply adding one to the fitness value of each individual changes their selection probabilities, as shown in Table 3.2.

Another issue with fitness-proportionate selection has to do with the spread of fitness values in the population. When the feature values of the individuals are very different, as in Table 3.2, the individuals with higher fitness values tend to be selected much more than the individuals with lower fitness values. This situation is depicted in Figure 3.9, and it clearly may lead to premature convergence, due to the very high selective pressure.

Rank-Based Selection Probabilities

Using rank-based selection probabilities instead of fitness-proportionate selection probabilities was proposed by [5] in an attempt to overcome the scaling problems inherent to fitness proportioned selection probabilities. The proposed strategy ranks individuals in the population according to their fitness values, and performs selection using rank-based selection probabilities. To understand the effect that rank-based se-

Table 3.2: Fitness proportionate selection scaling issue.

Individual	Fitness	Sel. Prob.	Fitness + 1	Sel. Prob.
1	10	0.1	11	0.1058
2	5	0.05	6	0.0577
3	70	0.7	71	0.6827
4	15	0.15	16	0.1538
Total	100	1	104	1

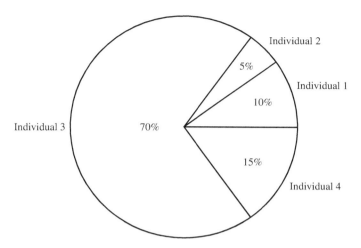

Figure 3.9: When the fitness of one individual dominates the roulette wheel.

lection has on the selection probabilities, consider the four hypothetical individuals in Table 3.3. For each individual the table lists its fitness value (Fitness), fitness proportionate selection probability (FP Probability), rank (Rank) and rank-based selection probability (RB Probability).

Table 3.3: Comparing fitness proportionate and ranking selection probabilities.

Individual	Fitness	FP Probability	Rank	RB Probability
1	10	0.1	2	0.2
2	5	0.05	1	0.1
3	70	0.7	4	0.4
4	15	0.15	3	0.3
Total	100	1	10	1

Organizing the selection probabilities as in Figure 3.10 makes it easier to see that selecting individuals according to their ranks attenuates the problem that a super fit individual causes when using fitness proportionate selection probabilities (the selection probabilities in plot (b) are much more evenly distributed than in plot (a)). Hence, rank-based selection reduces selective pressure and increases the chances of individuals with lower fitness values to be selected.

Linear Ranking Selection Probabilities

The linear ranking method [38] is a generalization of rank-based selection. The individual with the highest fitness is given a rank of $1 < s \leq 2$ and the individual with the

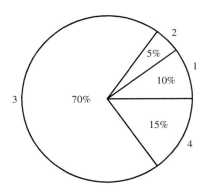

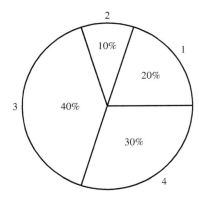

(a) Fitness proportionate selection probabilities.

(b) Rank-based selection probabilities

Figure 3.10: Comparing fitness proportionate and rank based selection probabilities for the individuals in Table 3.3.

worst fitness is given a rank of $2 - s$. The ranking of the i-*th* individual $\mathbf{x}_i$ is calculated by interpolation according to $r(\mathbf{x}_i) = s - \frac{2(i-1)(s-1)}{(N-1)}$, $i = 1, \ldots, N$.

The scalar parameter s controls the selective pressure. Increasing the value of s increases the selection probabilities of individuals with higher fitness thus increasing selective pressure. If $s = 2$, the worst individual gets no chance of reproduction at all, since its rank will be equal to zero. Note that if $s > 2$ then the worse individuals will receive negative ranking values, something that does not make sense. The Python code for linear fitness ranking is shown in Listing 3.11.

```
1 # -------------------------------------------------------------
2 #                   Fitness Linear Ranking
3 #     Computes the ranks of the individuals in the population
4 # -------------------------------------------------------------
5 # Inputs:
6 #     pop_chrom    - individuals in the population
7 #     pop_fit      - fitness values of the individuals
8 # Outputs:
9 #     newpop_chrom - individuals sorted in descending ranking order
10 #     newpop_fit   - ranks of the individuals
11 # Usage:
12 #     pop_chrom = np.array([1, 2, 3, 4])
13 #     pop_fit = np.array([10, 5, 70, 15])
14 #     npop_ch, npop_f = fitness_linear_ranking(pop_chrom, pop_fit)
15 # -------------------------------------------------------------
16 # file: fitness_linear_ranking.py
17 # -------------------------------------------------------------
18 import numpy as np
19 # -------------------------------------------------------------
20 def fitness_linear_ranking(pop_chrom, pop_fit):
21     # NUmber of individuals in the population
22     M = np.shape(pop_fit)[0]
23     # Fitness of the best individual
```

```
24    # Attention to the valid interval --> 1< s <= 2"
25    s = 1.5
26    # sort in descending fitness order
27    sorted_idx = np.argsort(-pop_fit)
28    # Sorted population according to ranks
29    newpop_chrom = np.zeros_like(pop_chrom)
30    # Ranks of the sorted individuals
31    newpop_fit = np.zeros_like(pop_fit, dtype = float)
32    # Fitness for intermediate individuals
33    for i in range(1,M+1):
34        newpop_chrom[i-1] = pop_chrom[sorted_idx[i-1]]
35        newpop_fit[i-1] = s - (2 * (i - 1) * (s - 1)) / (M - 1)
36    # Return the sorted individuals and their ranks
37    return newpop_chrom, newpop_fit
```

Listing 3.11: Fitness linear ranking.

Exponential Ranking Selection Probabilities

The exponential ranking method [38] can achieve high selective pressures while still giving some chance to the worst individuals in the population. In this method the individuals are ranked according to s^{i-1}, $i = 1, \ldots, N$, where typically $s = 0.99$. The selection pressure is proportional to $1 - s$. The Python code for exponential fitness ranking is shown in Listing 3.12.

```
 1 # ----------------------------------------------------------------
 2 #                 Fitness Exponential Ranking
 3 # ----------------------------------------------------------------
 4 #   pop_chrom    - individuals in the population
 5 #   pop_fit      - fitness values of the individuals
 6 # Outputs:
 7 #   newpop_chrom - individuals sorted in descending ranking order
 8 #   newpop_fit   - ranks of the individuals
 9 # Usage:
10 #   pop_chrom = np.array([1, 2, 3, 4])
11 #   pop_fit = np.array([10, 5, 70, 15])
12 #   np_ch, np_f = fitness_exponential_ranking(pop_chrom, pop_fit)
13 # ----------------------------------------------------------------
14 # file: fitness_exponential_ranking.py
15 # ----------------------------------------------------------------
16 import numpy as np
17 # ----------------------------------------------------------------
18 def fitness_exponential_ranking(pop_chrom, pop_fit):
19     # number of individuals in the population
20     N = np.shape(pop_chrom)[0]
21     # fitness of the best individual
22     s = 0.99
23     # sort in descending fitness order
24     sorted_idx = np.argsort(-pop_fit)
25     # sorted population
26     newpop_chrom = np.zeros_like(pop_chrom)
27     # rank values
28     newpop_fit = np.zeros_like(pop_fit, dtype=float)
29     # compute the ranks
30     for i in range(1,N+1):
```

```
31          newpop_chrom[i-1] = pop_chrom[sorted_idx[i-1]]
32          newpop_fit[i-1] = s**(i-1)
33    # return the sorted population and the corresponding
34    # ranks
35    return newpop_chrom, newpop_fit
```

Listing 3.12: Fitness exponential ranking.

3.5.2 Sampling

Roulette-Wheel Sampling

Many selection methods employ the concept of a roulette wheel mechanism to probabilistically sample individuals based on some measure of their fitness. Roulette-wheel sampling was proposed by Holland [44]. It samples individuals according to their fitness proportionate selection probabilities, that were seen in Section 3.5.1.

The area of the roulette wheel is given by the sum of the fitness values of all individuals in the current population. Each individual then receives a slice of the wheel, with the area of each slice corresponding to the individuals' fitness value, as shown in Figure 3.11. Individuals with higher fitness values occupy larger areas in the wheel, which means that they have more chances of being selected than individuals with lower fitness values.

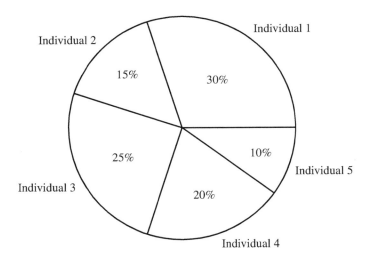

Figure 3.11: Roulette wheel example.

Let us illustrate the application of roulette-wheel selection with a hypothetical example. Suppose there are five individuals with the fitness values show in Table 3.4.

Table 3.4: Five hypothetical individuals and their fitness values.

Individual	Fitness Value
1	2
2	8
3	20
4	18
5	6
Total	54

Using the fitness values of the individuals as the areas of their slices of the wheel has some issues, such as having to deal with negative fitness values. Instead of directly using the fitness values, a better approach is to compute the fitness-proportionate probabilities of the individuals using linear scaling. The computed values are then used as the areas of the slices of the circle given to each individual. The fitness-proportionate selection probabilities are shown in Table 3.5.

Table 3.5: Five hypothetical individuals and their fitness-proportionate selection probabilities.

Individual	Fitness Value	FP Probabilities
1	2	0.0625
2	8	0.15625
3	20	0.34375
4	18	0.3125
5	6	0.125
Total	54	1

The next step is to sort the individuals in descending fitness value order and calculate the cumulative sum of the fitness-proportionate selection probabilities for each individual. The result of this step is shown in Table 3.6.

Table 3.6: Five hypothetical individuals, their fitness-proportionate selection probabilities and the corresponding cumulative sums.

Individual	FV	FP Probabilities	Cumulative Sum
3	20	0.34375	1
4	18	0.3125	0.65625
2	8	0.15625	0.34375
5	6	0.125	0.1875
1	2	0.0625	0.0625
Total	54	1	1

With the cumulative sums calculated, its time to sample the individuals. The roulette-wheel sampling will work according to Algorithm 3.7.

Algorithm 3.7. Selecting an Individual

1: **procedure** ROULETTE-WHEEL SELECTION
2:     $R \leftarrow$ uniform random number
3:     **if** $0.65625 < R \leq 1$ **then**
4:         select individual 3
5:     **end if**
6:     **if** $0.34375 < R \leq 0.65625$ **then**
7:         select individual 4
8:     **end if**
9:     **if** $0.1875 < R \leq 0.34375$ **then**
10:         select individual 2
11:     **end if**
12:     **if** $0.0625 < R \leq 0.1875$ **then**
13:         select individual 5
14:     **end if**
15:     **if** $0 \leq R \leq 0.0625$ **then**
16:         select individual 1
17:     **end if**
18: **end procedure**

Python code for roulette-wheel sampling is given in Listing 3.13.

```
#  ----------------------------------------------------------------
#                    Roulette-Wheel Sampling
#  ----------------------------------------------------------------
# This function can be used with both discrete and real-valued
# representations
#  ----------------------------------------------------------------
# file: sampling_rw.py
#  ----------------------------------------------------------------
import numpy as np
def sampling_rw(pop_chrom, pop_fit):
    # number of chromosomes
    M = np.shape(pop_chrom)[0]
    # sort in ascending order
    sorted_idx = np.argsort(pop_fit)
    # temporary population
    temp_pop_chrom = pop_chrom[sorted_idx]
    temp_pop_fit   = pop_fit[sorted_idx]
    # cumulative sum of ordered fitness values
    cumsum = np.zeros(M)
    cumsum[0] = temp_pop_fit[0]
    for i in range(1,M):
        for j in range(i+1):
            cumsum[i] = cumsum[i] + temp_pop_fit[j]
    # sample from uniform distribution
```

```
25    R = np.random.uniform(0,1) # in [0,1]
26    # select first parent
27    parent1_idx = 0
28    for i in range(M):
29        if R < cumsum[i]:
30            parent1_idx = i
31            break
32    # select second parent
33    parent2_idx = parent1_idx
34    while parent2_idx == parent1_idx:
35        R = np.random.uniform(0,1) # in [0,1]
36        for i in range(M):
37            if R < cumsum[i]:
38                parent1_idx = i
39                break
40    parent1 = temp_pop_chrom[parent1_idx]
41    parent2 = temp_pop_chrom[parent2_idx]
42    return parent1, parent2
```

Listing 3.13: Roulette-wheel sampling.

This sampling strategy has a significant drawback. As stated in [38], since each parent is chosen separately, there is no way to make sure that any particular individual, the best one in particular, will be chosen in any given generation. This sampling error is a source of noise in the optimization process.

Stochastic Universal Sampling

Stochastic Universal Sampling (SUS) [6] was proposed as a solution to the sampling error that characterizes roulette-wheel sampling. With roulette wheel there is always a chance that the best individual is not selected, not even after a good number of wheel spins. For example, in Figure 3.11, the best individual has a probability of selection of 0.3 whenever the wheel is spun, but its probability of not being selected is 0.7!. The probability that the best individual is not selected in k spins of the wheel is 0.7^k, which can be unacceptable depending on the situation.

The solution proposed in this method is that instead of spinning the roulette wheel n times to select n parents, use a spinner with n uniformly-spaced pointers over the wheel and spin it once. This gives n parents with a single spin, as shown in Figure 3.12, where $n = 2$ parents are simultaneously selected.

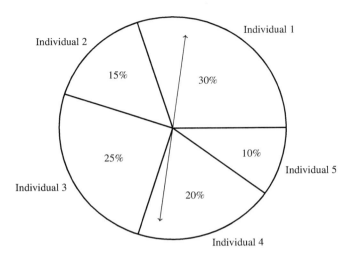

Figure 3.12: Stochastic Universal Sampling selecting $n = 2$ parents simultaneously.

Python code for stochastic universal sampling is given in Listing 3.14.

```
1 # -------------------------------------------------------------
2 #              Stochastic Universal Sampling
3 # -------------------------------------------------------------
4 # Selects two parents using stochastic universal sampling
5 # -------------------------------------------------------------
6 # Inputs:
7 #   pop_chrom   - individuals of the population
8 #   pop_fit     - corresponding fitness values
9 # Outputs:
10 #   parent1    - chromosome of the first parent
11 #   parent2    - chromosome of the second parent
12 # -------------------------------------------------------------
13 #  file: sampling_sus.py
14 # -------------------------------------------------------------
15 import numpy as np
16 # -------------------------------------------------------------
17 def sampling_sus(pop_chrom, pop_fit):
18     # number of individuals
19     M = np.shape(pop_chrom)[0]
20     # sort in ascending order
21     sorted_idx = np.argsort(pop_fit)
22     # temporary population
23     temp_pop_chrom = pop_chrom[sorted_idx]
24     temp_pop_fit   = pop_fit[sorted_idx]
25     # cumulative sum of ordered fitness values
26     cumsum = np.zeros(M)
27     cumsum[0] = temp_pop_fit[0]
28     for i in range(1,M):
29         for j in range(i+1):
30             cumsum[i] = cumsum[i] + temp_pop_fit[j]
31     N = 2 # number of offspring to keep
32     F = sum(temp_pop_fit) # total fitness of the population
33     P = F / N # distance between the pointers (F/N)
```

```
34    # sample from uniform distribution a starting point for
35    # the pointers
36    start = P*np.random.uniform(0,1) # in [0,P]
37    ptr = np.zeros(N)
38    # compute ending points for both pointers
39    for id in range(N):
40        ptr[id]= start + id * P
41    # select first parent id
42    parent1_idx = sorted_idx[0]
43    for i in range(M):
44        if (ptr[0] < cumsum[i]):
45            parent1_idx = i
46            break
47    # select second parent id
48    parent2_idx = sorted_idx[0]
49    for i in range(M):
50        if (ptr[1] < cumsum[i]):
51            parent2_idx = i
52            break
53    # pick the chromosomes corresponding to
54    # the parents' ids
55    parent1 = temp_pop_chrom[parent1_idx]
56    parent2 = temp_pop_chrom[parent2_idx]
57    # return the selected parents
58    return parent1, parent2
```

Listing 3.14: Stochastic universal sampling.

3.5.3   Selection of Individuals

Now that the strategies for computing selection probabilities and for sampling of individuals have been seen, it is possible to use them to actually select individuals from a population. The pseudocode for the selection of individuals is

---

Algorithm 3.8. Selection of Individuals

1: $X \leftarrow$ receive population of N individuals.
2: $F \leftarrow$ receive the corresponding fitness values.
3: P = compute_selection_probabilities(X,F)
4: (X_s, F_s)=sample(X,F,P)
5: Return X_s, F_s

Fitness Proportionate Selection Probabilities with Roulette Wheel Sampling

Let us see, for example, how to combine fitness proportionate selection probabilities with SUS. A function to compute fitness-proportionate with linear scaling selection probabilities and roulette-wheel sampling is given in Listing 3.15.

```
1  # ------------------------------------------------------------
2  #         Selection Linear Scaling Roulette Wheel
3  # ------------------------------------------------------------
```

```
 4 # Selection with fitness linear scaling with roulette wheel
 5 # sampling
 6 # ------------------------------------------------------------
 7 # Inputs:
 8 #    pop_chrom   - population of individuals
 9 #    pop_fit     - fitness value of each individual
10 # Outputs:
11 #    p1_chrom    - chromosome of the first parent
12 #    p2_chrom    - chromosome of the second parent
13 # ------------------------------------------------------------
14 # file: selection_linear_scaling_rw.py
15 # ------------------------------------------------------------
16 from operators_rep.selection.sampling_rw import sampling_rw
17 from operators_rep.selection.fitness_linear_scaling import \
18     fitness_linear_scaling
19 # ------------------------------------------------------------
20 def selection_linear_scaling_rw(pop_chrom, pop_fit):
21     # Fitness scaling
22     pop_fit = fitness_linear_scaling(pop_fit)
23     # Sampling
24     p1_chrom, p2_chrom = sampling_rw(pop_chrom, pop_fit)
25     return p1_chrom, p2_chrom
```

Listing 3.15: Fitness proportionate with linear scaling selection probabilities and roulette-wheel sampling.

Exponential Fitness Ranking Probabilities and SUS

As another example, let us see how to combine exponential fitness ranking probabilities and SUS. The Python code for a function that computes exponential ranking selection probabilities and selects individuals according to stochastic universal sampling is given in Listing 3.16.

```
 1 # ------------------------------------------------------------
 2 # Selection by Exponential Ranking and Stochastic Universal
 3 #                     Sampling
 4 # ------------------------------------------------------------
 5 # Inputs:
 6 #    pop_chrom   - population of individuals
 7 #    pop_fit     - fitness value of each individual
 8 # Outputs:
 9 #    p1_chrom    - chromosome of the first parent
10 #    p2_chrom    - chromosome of the second parent
11 # ------------------------------------------------------------
12 # file: selection_exponential_ranking_sus.py
13 # ------------------------------------------------------------
14 from operators_rep.selection.fitness_exponential_ranking import \
15     fitness_exponential_ranking
16 from operators_rep.selection.sampling_sus import sampling_sus
17 # ------------------------------------------------------------
18 def selection_exponential_ranking_sus(pop_chrom, pop_fit):
19     # Fitness scaling
20     pop_chrom, pop_fit = fitness_exponential_ranking(pop_chrom,
21         pop_fit)
22     # Sampling
```

```
22    p1_chrom, p2_chrom = sampling_sus(pop_chrom, pop_fit)
23    return p1_chrom, p2_chrom
```

Listing 3.16: Exponential ranking selection probabilities with stochastic universal sampling.

Tournament Selection

In tournament selection, $n > 2$ individuals are chosen at random from the current population and the individual with the best fitness value is always selected. This method selects one individual at a time, thus for selecting two parents this method has to be executed twice. Selective pressure is given by 2^{n-1}[[77], Section 8.7.6], thus being directly proportional to the number of individuals that participate in the tournament.

As tournament selection picks one individual at a time, it suffers from the same sampling errors as the roulette-wheel sampling strategy. The advantage of tournament selection is that it is particularly suitable to parallel processing. The code for this selection method is in Listing 3.17.

```
 1 # -----------------------------------------------------------------
 2 #                    Selection by Tournament
 3 # -----------------------------------------------------------------
 4 # Inputs:
 5 #    pop_chrom    - population of individuals
 6 #    pop_fit      - fitness value of each individual
 7 # Outputs:
 8 #    p1_chrom     - chromosome of the first parent
 9 #    p2_chrom     - chromosome of the second parent
10 # -----------------------------------------------------------------
11 # file: selection_tournament.py
12 # -----------------------------------------------------------------
13 import numpy as np
14 import random
15 # -----------------------------------------------------------------
16 def selection_tournament(pop_chrom, pop_fit):
17     # number of individuals in the population
18     M = np.shape(pop_chrom)[0]
19     if M <= 3:
20         print('selection_tournament --> M must be bigger than 3')
21         exit()
22     # randomly select num_indvs individuals without replacement
23     num_indvs = 3 # this number could be a formal parameter
24     inds = random.sample(range(1, M), num_indvs)
25     selected_indvs = pop_chrom[inds]
26     selected_fits = pop_fit[inds]
27     # sort in descending order
28     sorted_idx = np.argsort(-selected_fits)
29     # pick the two most fit individuals
30     ind_p1 = sorted_idx[0]
31     p1_chrom = selected_indvs[ind_p1]
32     ind_p2 = sorted_idx[1]
33     p2_chrom = selected_indvs[ind_p2]
34     # return selected parents
35     return p1_chrom, p2_chrom
```

Listing 3.17: Tournament selection.

3.6 Crossover (Recombination)

After the parents have been selected, it is time to decide how their genetic information will be combined to create new individuals. Crossover, also called recombination, is the process of exchanging genes between two chromosomes in order to produce one or more new individuals.

The application of crossover is controlled by a scalar parameter called *crossover probability*, represented by the symbol p_c, with $0 \leq p_c \leq 1$. The crossover probability p_c controls wether a given parent survives and gets introduced to the next generation, allowing individuals from different generations to coexist, as it happens in nature.

If $p_c = 1$, no parent survives and the next generation is comprised only of the children of the current generation. If $p_c = 0$, no child of the current generation survives, with the next generation being formed only by the individuals of the current population that were chosen as parents. When $0 < p_c < 1$, some parents pass to the next generation and therefore individuals of different generations end up coexisting.

To illustrate the effect of the crossover operator on the optimization process, we will use a genetic algorithm to minimize the bi-dimensional sphere function seen in Figure 3.5 for two different values of p_c. To isolate the effect of the crossover operator, the operators described in Sections 3.7 and 3.8 are not used. The selection method used will be fitness proportionate selection with linear scaling and stochastic universal sampling.

The situation where $p_c = 0$ is shown in Figure 3.13. The plot displays the convergence curve of the optimization process, which shows the evolution of the fitness of the best individual found in each generation. Figure 3.13 illustrates the fact that in the absence of any operation that creates new individuals, no search really occurs. Accordingly the convergence curve is flat.

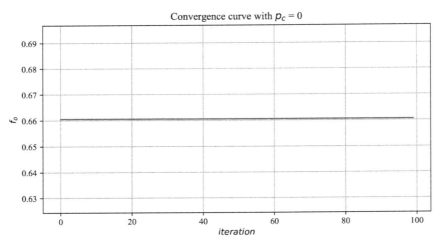

Figure 3.13: Bi-dimensional sphere function minimization with $p_c = 0$, no mutation and no elitism. The plot displays the fitness of the best individual found in each generation.

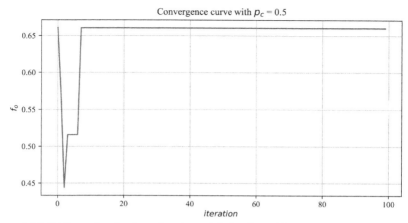

Figure 3.14: Bidimensional sphere function minimization with $p_c = 0.5$, no mutation and no elitism. The plot displays the fitness of the best individuals found in each generation.

When $p_c > 0$, as in Figure 3.14, the search process creates intermediate populations whose elements are re-combinations of their parents. There is thus a chance that the offspring have better fitness than their parents, and thus some progress towards the optimal value occurs. Nonetheless, there is also a chance that the offspring are worse than their parents. In the absence of elitism, there is no mechanism to ensure that the best individuals pass to the next generation. As a result, the convergence curve may display hills, valleys and plateaus.

There is a growing list of crossover methods [35]. In what follows some of the most widely used crossover methods are described.

3.6.1 Recombination for Discrete Representations

The following recombination schemes have been conceived to work with discrete (binary and integer) representations.

Single-Point Crossover

In single-point crossover [61], the genes of two parents with M genes each are re-combined at a randomly selected point m, $2 < m < M$, in a way that the resulting offspring has the first m genes inherited from the first parent and the remaining $M - m$ genes inherited from the second parent. This scheme is illustrated in Figure 3.15 for chromosomes with $M = 6$ genes and crossover point $m = 2$.

Parents						Children					
0	1	0	1	1	1	0	1	1	0	0	0
1	0	1	0	0	0	1	0	0	1	1	1

Figure 3.15: Single-point crossover example in a binary evolutionary algorithm. The crossover point is $m = 2$.

Single-point crossover can also be used with integer representations, as shown in Figure 3.16.

Parents							Children					
15	5	10	20	40	45		15	5	37	9	75	14
18	72	37	9	75	14		18	72	10	20	40	45

Figure 3.16: Single-point crossover example with integer representation. The crossover point is $m = 2$.

The pseudocode for single-point crossover is shown in Algorithm 3.9. The p_c parameter defines the probability that the crossover will take place. As a result, there is always a chance that the children are simply copies of their parents. The Python code for Algorithm 3.9 is in Listing 3.18.

Algorithm 3.9. Single-point crossover

1: $P_1 \leftarrow$ receive first parent.
2: $P_2 \leftarrow$ receive second parent.
3: $p_c \leftarrow$ receive crossover probability.
4: $M \leftarrow$ compute number of genes of a parent.
5: $m \leftarrow$ randomly select m from $\{2, 3, \ldots, M-1\}$
6: $C_1 = \text{crossover}(P_1, P_2, m)$
7: $C_2 = \text{crossover}(P_2, P_1, m)$
8: $r_1 \leftarrow$ random number $r_1 \in [0, 1)$.
9: **if** $r_1 > p_c$ **then**
10:      $C_1 = P_1$
11: **end if**
12: $r_2 \leftarrow$ random number $r_2 \in [0, 1)$.
13: **if** $r_2 > p_c$ **then**
14:      $C_2 = P_2$
15: **end if**
16: Return C_1, C_2

```
 1 # ------------------------------------------------------------
 2 #                    Single Point crossover
 3 # ------------------------------------------------------------
 4 # Inputs
 5 #    parent1_chrom    - first parent
 6 #    parent2_chrom    - second parent
 7 #    pc               - crossover probability
 8 # Outputs:
 9 #    child1           - first offspring
10 #    child2           - second offspring
11 # ------------------------------------------------------------
12 # file: crossover_sp.py
13 # ------------------------------------------------------------
```

```python
import numpy as np
def crossover_sp(parent1_chrom, parent2_chrom, pc):
    # Compute the number of genes of the chromosomes
    num_genes = np.size(parent1_chrom)
    # Compute the crossover point
    high = num_genes - 1  # excludes the last bit
    low = 1               # excludes the first bit
    # random integers from low (inclusive) to high (exclusive).
    cross_pt = np.random.randint(low,high+1)  # Note that Python
                                              # indexing starts
                                              # in 0
    # Fist child
    part1 = parent1_chrom[0:cross_pt]
    part2 = parent2_chrom[cross_pt: num_genes]
    child1 = np.concatenate((part1, part2))
    # Second child
    part1 = parent2_chrom[0:cross_pt]
    part2 = parent1_chrom[cross_pt: num_genes]
    child2 = np.concatenate((part1, part2))
    # Decide if recombined children make it to the next
    # generation
    R1 = np.random.uniform()
    if R1 > pc:
        child1 = parent1_chrom  # do not recombinate
    R2 = np.random.uniform()
    if R2 > pc:
        child2 = parent2_chrom  # do not recombinate
    # Return the offspring
    return child1, child2
```

Listing 3.18: Single-point crossover method.

The offspring that results from single-point crossover is not very different from the parents, since there is only one crossover point. To increase the genetic diversity of the offspring, it is possible to define more than one crossover point.

Multiple-Point Crossover

In a multiple-point crossover, there can be more than two crossover points. The more crossover points, the more different the children are from their parents. Multiple-point crossover can be used with both binary and integer representations. An example of the commonly used double-point crossover [54] method is illustrated in Figure 3.17.

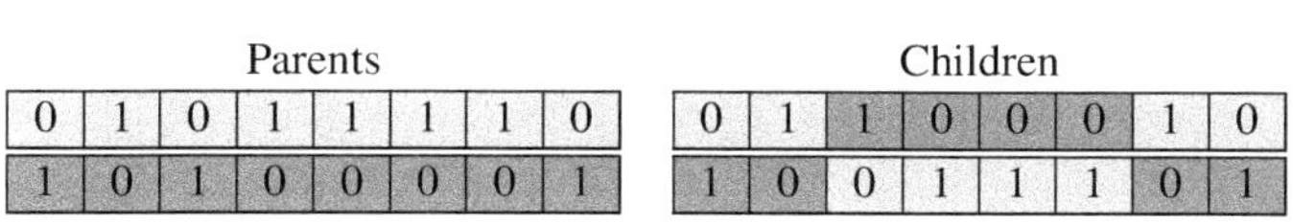

Figure 3.17: Two-point crossover example in a binary evolutionary algorithm.

The pseudocode for a two-point crossover method is shown in Algorithm 3.10. The corresponding Python code is in Listing 3.19.

Algorithm 3.10. Double-point crossover

1: $P_1 \leftarrow$ receive first parent.
2: $P_2 \leftarrow$ receive second parent.
3: $p_c \leftarrow$ receive crossover probability.
4: $M \leftarrow$ compute number of genes of a parent.
5: $m_1, m_2 \leftarrow$ randomly select two different crossover points from $\{2, 3, \ldots, M-1\}$
6: $C_1 = \text{crossover}(P_1, P_2, m_1, m_2)$
7: $C_2 = \text{crossover}(P_2, P_1, m_1, m_2)$
8: $r_1 \leftarrow$ random number $r_1 \in [0, 1)$.
9: **if** $r_1 > p_c$ **then**
10: $\qquad C_1 = P_1$
11: **end if**
12: $r_2 \leftarrow$ random number $r_2 \in [0, 1)$.
13: **if** $r_2 > p_c$ **then**
14: $\qquad C_2 = P_2$
15: **end if**
16: Return C_1, C_2

```
1  # -------------------------------------------------------------
2  #                 Double Point crossover
3  # -------------------------------------------------------------
4  # Inputs
5  #   parent1_chrom    - first parent
6  #   parent2_chrom    - second parent
7  #   pc               - crossover probability
8  # Outputs:
9  #   child1           - first offspring
10 #   child2           - second offspring
11 # -------------------------------------------------------------
12 # file: crossover_dp.py
13 # -------------------------------------------------------------
14 import numpy as np
15 def crossover_dp(parent1_chrom, parent2_chrom, pc):
16     # Compute the range of valid crossing points
17     valid_cp = np.arange(1, len(parent1_chrom))
18     # Sample two crossing points from valid_cp without repetition
19     samples = np.random.choice(valid_cp, 2, replace=False)
20     cross_pt1 = samples[0]
21     cross_pt2 = samples[1]
22     # Make sure that cross_pt1 < cross_pt2
23     if cross_pt1 > cross_pt2:
24         temp = cross_pt1
25         cross_pt1 = cross_pt2
26         cross_pt2 = temp
27     # First child
28     part1 = parent1_chrom[0:cross_pt1]
29     part2 = parent2_chrom[cross_pt1:cross_pt2]
30     part3 = parent1_chrom[cross_pt2:]
31     child1 = np.concatenate((part1, part2, part3))
32     # Second child
33     part1 = parent2_chrom[0:cross_pt1]
34     part2 = parent1_chrom[cross_pt1:cross_pt2]
```

```
35    part3 = parent2_chrom[cross_pt2:]
36    child2 = np.concatenate((part1, part2, part3))
37    # Decide if recombined children make it to the next
      generation
38    R1 = np.random.uniform()
39    if R1 > pc:
40        child1 = parent1_chrom   # do not recombinate
41    R2 = np.random.uniform()
42    if R2 > pc:
43        child2 = parent2_chrom   # do not recombinate
44    # Return the offspring
45    return child1, child2
```

Listing 3.19: Dual-point crossover method.

Uniform Crossover

In uniform crossover [61], each child feature has a 50% chance of coming from either of its two parents. Uniform crossover can produce more diverse offspring than the previous methods. It can be used with both discrete and integer representations. The pseudocode for uniform crossover is shown in Algorithm 3.11. The corresponding Python code is in Listing 3.20.

Algorithm 3.11. Uniform crossover

1: $P_1 \leftarrow$ receive first parent.
2: $P_2 \leftarrow$ receive second parent.
3: $p_c \leftarrow$ receive crossover probability.
4: $M \leftarrow$ compute number of genes of a parent.
5: **for** $i \in \{1, 2, \dots, M\}$ **do**
6:     $r \leftarrow$ random number $r \in [0, 1)$
7:     **if** $r < 0.5$ **then**
8:         $C_1[i] = P_1[i]$
9:         $C_2[i] = P_2[i]$
10:    **else**
11:        $C_1[i] = P_2[i]$
12:        $C_2[i] = P_1[i]$
13:    **end if**
14: **end for**
15: $r_1 \leftarrow$ random number $r_1 \in [0, 1)$.
16: **if** $r_1 > p_c$ **then**
17:     $C_1 = P_1$
18: **end if**
19: $r_2 \leftarrow$ random number $r_2 \in [0, 1)$.
20: **if** $r_2 > p_c$ **then**
21:     $C_2 = P_2$
22: **end if**
23: Return C_1, C_2

```
1  # -------------------------------------------------------------
2  #                 Uniform crossover
3  # -------------------------------------------------------------
4  # Inputs:
5  #   parent1_chrom    - first parent
6  #   parent2_chrom    - second parent
7  #   pc               - crossover probability
8  # Outputs:
9  #   child1           - first offspring
10 #   child2           - second offspring
11 # -------------------------------------------------------------
12 # file: crossover_uniform.py
13 # -------------------------------------------------------------
14 import numpy as np
15 # -------------------------------------------------------------
16 def crossover_uniform(parent1_chrom, parent2_chrom, pc):
17     # Number of genes of each parent
18     num_genes = np.size(parent1_chrom)
19     # Declare variables for the children
20     child1 = np.zeros(num_genes)
21     child2 = np.zeros(num_genes)
22     # uniform recombination
23     for ii in range(num_genes):
24         r = np.random.uniform()
25         # There is a 50% chance that a feature comes
26         # from a given parent
27         if r < 0.5:
28             child1[ii] = parent1_chrom[ii]
29             child2[ii] = parent2_chrom[ii]
30         else:
31             child1[ii] = parent2_chrom[ii]
32             child2[ii] = parent1_chrom[ii]
33     # Decide if recombined children make it to the
34     # next generation
35     R1 = np.random.uniform(low=0.0, high=1.0)
36     if R1 >= pc:
37         child1 = parent1_chrom  # do not recombinate
38     R2 = np.random.uniform()
39     if R2 >= pc:
40         child2 = parent2_chrom # do not recombinate
41     # Return the offspring
42     return child1, child2
```

Listing 3.20: Uniform crossover method.

3.6.2 Recombination for Real-valued Representations

The discrete operators just discussed could in principle be applied to real-valued representations, but in this case they would not add new genetic information to the population, because they would only produce different combinations of the parents. Each continuous value of the parents would be propagated without modification to the offspring, only in a different position. The following example will show why this is a problem.

Example 4 *If, for instance, the EA population is comprised of only two individuals, such as:*

■ $p_1 = [1, 2]$

■ $p_2 = [3, 4]$

Exchanging the last genes between those two individuals would result in

■ $p_1 = [1, 4]$

■ $p_2 = [3, 2]$

The new individuals are indeed different from the original ones, but if the crossover operation is applied again, the result would be

■ $p_1 = [1, 2]$

■ $p_2 = [3, 4]$

The resulting individuals are now identical to the original ones, bringing no new information to the population.

Some recombination methods conceived for working with real-valued representations are presented in what follows. The presented methods are just a small fraction of all the existing recombination methods. They were chosen because they are widely used and simple to apply.

Blending Methods

Blending methods [68] recombine genes from the two parents into the corresponding genes of the offspring. A single gene from one offspring $\mathbf{c} \in \mathbb{R}^M$ is a linear combination of the corresponding genes of the parents $\mathbf{p_1} \in \mathbb{R}^M$ and $\mathbf{p_2} \in \mathbb{R}^M$. Two offspring are produced according to

$$\mathbf{c}_{1_i} = \alpha\mathbf{p}_{1_i} + (1 - \alpha)\mathbf{p}_{2_i} \tag{3.6}$$
$$\mathbf{c}_{2_i} = \alpha\mathbf{p}_{2_i} + (1 - \alpha)\mathbf{p}_{1_i} \tag{3.7}$$

where $\alpha \in [0, 1]$ is a random number, $\mathbf{c}_{1_i}$, $i = 1, 2, \ldots, M$, is the value of the ith gene of $\mathbf{c}_1$, $\mathbf{p}_{1_i}$ is the value of the ith gene of the first parent, and $\mathbf{p}_{2_i}$ is the value of the ith gene of the second parent.

Different blending methods result from different ways of calculating α. Listing 3.21 follows the algorithm proposed in [68], which samples α from a standard normal distribution.

```
1 # ------------------------------------------------------------
2 # Blending Crossover
3 # ------------------------------------------------------------
4 # Inputs
5 #   p1    - first parent
```

```
 6 #    p2   - second parent
 7 #    pc   - crossover probability
 8 # Outputs:
 9 #    child1 - first offspring
10 #    child2 - second offspring
11 # -----------------------------------------------------------
12 # file: crossover_rv_blending.py
13 # -----------------------------------------------------------
14 import numpy as np
15 # -----------------------------------------------------------
16 def blending_crossover(p1, p2, pc):
17     n_dim = len(p1)
18     # perform crossover?
19     if np.random.rand() < pc:
20         # alpha - random vector in [0,1]
21         alpha = np.random.rand(n_dim)
22         # blending
23         child1 = alpha * p1 + (1 - alpha) * p2
24         child2 = alpha * p2 + (1 - alpha) * p1
25     else:
26         # no crossover
27         child1 = p1
28         child2 = p2
29     return child1, child2
```

Listing 3.21: Real-valued blending crossover method.

Intermediate Recombination

Intermediate recombination [62] is a method of producing children located around and between the parents, favoring exploitation instead of exploration. The offspring is produced according to

$$\mathbf{c}_{1_i} = \mathbf{p}_{1_i} \times \alpha(\mathbf{p}_{2_i} - \mathbf{p}_{1_i}) \tag{3.8}$$

$$\mathbf{c}_{2_i} = \mathbf{p}_{2_i} \times \alpha(\mathbf{p}_{1_i} - \mathbf{p}_{2_i}) \tag{3.9}$$

where $\alpha \in [-0.25, 1.25]$ is a random number, $\mathbf{c}_{1_i}$, $i = 1, n$, is the value of the ith gene of $\mathbf{c}_1$, and $\mathbf{p}_{1_i}$ is the value of the ith gene of the first parent.

```
 1 # -----------------------------------------------------------
 2 # Intermediate Crossover
 3 # -----------------------------------------------------------
 4 # Inputs
 5 #    p1   - first parent
 6 #    p2   - second parent
 7 #    pc   - crossover probability
 8 # Outputs:
 9 #    child1 - first offspring
10 #    child2 - second offspring
11 # -----------------------------------------------------------
12 # file: crossover_rv_intermediate.py
13 # -----------------------------------------------------------
14 import numpy as np
15 # -----------------------------------------------------------
16 def intermediate_crossover(p1, p2, pc):
```

```
17    n_dim = len(p1)
18    # perform crossover?
19    if np.random.rand() < pc:
20        child1 = np.zeros(n_dim)
21        child2 = np.zeros(n_dim)
22        for id in range(n_dim):
23            # alpha - random vector in [a,b]
24            b = 1.25
25            a = -0.25
26            alpha = (b-a)*np.random.random_sample() + a
27            # blending
28            child1[id] = p1[id] * alpha * (p2[id] - p1[id])
29            child2[id] = p2[id] * alpha * (p1[id] - p2[id])
30    else:
31        # no crossover
32        child1 = p1
33        child2 = p2
34    return child1, child2
```

Listing 3.22: Real-valued intermediate crossover method.

Simulated Binary Crossover (SBX)

The idea of the Simulated Binary Crossover (SBX) operator[47] is to be a crossover operator applicable to real-valued vectors that preserve some properties of the single-point binary crossover operator described in Section 3.6.1.

The concept that underpins the SBX operator is the *spread factor*. The spread factor is defined as the absolute value of the ratio of the distance between the two offspring and the distance between the two parents. Thus, the spread factor between children $\mathbf{c}_i \in \mathbb{R}^M, i = 1, 2$ and parents $\mathbf{p}_i \in \mathbb{R}^M, i = 1, 2$ is given by:

$$\beta = \left| \frac{\mathbf{c}_1 - \mathbf{c}_2}{\mathbf{p}_1 - \mathbf{p}_2} \right|. \tag{3.10}$$

If $\beta < 1$, then the SBX crossover operation is a contraction, because the children are closer to each other than the parents are, being located between the parents. If $\beta > 1$ the operation is an expansion, because the children are farther apart from each other than the parents are, with the parents located between the children. Finally, if $\beta = 1$, the operation is said to be stationary, with the parents being equal to the children.

The first step in creating the offspring is defining a random value for β. This is done according to

$$\beta = \begin{cases} (2u)^{\frac{1}{\eta_c+1}}, & \text{if } u \leq 0.5 \\ \left(\frac{1}{2(1-u)}\right)^{\frac{1}{\eta_c+1}}, & \text{otherwise} \end{cases} \tag{3.11}$$

where $u \in [0, 1]$ is a random number and $n_c > 0$ is a user-defined parameter, called *distribution index*, that controls the probability distribution of β. Larger values of η_c, such as $\eta_c = 5$, increase the probability of creating children located closer to the parents, favoring exploitation. Smaller values of n_c, such as $\eta_c = 2$, increase the probability of creating children that are more distant to their parents, favoring exploration and increasing diversity.

Once β has been calculated using Equation (3.11), the two offspring are calculated as

$$\mathbf{c}_1 = 0.5[(1+\beta)\mathbf{p}_1 + (1-\beta)\mathbf{p}_2)] \tag{3.12}$$

$$\mathbf{c}_2 = 0.5[(1-\beta)\mathbf{p}_1 + (1+\beta)\mathbf{p}_2)]. \tag{3.13}$$

A Python implementation of the SBX crossover is shown in Listing 3.23. The SBX function receives the two parents as parameters, as the value of η_c and the value of the crossover rate p_c. It then returns the two children.

```python
# -------------------------------------------------------------
# SBX: Simulated Binary Crossover
# -------------------------------------------------------------
# Inputs:
#    p1 - first parent
#    p2 - second parent
#    pc - crossover probability
#    eta - distribution index
# Outputs:
#    c1 - first offspring
#    c2 - second offspring
# -------------------------------------------------------------
# file: crossover_rv_sbx.py
# -------------------------------------------------------------
import numpy as np
import random
# -------------------------------------------------------------
def sbx_crossover(p1,p2, pc,eta=2):
    # number of elements of the parents
    n_dim = len(p1)
    # perform crossover ?
    if np.random.rand() < pc:
        # storage for the offspring
        c1 = np.zeros(n_dim)
        c2 = np.zeros(n_dim)

        for i in range(n_dim):
            # SBX crossover
            u = random.random()
            if u <= 0.5:
                beta = 2. * u
            else:
                beta = 1. / (2. * (1. - u))
            beta = beta**(1. / (eta + 1.))
            # new offspring
            c1[i] = 0.5 * (((1 + beta) * p1[i]) +
                          ((1 - beta) * p2[i]))
            c2[i] = 0.5 * (((1 - beta) * p1[i]) +
                          ((1 + beta) * p2[i]))
    else:
        # no crossover
        c1 = p1
```

```
43        c2 = p2
44    return c1,c2
```

Listing 3.23: Real-valued Simulated Binary Crossover (SBX) implementation.

3.7 Mutation

Mutation is the operation that brings new features to the population of an evolutionary algorithm. It is implemented by applying random changes to some of the genes of an individual. With some luck, these random changes will produce an individual with a better fitness value than the original individual. Let us illustrate the mutation process with an example.

Suppose we have a binary chromosome and we want to apply mutation to its second bit. As we are dealing with a binary chromosome, the only thing we need to do is to flip the value of the second bit. If it is one, we flip it to zero and the other way round. The resulting individual will be exactly equal to the original individual, but with its second bit flipped, as seen in Figure 3.18.

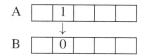

Figure 3.18: Example of mutation in a binary chromosome.

The number of genes of a chromosome that will undergo mutation is controlled by a scalar parameter called *probability of mutation*, represented by the symbol p_m, with $0 \leq p_m \leq 1$. To determine if a given gene of an individual will undergo mutation, we generate a random number in the closed interval $[0, 1]$. If the number is less than p_m, the gene is mutated, otherwise, it is left intact. This is done for every gene of the chromosome. To illustrate the effect of p_m, let us use a genetic algorithm to minimize the bi-dimensional sphere function, first with $p_m = 0.1$, then $p_m = 1$. Crossover and elitism are not applied, so that the only operation driving the search process is mutation.

With a low mutation rate such as $p_m = 0.1$, there may be not enough exploration to find even a reasonable candidate solution. That is the situation shown in Figure 3.19, where the final best candidate solution is worse than the initial best candidate solution. It is important to remember that there is no elitism, thus the initial best candidate solution was lost.

With $p_m = 1$, as show in Figure 3.20, there was enough exploration to find good candidate solutions. The convergence curve variation indicates that the best solution is constantly being lost from one generation to the next, as expected in the absence of elitism. Though the optimization process was able to find good candidate solutions using only mutation, it is important to emphasize this will not always be the case, specially when the dimensionality of the problem is higher.

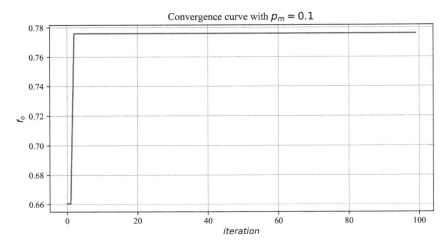

Figure 3.19: Bi-dimensional sphere function minimization with $p_m = 0.1$. The plot displays the fitness of the best individual found in each generation.

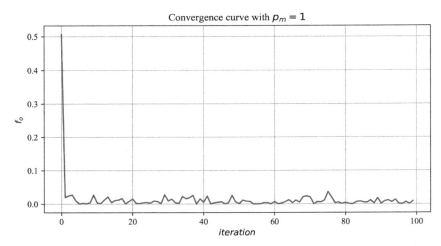

Figure 3.20: Bi-dimensional sphere function minimization with $p_m = 1$. The right displays the fitness of the best individual found in each generation.

3.7.1 Mutation for Binary Representations

The pseudocode for the binary mutation is given in Algorithm 3.12, and the corresponding Python code is in Listing 3.24.

Algorithm 3.12. Binary mutation

1: $X \leftarrow$ receive individual to undergo mutation.
2: $p_m \leftarrow$ receive mutation probability.
3: **if** $p_m == 0$ **then**
4:     Return X ▷ No mutation takes place.
5: **end if**
6: $M \leftarrow$ number of genes of X.
7: **for** $i \in \{1, 2, \ldots, M\}$ **do**
8:     $r \leftarrow$ random number in $[0, 1)$
9:     **if** $r < p_m$ **then**
10:         $Y[i] = \text{flip\_bit}(X[i])$ ▷ The ith bit of X undergoes mutation.
11:     **else**
12:         $Y[i] = X[i]$
13:     **end if**
14: **end for**
15: Return Y

```
# ------------------------------------------------------------
#                      Binary  Mutation
# ------------------------------------------------------------
# Inputs:
#   x              - individual to undergo mutation
#   pm             - mutation probability
# Outputs:
#   mutated_x      - mutated individual
# ------------------------------------------------------------
# file: mutation_binary.py
# ------------------------------------------------------------
import numpy as np
# ------------------------------------------------------------
# Auxiliary function to flip a bit
def flip_bit(bit):
    if bit==0:
        bit = 1
    else:
        bit = 0
    return bit
# Binary mutation function
def mutation_binary(x, pm):
    # if pm=0, no mutation is performed
    if pm == 0:
        return x
    # Compute the number of genes in x
    M = np.size(x)
    # This is because in Python arguments are passed
    # by reference, not by value
    mutated_x = np.copy(x)
    # Mutate each gene
    for k in range(M):
        r = np.random.uniform()
        if r < pm:
```

```
35        mutated_x[k] = flip_bit(x[k])
36    # Return mutated individual
37    return mutated_x
```

Listing 3.24: Binary mutation method.

3.7.2 Mutation for Real-valued Representations

In case of using real-valued representation for the chromosomes, the genes of an individual are floating point numbers, and floating point numbers cannot simply be flipped. In this situation, mutation can be performed either by perturbing the gene values or by randomly selecting new values within the bounds of the search space.

Uniform Mutation

Uniform/Usual mutation [26] randomly selects one variable k of the n-dimensional individual being mutated and sets it equal to a uniform random number in the interval $[\mathbf{a}, \mathbf{b}]$ that defines the valid search space. Listing 3.25 shows the Python implementation of the uniform mutation scheme.

```
1 # ------------------------------------------------------------
2 #                    Uniform Mutation
3 # Analogous to the binary (bit flipping) mutation and random
4 # resetting mutation
5 # ------------------------------------------------------------
6 # Inputs:
7 #    x   - n-dimensional individual to be mutated
8 #    pm  - probability that a gene will undergo mutation
9 #    a   - lower bound for the values of the genes
10 #    b   - upper bound for the values of the genes
11 # Output:
12 #    mutated_x - mutated individual
13 # ------------------------------------------------------------
14 # file: mutation_uniform_rv.py
15 # ------------------------------------------------------------
16 import numpy as np
17 # ------------------------------------------------------------
18 def mutation_uniform_rv(x, pm, a, b):
19     # No mutation is performed
20     if pm == 0:
21         return x
22     # Number of genes of the individual
23     num_genes = np.size(x)
24     # Create the mutated individual
25     mutated_x = np.copy(x)
26     # Uniform mutation
27     for k in range(num_genes):
28         # Generate a random number
29         r = np.random.uniform()
30         # Mutate this gene?
31         if r < pm:
32             # Generate a uniformly distributed random
33             # number in [a,b]
34             mutated_x[k] = np.random.uniform(a[k],b[k],1)
```

```
35      # Return the mutated chromosome
36      return mutated_x
```

Listing 3.25: Real-coded mutation by uniform random perturbations.

As an example, Figure 3.21 displays the probability distribution of the mutated individuals produced by uniform mutation, assuming that the parent is $p = 3.0$ and that $p \in [1, 8]$. As expected, the mutated individuals are uniformly distributed in the interval $[1, 8]$.

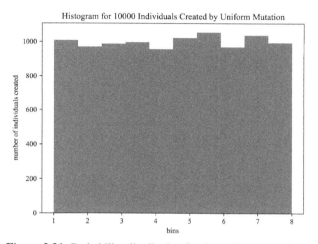

Figure 3.21: Probability distribution for the uniform mutation.

Gaussian Mutation

Gaussian mutation works by adding a Gaussian distributed random vector to the individual being mutated. There are many possible interpretations for this paradigm, a simple one is given in Listing 3.26, which shows the Python implementation of a mutation scheme that works by adding zero-mean Gaussian perturbations to the individual. The strength of the perturbation depends on the upper and lower bounds of the search space. A much more complex and sophisticated Gaussian mutation is given in [26].

```
 1 # ------------------------------------------------------------------
 2 #               Gaussian Mutation
 3 # ------------------------------------------------------------------
 4 # This function can be used only with real-valued representations
 5 # ------------------------------------------------------------------
 6 # Inputs:
 7 #    x   - n-dimensional individual to be mutated
 8 #    pm  - probability that a gene will undergo mutation
 9 #    a   - lower bound for the values of the genes
10 #    b   - upper bound for the values of the genes
11 # Output:
12 #    mutated_x - mutated individual
13 # ------------------------------------------------------------------
```

```
14 # file: mutation_gaussian_rv.py
15 # ------------------------------------------------------------
16 import numpy as np
17 def mutation_gaussian_rv(x, pm, a, b):
18     # No mutation is performed
19     if pm == 0:
20         return x
21     num_genes = np.size(x)
22     # create the mutated individual
23     mutated_x = np.copy(x)
24     # Uniform mutation
25     for k in range(num_genes):
26         # Generate a random number
27         r = np.random.uniform()
28         # Mutate this gene?
29         if r < pm:
30             # mutation by adding random perturbation
31             # from a Gaussian distribution with zero mean
32             mutated_x[k] = \
33                 0.9*mutated_x[k] + \
34                 0.1*((b[k] - a[k]) * np.random.randn())
35             # keep the mutated individual in [a,b]
36             mutated_x[k] = np.clip(mutated_x[k],a[k],b[k])
37     # Return the mutated individual
38     return mutated_x
```

Listing 3.26: Real-coded mutation by Gaussian perturbations.

As an example, Figure 3.22 displays the probability distribution of the mutated individuals produced by Gaussian mutation, assuming that the parent is $p = 3.0$ and that $p \in [1, 8]$. As expected, the mutated individuals follow a normal distribution centered around $c = 3.0$.

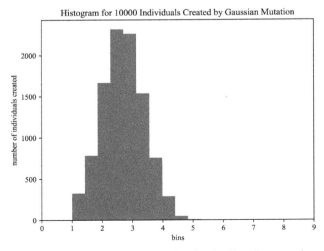

Figure 3.22: Probability distribution for the Gaussian mutation.

Polynomial Mutation

In a polynomial mutation ([25], [26]), a polynomial probability distribution is used to create mutated solutions in the vicinity of a parent solution. The probability distribution is adjusted so that the mutated solutions remain inside the interval $[\mathbf{a}, \mathbf{b}]$ that defines the search space.

For a given parent solution $\mathbf{p} \in \mathbb{R}^M$ located in $[\mathbf{a} \in \mathbb{R}^M, \mathbf{b} \in \mathbb{R}^M]$, the mutated solution $\mathbf{c} \in \mathbb{R}^M$ is created as follows:

$$c_i = \begin{cases} p_i + \delta_L(p_i - a_i), & \text{for } u \leq 0.5 \\ p_i + \delta_R(b_i - p_i), & \text{for } u > 0.5 \end{cases} \tag{3.14}$$

where $u \in [0, 1]$ is a uniform random number, $i = \{1, \ldots, M\}$, c_i is the ith component of $\mathbf{c}$ and p_i is the ith component of $\mathbf{p}$. Parameters δ_L and δ_R are computed according to

$$\delta_L = (2u)^{(1/(1+\eta_m))} - 1, \text{ for } u \leq 0.5 \tag{3.15}$$

$$\delta_R = 1 - (2(1-u))^{(1/(1+\eta_m))}, \text{ for } u > 0.5, \tag{3.16}$$

where η_m is the user-defined *distribution index* parameter that the authors of the algorithm recommend to be in $[20, 100]$.

```
1  # -------------------------------------------------------------
2  #                  Polynomial Mutation
3  # -------------------------------------------------------------
4  # Inputs:
5  #    x             - individual to be mutated
6  #    pm            - probability that a gene will undergo mutation
7  #    a             - lower bound for the search scape
8  #    b             - upper bound for the search scape
9  #    eta_m         - distribution index in [20,100]
10 # Outputs:
11 #    mutated_x     - mutated individual
12 # -------------------------------------------------------------
13 # file: mutation_polynomial_rv.py
14 # -------------------------------------------------------------
15 import numpy as np
16 def mutation_polynomial_rv(x, pm, a, b, eta_m = 20):
17     # No mutation is performed
18     if pm == 0:
19         return x
20     # Decide if mutation will occur
21     # if r < pm   --> perform mutation
22     # if r >= pm  --> do not perform mutation
23     r = np.random.uniform()
24     if r < pm:
25         # number of genes
26         n_var =len(x)
27         # create the mutated individual
28         mutated_x = np.copy(x)
29         # polynomial mutation
30         for k in range(n_var):
31             u = np.random.uniform()
```

```
32      if u <= 0.5:
33          sig_L = (2 * u) ** (1 / (1+eta_m)) - 1
34          mutated_x[k] = mutated_x[k] + \
35                         sig_L*(mutated_x[k] - a[k])
36      else:
37          sig_R = 1 - (2 * (1 - u)) ** (1 / (1 + eta_m))
38          mutated_x[k] = mutated_x[k] + \
39                         sig_R * (b[k] - mutated_x[k])
40  else:
41      # Do not perform mutation
42      mutated_x = x
43  # Return the mutated individual
44  return mutated_x
```

Listing 3.27: Real-coded mutation by polynomial mutation.

As an example, Figure 3.23 displays the probability distribution of the mutated individuals produced by the polynomial mutation operator, assuming that the parent individual is $p = 3.0$, $p \in [1, 8]$, and $\eta_m = 20$.

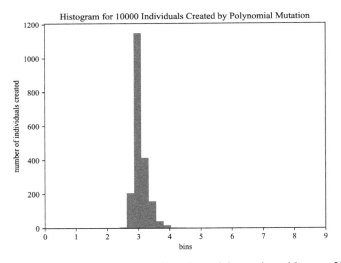

Figure 3.23: Probability distribution for polynomial mutation with $\eta_m = 20$.

Figure 3.24 displays the probability distribution of the mutated individuals produced by the polynomial mutation operator, assuming now that $\eta_m = 80$.

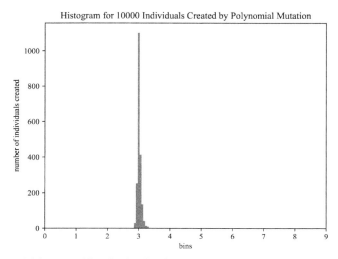

Figure 3.24: Probability distribution for polynomial mutation with $\eta_m = 80$.

Comparing Figures 3.23 and 3.24, it is clear from the spread of the mutated individuals that lower values of η_m favor exploration, while higher values favor exploitation.

3.7.3 Mutation for Integer Representations

Random Resetting

In this mutation strategy a random value from the list of permissible values for the genes is assigned to a randomly chosen gene.

```
 1 #  -----------------------------------------------------------------
 2 #              Random Resetting Mutation
 3 #  -----------------------------------------------------------------
 4 # Inputs:
 5 #     x      - n-dimensional individual to be mutated
 6 #     v      - vector of permissible values for the genes
 7 #     pm     - probability that a gene will undergo mutation
 8 # Outputs:
 9 #     mutated_x - mutated individual
10 #  -----------------------------------------------------------------
11 # file: mutation_rand_reset_int.py
12 #  -----------------------------------------------------------------
13 import numpy as np
14 #  -----------------------------------------------------------------
15 def mutation_rand_reset(x,v, pm):
16     # No mutation is performed
17     if pm == 0:
18         return x
19     # Create the mutated individual
20     mutated_x = np.copy(x)
21     # Dimensionality
```

```
22    numVar = len(x)
23    # Random changes
24    for ll in range(numVar):
25        if np.random.rand() < pm:
26            mutated_x[ll] = np.random.choice(v)
27    # return the mutated individual
28    return mutated_x
```

Listing 3.28: Random resetting mutation.

3.8 Elitism

Elitism is the idea of preserving the best individuals found so far in the optimization process, allowing them to survive from one generation to the next. The elite solutions do not undergo any change, being transferred directly to the population of the next generation. This is an interesting strategy, since it allows evolutionary algorithms to preserve good solutions that could otherwise be lost due to the randomness inherent to many selection methods.

Elitism is controlled by a scalar parameter called *elitism rate*, which is the percentage of the best solutions of a population that are directly transferred to the next generation. In other words, the elitism rate defines the number of elite chromosomes. The elitism rate is represented by the symbol e_r, with $0 \leq e_r \leq 1$.

To illustrate the effects of elitism, lets minimize the bi-dimensional sphere function, first with $e_r = 0.1$, then with $e_r = 1$. The experiment in which elitism, mutation and crossover rates were all zero is show in Figure 3.13. In that situation, there was no progress in the optimization process because no genetic operators that could produce new individuals (new genetic information) were acting on the population. The experiment described in this section uses $p_m = 0.1$, in order to allow the creation of new individuals.

Figure 3.25 shows that the optimization process succeeded in finding the optimal solution. As expected, the convergence curve shows monotonic increase, indicating that the best elements found during the optimization process survived across generations. The experiment confirms that some degree of elitism is necessary.

A very high elitism rate though can end up inhibiting the search process, because too many individuals from a given generation are transferred to the next generation. This reduces genetic diversity, thus reducing the chances of finding better individuals. In Figure 3.19, where $e_r = 0$, the best individual of the initial population was lost, because there was no elitism. In Figure 3.26, where $e_r = 1$, the best individual of the initial population was preserved, but no better individuals were created, because of the loss of genetic diversity resulting from the extremely high elitism rate.

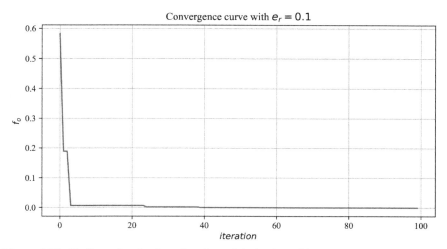

Figure 3.25: Bi-dimensional sphere function minimization with $p_m = 0.1$ and $e_r = 0.1$. The plot displays the fitness of the best individual found in each generation.

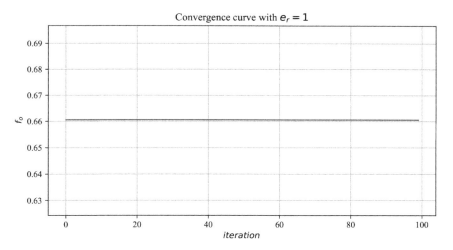

Figure 3.26: Bi-dimensional sphere function minimization with $p_m = 0.1$ and $e_r = 1$. The plot displays the fitness of the best individual found in each generation.

Elitism thus is a necessary genetic operator, but a very high elitism rate can hinder the optimization process. Listing 3.29 presents a Python implementation of elitism.

```
1 # ----------------------------------------------------------------
2 #                         Elitism
3 # Implements elitism by replacing the worst M of the N
4 # children received  with the M elite individuals of the
5 # last generation (pop_chrom)
6 # ----------------------------------------------------------------
```

```
 7 # Inputs:
 8 #   pop_chrom       - individuals of the last generation
 9 #   pop_fit         - fitness values of the individuals
10 #   children_chrom  - new individuals
11 #   children_fit    - fitness values of the new individuals
12 # Outputs:
13 #   new_pop_chrom   - new population
14 #   new_pop_fit     - fitness of the new population
15 # -----------------------------------------------------------
16 # file: elitism.py
17 # -----------------------------------------------------------
18 import numpy as np
19 def elitism(pop_chrom, pop_fit, children_chrom, children_fit, er)
        :
20     # Compute number of individuals in the population
21     N = np.shape(pop_chrom)[0]
22     # Compute number of elite chromosomes
23     M = int(np.ceil(N * er))
24     # Sort the N children in descending fitness order
25     ids_sorted = np.argsort(-children_fit)
26     # Keep only the best N - M children
27     ids_sorted = ids_sorted[0:(N - M)]
28     children_chrom = children_chrom[ids_sorted]
29     children_fit = children_fit[ids_sorted]
30     # Pick the best M individuals of the current population
31     ids_sorted = np.argsort(-pop_fit)
32     ids_sorted = ids_sorted[0:M]
33     best_pop_chrom = pop_chrom[ids_sorted]
34     best_pop_fit = pop_fit[ids_sorted]
35     # Replace the worst M children with the M elite chromosomes
         of the
36     # last generation
37     new_pop_chrom = np.vstack((children_chrom, best_pop_chrom))
38     new_pop_fit = np.hstack((children_fit,best_pop_fit))
39     # Return the new population and the corresponding fitness
         values
40     return new_pop_chrom, new_pop_fit
```

Listing 3.29: Elitism operation.

SINGLE-OBJECTIVE EVOLUTIONARY ALGORITHMS

Now that the central ideas of optimization and of evolutionary algorithms have been seen, it is time to discuss some important single-objective evolutionary algorithms. First, the discussion focuses on Ant Colony Optimization (ACO) and Particle Swarm Optimization (PSO), two widely used representatives of the swarm intelligence approach. The class of evolution strategies algorithms is discussed next, including Natural Evolution Strategies (NES) and Covariance Matrix Adaptation Evolution Strategies (CMAES). Then the presentation focuses on Genetic Algorithms (GAs), perhaps the most widely used class of evolutionary algorithms. Finally, the Differential Evolution (DE) approach is discussed.

Chapter 4

Swarm Optimization

Collective intelligence is one of the most striking phenomena in nature. Simple animals that individually exhibit only a handful of simple behaviors are capable of impressive collective behaviors. Bees, for instance, are capable of building complex colonies with very efficient labor distribution among its members, while schools of fish are capable of performing impressive maneuvers when trying to escape predators.

The collective behavior of ants when searching for food is particularly interesting. According to [53], in the beginning of the search process, scout ants walk around in a seemingly chaotic way, returning to the nest when they get tired. When one of them finds food, it takes a piece of the food back to the nest leaving a trail of pheromones (a scent-emanating volatile substance). Other ants then start following that trail, initially without much order, because of the low quantity of pheromones in the trail. As large numbers of ants start going after the food, they end up finding lots of different paths to the food source and back to the nest. Since pheromones are volatile, shorter trails tend to have stronger scents. As a result, more ants follow the shortest trail and leave their scent marks, reinforcing the trail. This collective behavior thus acts as an optimization process, because ants concentrate their efforts in the shortest trails. That study also found that the experience of individual ants contributes to their foraging success. Older ants have a better knowledge of the nests surroundings, being more efficient food scouts than younger ants.

The foraging strategy of ants has thus two very interesting components. The first is a social component, which is due to the fact that the pheromone trails end up communicating the location of the food found by one scout to the other ants of the nest. The other is an individual component, which accounts for the fact that the experience of the individual makes a difference when scouting for food. These components, also found in the group behavior of other animals, are incorporated in the search strategy of algorithms such as ACO and PSO.

Both ACO and PSO have been recently applied to interesting real-world problems. ACO has been applied to the optimization of task offloading for IoT-based applications in fog computing [45], to the route optimization for last-mile distribution of rural e-commerce logistics [56], and to the robust scheduling of hot rolling production [93]. PSO has been applied to the problem of cell range expansion for heterogeneous mobile networks [52], to the scheduling of workflows with composite tasks [78], and to the optimization of the shape and electric performance improvement of insulators [30], just to cite a few.

Though some researchers claim that swarm-intelligence algorithms are not exactly evolutionary algorithms, many other researchers consider them to be EAs. If at some point in the future there is consensus that they are not, at least they are interesting and effective population-based, biologically-inspired, optimization heuristics, that is why they are discussed here.

4.1 Ant Colony Optimization

ACO [19] is a single-objective population-based metaheuristic in which a colony of artificial ants cooperate in the search for solutions to discrete optimization problems. The ACO metaheuristic can be applied to any combinatorial optimization problem, provided that a proper representation of the candidate solutions is found. Henceforth, any algorithms that fit into the ACO metaheuristic will be called ACO algorithms. The ACO metaheuristic will be discussed in the context of the TSP problem.

The ACO Metaheuristic

An ACO algorithm is comprised of two main steps: build solutions and update pheromones. Procedures called artificial ants concurrently build paths (solutions) that start at a given city, visit all other cities only once and then return to the start city. Ants decide which city will be visited next according to a stochastic policy that takes into account pheromone trails.

After the solutions are built, the pheromone trails of the arcs that form the solutions are updated. The pheromone trail in a given arc decays as a result of pheromone evaporation, but it is made stronger by the deposition of pheromones by the ants that traverse the arc. Arcs with higher pheromone levels tend to be chosen more often by ants, while arcs will lower pheromone levels tend to be chosen less.

The basic ACO algorithm (an algorithm that fits into the ACO metaheuristic) is shown in Algorithm 4.1.

Algorithm 4.1. Ant Colony Optimization
1: **procedure** ACO
2:      **while** termination criterion not satisfied **do**
3:           build candidate solutions
4:           update the pheromone quantity of all solutions
5:      **end while**
6:      return the best solution
7: **end procedure**

The first ACO algorithm was Ant System (AS) [29], and it was introduced in the context of the TSP. This section adopts the same approach to present the Elitist AS algorithm, which is an extension of the AS algorithm. Let us thus consider again the TSP problem described in Section 2.9 and depicted in Figure 4.1.

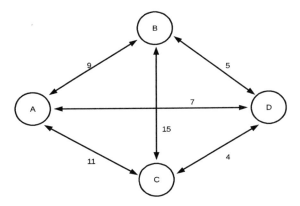

Figure 4.1: The cities that have to be visited by the travelling business person.

The set of components of the TSP problem is $S = \{A,B,C,D\}$, and the possible solutions are

$$
\begin{aligned}
S_1 &= (A,B,C,D,A) \\
S_2 &= (A,B,D,C,A) \\
S_3 &= (A,C,B,D,A) \\
S_4 &= (A,C,D,B,A) \\
S_5 &= (A,D,B,C,A) \\
S_6 &= (A,D,C,B,A)
\end{aligned}
$$

The Ant System

AS starts by placing ants on randomly chosen cities. Each ant then starts building a candidate solution (a path that starts and ends at the same city and visits all other cities of the TSP once) by picking edges l_{ij} that connect cities i and j. The probability that the kth ant, located at city i, takes a path to a city j that it has not visited yet is given by (4.1)

$$p_{i,j}^k(t) = \frac{\tau_{i,j}^\alpha(t) \cdot \eta_{i,j}^\beta}{\sum_{j \in J^k} \tau_{i,j}^\alpha(t) \cdot \eta_{i,j}^\beta} \tag{4.1}$$

where

- $p_{i,j}^k(t)$ is the probability that ant k chooses edge $l_{i,j}$ at iteration t;

- J^k is the list of cities ant k has yet to visit;

- $\tau_{i,j}^\alpha(t)$ is the intensity of the pheromone trail of edge $l_{i,j}$ at iteration t;

- $\eta_{i,j} = 1/d_{i,j}$ is the heuristic desirability of going from city i directly to city j. $d_{i,j}$ is never zero, since there is no path from a city to itself.

- α and β are parameters that respectively define the relative importance of τ and η.

The ant keeps adding cities to its candidate solution until all cities have been visited only once and the ant returns to the city where it started. After all ants have built their candidate solutions S^k, the quantity of pheromone on edge $l_{i,j}$ is updated according to

$$\tau_{i,j}(t+1) = (1-\rho) \cdot \tau_{i,j}(t) + \sum_{k=1}^m \Delta\tau_{i,j}^k, \quad \forall(i,j) \in S^k \tag{4.2}$$

with

$$\Delta\tau_{i,j}^k = \begin{cases} \frac{1}{L^k} & if\ l_{i,j} \in S^k \\ 0 & otherwise \end{cases} \tag{4.3}$$

where,

- m is the total number of ants.

- $0 < \rho \leq 1$ is the evaporation rate of the pheromone;

- $\Delta\tau_{i,j}^k$ is the quantity of pheromone that is to be deposited on edge $l_{i,j}$ by the kth ant;

- S^k is the solution found by the kth ant.

- L^k is the length of solution S^k, computed as the sum of the lengths of all arcs $l_{i,j} \in S^k$.

The AS Parameters. The parameters that the user must tune are

- m - the number of ants;

- ρ - the decay rate of the pheromones

- α - the importance given to the quantity of pheromones on a given edge (see (4.1)).

- β - the importance given to the quality of a given edge (see (4.1))

The Elitist AS

The Elitist AS is a powerful extension of the AS algorithm. The extension makes use of the idea of elitism discussed in Section 3.8 to increase the desirability of the arcs belonging to the best solution found since the start of the optimization process. This is accomplished by adding more pheromones to those arcs. The pheromone update equation becomes

$$\tau_{i,j}(t+1) = (1-\rho) \cdot \tau_{i,j}(t) + \sum_{k=1}^{m} \Delta\tau_{i,j}^k + w\Delta\tau_{i,j}^\star \tag{4.4}$$

where $\Delta\tau_{i,j}^k$ is defined as in equation (4.3), w is a user-defined parameter that defines the weight given to the best solution so far $S^\star$ with corresponding length $L^\star$, and $\Delta\tau_{i,j}^\star$ is given by

$$\Delta\tau_{i,j}^\star = \begin{cases} \frac{1}{L^\star} & if \ l_{i,j} \in S^\star \\ 0 & otherwise \end{cases} \tag{4.5}$$

Though equation (4.5) features only one elite solution $S^\star$, the Elitist AS usually allows more than one elite solution. The smaller this number, the more elitist the algorithm becomes. The code for the Elitist AS algorithm is presented in the following listings.

Listing 4.1 shows how to code the graph object that is used to represent the TSP problem. The architecture of the graph as well as the cost of each edge is coded in the *cost_matrix* parameter. The only method that the graph object has is *calc_path_cost*, which is responsible for calculating the cost of the path it receives as formal parameter.

```
#    -------------------------------------------------
# Graph - class that implements the graph where the
# search occurs
#    -------------------------------------------------
# file: graph.py
#    -------------------------------------------------
class Graph(object):
    def __init__(self, cost_matrix):#, rank: int):
        self.cost_matrix = cost_matrix
        self.n_nodes = len(cost_matrix)

    # calculate the cost of a given solution
```

```
13    def calc_path_cost(self, path):
14        total_cost = 0
15        for edge in path:
16            total_cost += self.cost_matrix[edge]
17        return total_cost
```

Listing 4.1: TSP graph used by the Elitist AS algorithm.

The ants are implemented according to Listing 4.2. Ants are responsible for creating candidate solutions. An ant selects its path according to the probabilities given by (4.1), they thus must have access to the graph object, to the *pheromone matrix* and to the parameters α and β of the ACO. An ant must also know where it is initially placed in the graph, that is why they receive parameter start_node.

```
 1 # -----------------------------------------------------
 2 #                      Ant
 3 # Class that implements the artificial ants used by elitist_AS
 4 # -----------------------------------------------------
 5 # file: ant.py
 6 # -----------------------------------------------------
 7 from numpy.random import choice as np_choice
 8 import numpy as np
 9 # -----------------------------------------------------
10 class Ant(object):
11     def __init__(self,start_node, graph, pheromone_matrix,
12                  alpha, beta   ):
13        self.pheromone_matrix = pheromone_matrix
14        self.graph = graph
15        self.start_node = start_node
16        self.alpha = alpha
17        self.beta = beta
18        # consistency check for the start_node parameter
19        if start_node <0 or start_node > (graph.n_nodes - 1):
20            print("start node must be in [0,{}]".format(graph.
    n_nodes-1))
21            exit()
22
23        # ---------------------------------------------------
24        # Select an edge that leads to a non-visited node
25        # ---------------------------------------------------
26     def select_edge(self, edges_pheromone, edges_costs, visited):
27        pheromone = np.copy(edges_pheromone)
28        # zeroes the probability of revisiting a node
29        pheromone[list(visited)] = 0
30        # probability of selecting each edge that leads
31        # to a non-visited node
32        row = (pheromone ** self.alpha) * \
33              (( 1.0 / edges_costs) ** self.beta)
34        prob_edges = row / row.sum()
35        # selects an edge
36        move = np_choice(range(self.graph.n_nodes),
37                         1, p=prob_edges)[0]
38        return move
39        # ---------------------------------------------------
40        # Generate a single round-trip path starting in the
```

```
41    # node defined by variable start_node
42    # ---------------------------------------------------
43    def gen_path(self):
44        path = []
45        # create a set for storing the cities
46        # already visited
47        visited = set()
48        # add the initial city to the set
49        visited.add(self.start_node)
50        # store the current position of the ant
51        prev = self.start_node
52        for i in range(self.graph.n_nodes - 1):
53            # select an edge to a non-visited node
54            edge = self.select_edge(
55                self.pheromone_matrix[prev],
56                self.graph.cost_matrix[prev], visited)
57            # add the selected path to the solution
58            # being constructed
59            path.append((prev, edge))
60            # move the ant to the city at the end
61            # of the chosen path
62            prev = edge
63            # mark the current position of the and
64            # as visited
65            visited.add(edge)
66        # going back to where the ant started
67        path.append((prev, self.start_node))
68        return path
```

Listing 4.2: Ants used by the Elitist AS algorithm.

The Elitist AS algorithm is implemented in Listing 4.3. It is in the *run* method that the algorithm performs the optimization. It starts by instantiating n_{ants} ants, who produce n_{ants} candidate solutions. Then it allows the pheromones on all edges to evaporate and then spreads pheromones on the edges that were part of the candidate solutions. These two operations are performed according to (4.4). The method also keeps track of the best solution found so far.

```
 1 # ---------------------------------------------------
 2 #               elitist_AS
 3 #   Class that implements the elitist_AS algorithm "elitist
 4 #   ant system" version
 5 # ---------------------------------------------------
 6 # Inputs:
 7 #   graph          - Graph of the TSP problem
 8 #   start_node     - Start node for all ants
 9 #   n_ants         - Number of ants
10 #   n_best         - number of elite solutions
11 #   n_iterations   - Number of optimization iterations
12 #   rho            - pheromone evaporation rate
13 #   alpha          - importance of the distance between
                         cities
14 #   beta           - importance of the pheromone trail
15 #   w              - weight for the extra pheromone deposit
16 #                      for elite solutions
```

```
17 # Outputs:
18 #   all_time_cheapest_path - shortest path found
19 # ------------------------------------------------------
20 #   Implemented as a minimization algorithm
21 # ------------------------------------------------------
22 # file: elitist_as.py
23 # ------------------------------------------------------
24 import numpy as np
25 from aco_rep.algs.ant import Ant
26 # ------------------------------------------------------
27 class elitist_AS(object):
28     def __init__(self, graph, start_node, n_ants, n_best,
        n_iterations, rho, alpha, beta, w):
29         self.graph = graph
30         self.costs = graph.cost_matrix
31         self.start_node = start_node
32         self.n_ants = n_ants
33         self.n_best = n_best
34         self.n_iterations = n_iterations
35         self.rho = rho
36         self.alpha = alpha
37         self.beta = beta
38         self.w    = w
39         # uniform distribution of pheromones
40         self.pheromone_matrix = np.ones(self.costs.shape)
41     # ------------------------------------------------------
42     # Perform the optimization
43     # ------------------------------------------------------
44     def run(self):
45         # storage for the all-time best solution
46         all_time_cheapest_path = [[], np.inf]
47         for i in range(self.n_iterations):
48             # generate candidate solutions
49             candidate_sols = self.gen_candidate_solutions()
50             # decay pheromone level on all edges
51             self.pheromone_matrix = (1-self.rho)* \
52                     self.pheromone_matrix
53             # add pheromone to the arcs that comprise all
54             # candidate solutions
55             self.update_pheromone(candidate_sols,
56                     self.n_ants, w = 1.0)
57             # reinforce pheromone on the arcs that comprise
58             # the elite candidate solutions
59             self.update_pheromone(candidate_sols,
60                     self.n_best, w = self.w)
61             # find the candidate solution with best cost
62             cheapest_path = min(candidate_sols,
63                             key=lambda x: x[1])
64             # update the best solution found so far
65             if cheapest_path[1] < all_time_cheapest_path[1]:
66                 all_time_cheapest_path = cheapest_path
67         # return the best solution found
68         return all_time_cheapest_path
69     # ------------------------------------------------------
70     # Update the pheromone intensity for the paths that
71     # comprise candidate solutions
72     # ------------------------------------------------------
```

```
73  def update_pheromone(self, candidate_sols, n_sols,w):
74      # sort paths in ascending order of path cost
75      sorted_paths = sorted(candidate_sols, key=lambda x: x[1])
76      # the pheromone trail is updated only for
77      # the n_sols paths
78      for path, dist in sorted_paths[:n_sols]:
79          # for each edge in the path
80          for edge in path:
81              # update the pheromone quantity
82              self.pheromone_matrix[edge] = \
83                  self.pheromone_matrix[edge] + \
84                  (w / self.costs[edge])
85  # -----------------------------------------------------
86  # Generate one candidate solution for each ant
87  # -----------------------------------------------------
88  def gen_candidate_solutions(self):
89      all_paths = []
90      # for each ant
91      for i in range(self.n_ants):
92          ant = Ant(start_node=self.start_node,
93                    graph = self.graph,
94                    pheromone_matrix = self.pheromone_matrix,
95                    alpha = self.alpha, beta = self.beta)
96          # generate a round-trip path
97          # starting in the first node
98          path = ant.gen_path()
99          # add the round-trip path to
100         # the set of candidate soutions
101         all_paths.append((path,
102                 self.graph.calc_path_cost(path)))
103     # returns the set of new candidate solutions
104     return all_paths
```

Listing 4.3: Python code for the Elitist AS algorithm.

Example 5 *Let us show how to use the Elitist AS code to solve the TSP problem shown in Figure 4.1. As the number of feasible solutions is small, it is possible to enumerate them and calculate their costs, as done bellow. It is thus possible to check if the algorithm will return one of the two best answers.*

$$S_1 = (A, B, C, D, A)$$
$$S_2 = (A, B, D, C, A)$$
$$S_3 = (A, C, B, D, A)$$
$$S_4 = (A, C, D, B, A)$$
$$S_5 = (A, D, B, C, A)$$
$$S_6 = (A, D, C, B, A)$$

$$f(S_1) = 35$$
$$f(S_2) = 29$$
$$f(S_3) = 38$$
$$f(S_4) = 29$$
$$f(S_5) = 38$$
$$f(S_6) = 35$$

To use the algorithm, the first step is to define a graph that represents the TSP. To this end, write a square matrix where each line corresponds to one of the cities (line 1 corresponds to city A, line 2 to city B, etc). Each row also corresponds to one city, such that position (i, j) of the matrix corresponds to the length (cost) of the edge that links city i to city j. The matrix is thus:

$$\begin{bmatrix} \infty & 9 & 11 & 7 \\ 9 & \infty & 15 & 5 \\ 11 & 15 & \infty & 4 \\ 7 & 5 & 4 & \infty \end{bmatrix}$$

where the infinite values in the main diagonal mean that there are no edges that link a city to herself. Once the matrix of distances is written, just define values for the parameters needed by the algorithm, as show in Listing 4.4.

```
1  # -----------------------------------------------------------
2  #         elitist_AS Solves TSP with 4 Cities
3  # -----------------------------------------------------------
4  # file: run_elitist_as_4_cities.py
5  # -----------------------------------------------------------
6
7  import numpy as np
8  from aco_rep.algs.elitist_as import elitist_AS
9  from aco_rep.graph import Graph
10
11 # 1 - Write the matrix of costs
12 # The cost of going from a city to herself
13 # is infinite, meaning that  there is no
14 # edge linking a city to herself
15 cost_matrix = np.array([[np.inf, 9, 11, 7],
16                         [9, np.inf, 15, 5],
17                         [11, 15, np.inf, 4],
18                         [7, 5, 4, np.inf]])
19
20 # 2 - Instantiate the graph
21 graph = Graph(cost_matrix=cost_matrix)
22 # 3 - Instantiate the elitist_AS
23 node_0 = 0        # start at city A (Python starts enumerating with
                        zero)
24 n_ants = 20       # number of antes
25 n_best = 2        # number of best candidate solutions that get
26                   # extra pheromone deposit
27 w = 0.1           # weight for the extra pheromone deposit on
28                   # the paths of the elite solutions
29 n_gen = 50        # number of generations of ants
```

```
30 rho = 0.5         # pheromone evaporation rate
31 alpha = 0.5       # importance of pheromone level on an edge on an
32                   # ant's decision to pick the path
33 beta = 0.5        # importance of the cost of an edge on an ant's
34                   # decision to pick the path
35 aco = elitist_AS(graph, node_0, n_ants, n_best, n_gen,
36                  rho, alpha=alpha, beta=beta, w = w)
37 # 4 - Solve the problem
38 shortest_path = aco.run()
39 # 5 - Print the results
40 print ("shorted_path: {}".format(shortest_path))
```

Listing 4.4: Using Elitist AS to solve the TSP.

4.2   Particle Swarm Optimization

The PSO [48] algorithm is a single-objective population-based metaheuristic inspired by the collective behavior of birds in their search for food or for shelter, designed to handle optimization problems with continuous search spaces. PSO makes almost no assumptions about the optimization problem and has the ability to search very large spaces using distributed candidate solutions called *particles*.

Particles are stochastic procedures that simulate birds working together in a flock in the search for food or for shelter. PSO simulates some of the benefits that birds obtain when they join a flock, such as the fact that more ears and eyes increase the chance of finding food. The disadvantages of being in a flock, such as the fact that a larger flock requires more food and thus increases the competition between individuals, perhaps resulting in the death of some weaker birds, are not simulated. In PSO, weaker individuals do not die, as they do in genetic algorithms. The initial population of particles survives until the end of the optimization process, with particles trying to make themselves stronger with each generation.

The PSO Algorithm

At any given iteration k, the ith particle has position $\mathbf{x}_i^k$ and velocity $\mathbf{v}_i^k$, with position $\mathbf{x}_i^k$ representing a candidate solution to the problem. Each particle keeps track of the best solution it has found so far, $\mathbf{pbest}_i^k$, and of the global best (the best solution found so far by the successive populations), $\mathbf{gbest}^k$.

The movement of the particles in the search space is controlled by the velocity vector. The velocity of the ith particle at iteration $k+1$ is given by

$$\mathbf{v}_i^{k+1} = w\mathbf{v}_i^k + c_1 r_1 \left(\mathbf{pbest}_i^k - \mathbf{x}_i^k \right) + c_2 r_2 \left(\mathbf{gbest}^k - \mathbf{x}_i^k \right), \qquad (4.6)$$

where term $w\mathbf{v}_i^k$ accounts for the inertia of the particle, term $c_1 r_1 \left(\mathbf{pbest}_i^k - \mathbf{x}_i^k \right)$ accounts for the role of the memory of the individual (the particle is attracted to the best position it found) and term $c_2 r_2 \left(\mathbf{gbest}^k - \mathbf{x}_i^k \right)$ accounts for the role of cooperation between particles (the particle is attracted to the best solution found by the swarm). Constants c_1 and c_2 are respectively called *cognitive* and *social* scaling parameters or simply *acceleration coefficients*, while r_1 and r_2 are random numbers in the range $[0, 1]$ drawn from a uniform distribution. The inertia weight w parameter was introduced by [76]. To get the original PSO of [48], just put $w = 1$.

Allowing a particle to move at unbounded speeds may be harmful to the optimization process, because the particle can jump erratically in the search space without being able to explore its vicinity. It is good practice to impose upper and lower bounds on the velocity vector as well as on the particle position.

After updating the velocity, the position of the particle is updated according to

$$\mathbf{x}_i^{k+1} = \mathbf{x}_i^k + \mathbf{v}_i^{k+1}. \tag{4.7}$$

The complete pseudocode of the modified PSO [76] is given in Algorithm 4.2.

Algorithm 4.2. Particle Swam Optimization

1: **procedure** PSO
2:     $N \leftarrow$ number of particles
3:     $w \leftarrow$ velocity inertia
4:     $c_1 \leftarrow$ cognitive scaling parameter
5:     $c_2 \leftarrow$ social scaling parameter
6:     Create a population of N random particles
7:     **while** termination criterion not satisfied **do**
8:         **for** each of the N particles **do**
9:             Update the particle velocity using equation 4.6
10:            Bound the particle velocity
11:            Update the particle position using equation 4.7
12:            Bound the particle position
13:        **end for**
14:        **for** each of the N particles **do**
15:            Calculate the fitness value of the particle
16:            Update *pbest* if required
17:            Update *gbest* if required
18:        **end for**
19:     **end while**
20:     return *pbest* and *gbest*
21: **end procedure**

Parameter w. Parameter w tunes the balance between exploration and exploitation. The past velocity $\mathbf{v}_i^k$ serves as a memory of the previous direction of movement, thus higher values of w favor exploitation. Parameter w is usually linearly decreased from 0.9 to 0.4 as the optimization advances.

Parameter c_1. This parameter controls the intensity with which the particle is attracted towards its personal best position. Higher values of c_1 reinforce the memory of a particle's best position and thus prevents it from wandering.

Parameter c_2**.** This parameter controls the sharing of information between particles. Higher c_2 values reinforce the attraction towards the best particle found by the swarm, meaning that each particle learns more from others in the swarm.

Python Listing

A Python implementation of the modified PSO algorithm for maximization is given in Listing 4.5.

```
 1 # --------------------------------------------------------
 2 #                    PSO
 3 #         Particle Swarm Optimization
 4 # --------------------------------------------------------
 5 #   Implemented as a Maximization Algorithm
 6 # --------------------------------------------------------
 7 # Inputs:
 8 # fit         - function to be maximized
 9 # maxiters    - maximum number of optimization iterations
10 # lb          - lower bound vector for solutions
11 # ub          - upper bound vector for solutions
12 # noP         - number of particles
13 # c1          - cognitive scaling
14 # c2          - social scaling
15 # w_min       - minimum value for the velocity inertia
16 # w_max       - maximum value for the velocity inertia
17 # Outputs:
18 #    gbest_pos   - global best position found
19 #    gbest_val   - fit(gbest_pos)
20 #    gbest_val_h - history of global best values
21 # --------------------------------------------------------
22 # file: pso.py
23 # --------------------------------------------------------
24 import math
25 import numpy as np
26 # --------------------------------------------------------
27 def pso(fit, maxiters, lb, ub, noP, c1, c2, w_min, w_max):
28     # Dimensionality of the search space
29     nVar = len(lb)
30     # Maximum and minimum values for the particles' velocities
31     vMax = np.multiply((ub - lb), 0.2)
32     vMin = -vMax
33     # Initialize the inertia parameter
34     w = w_max
35
36     # Storage for position and velocity of particles
37     position = np.zeros((noP,nVar))
38     velocity = np.zeros((noP, nVar))
39
40     # Storage for the individual best and the global best
       solutions
41     pbest_pos = np.zeros((noP,nVar))
42     pbest_val = np.zeros(noP)
43
44     # Initialization of particles
45     for k in range(noP):
46         # Random position within [lb, ub]
```

```
47      position[k] = np.multiply((ub - lb),
48                                np.random.rand(nVar)) + lb
49      # Zero initial velocity
50      velocity[k] = np.zeros((1, nVar))
51      # All-Zero individual best solutions
52      pbest_pos[k] = np.zeros((1, nVar))
53      # Minus infinity value for the initial individual best
54      # solution
55      pbest_val[k] = -math.inf # for maximization
56
57  # Global best found so far
58  gbest_pos = np.zeros(nVar)
59  gbest_val = -math.inf # for maximization
60  gbest_val_h = np.zeros((maxiters, nVar)) # stores the global
    best at each iteration
61
62  # main loop
63  for id_iter in range(maxiters):
64      for k in range(noP):
65          # Update particle velocity
66          r1 = np.random.rand( nVar)
67          r2 = np.random.rand(nVar)
68          velocity[k] = w * velocity[k] + \
69                      np.multiply(c1,np.multiply( r1,
70                              (pbest_pos[k] - position[k]))) \
71                      + np.multiply(c2,np.multiply(r2,
72                              (gbest_pos - position[k])))
73          # Bound velocity
74          index1 = np.where(velocity[k] > vMax)
75          index2 = np.where(velocity[k] < vMin)
76          if np.array(index1).size>0:
77              velocity[k][index1] = vMax[index1]
78          if np.array(index2).size>0:
79              velocity[k][index2] = vMin[index2]
80          # Update particle position
81          position[k] = position[k] + velocity[k]
82          # Bound position
83          index1 = np.where(position[k] > ub)
84          index2 = np.where(position[k] < lb)
85          if np.array(index1).size > 0:
86              position[k][index1] = ub[index1]
87          if np.array(index2).size > 0:
88              position[k][index2] = lb[index2]
89
90      for k in range(noP):
91          # calculate the objective value of the k-th particle
92          current_pos = position[k]
93          current_val = fit(current_pos)
94          # Update pbest - maximization
95          if current_val > pbest_val[k]:
96              pbest_pos[k] = current_pos
97              pbest_val[k] = current_val
98          # Update gbest - maximization
99          if current_val > gbest_val:
100             gbest_pos = current_pos
101             gbest_val = current_val
102     # store the global best of the current iteration
```

```
103    gbest_val_h[id_iter] = gbest_val
104    # Update w
105    w = w_max - id_iter * ((w_max - w_min) / maxiters)
106  # Return the global best solution found
107  return gbest_pos, gbest_val, gbest_val_h
```

Listing 4.5: Modified PSO algorithm.

Example 6 *This example shows how to use PSO to minimize a real-valued 20-dimensional sphere (3.2). The first thing to do is write the objective function and the fitness function. These are the same functions already discussed in Section 3.3, whose codes are respectively shown in Listing 3.4 and Listing 3.5.*

After that, just write a piece of code to properly call the PSO algorithm, as given in Listing 4.6. The code in the end of the program is just for plotting the convergence curve shown in Figure 4.2. It is not necessary to solve the problem.

```
1  # -----------------------------------------------------
2  #      PSO Algorithm Minimizing a Sphere
3  # -----------------------------------------------------
4  # file: fig_pso_sphere.py
5  # -----------------------------------------------------
6  # Import the necessary libraries and functions
7  import numpy as np
8  from pso_rep.pso import pso
9  import matplotlib.pyplot as plt
10 from fitnessf_max.fitnessf_sphere_rv import \
11     fitness_sphere_rv
12 # -----------------------------------------------------
13 # Plot the convergence curve
14 # -----------------------------------------------------
15 def plot_convergence_curve(fig_name,title_str,fbest_h,
16                            fig_size_x = 8,fig_size_y = 4,
17                            dpi=1000):
18     num_vals = len(fbest_h)
19     t = np.linspace(0, num_vals-1, num_vals)
20     fig, ax = plt.subplots(figsize=(fig_size_x,fig_size_y),
21                            dpi=dpi) # figura 800x600 pixels
22     ax.plot(t, fbest_h,c='0.35')
23     #ax.set_xlabel(r'$\mathit{iteration}$', fontsize=18)
24     #ax.set_ylabel(r'$f_o$', fontsize=18)
25     ax.set_xlabel(r'$\mathit{iteration}$')
26     ax.set_ylabel(r'$f_o$')
27     ax.set_title(title_str)
28     ax.grid(True)
29     plt.savefig(fig_name,format="eps",dpi=dpi)
30 # -----------------------------------------------------
31 # Minimization
32 # -----------------------------------------------------
33 # 1 - Define the upper and lower bounds of the search space
34 ndim = 20                # Number of dimensions of the problem
35 lb = -5*np.ones(ndim)    # Bounds of the search space
36 ub = 5*np.ones(ndim)
37
38 # 2 - Define the parameters for the optimization
39 noP = 50         # Number of particles
```

```
40 maxIters = 300  # Number of optimization iterations
41
42 # 3 - Parameters for the PSO
43 c1 = np.ones(ndim)  # Cognitive scaling parameter
44 c2 = np.ones(ndim)  # Social scaling parameter
45 w_min = 0.4*np.ones(ndim) # Minimum inertia
46 w_max = 0.9*np.ones(ndim) # Maximum inertia
47
48 # 4 - Define the cost function
49 fcost = fitness_sphere_rv
50
51 # 5 - Run the PSO algorithm
52 np.random.seed(123)
53 xbest, fbest, fbest_h = pso(fcost,maxIters,lb,ub,noP,c1,c2,w_min,
     w_max)
54
55 # 6 - Print the results
56 print('xbest: {}'.format(xbest))
57 print('fbest: {}'.format(fbest))
58
59 # 7 - Plot the convergence curve-------------------------
60 from auxiliary.plot_convergence_curve \
61     import plot_convergence_curve
62 fig_file= 'figure_4_2.eps'
63
64 title_str=\
65 "PSO Minimizing a " + str(ndim) + "-dimensional Sphere"
66 plot_convergence_curve(fig_file,title_str,fbest_h)
```

Listing 4.6: Minimization of a 20-d sphere function with PSO.

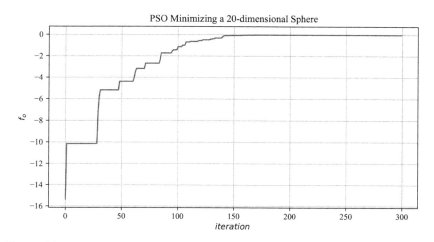

Figure 4.2: Convergence curve of PSO solving the real-valued sphere function (see (3.2)).

Chapter 5

Evolution Strategies

Evolution Strategies (ES) [70] is a class of evolutionary optimization algorithms that rely on stochastic variations and selection mechanisms to generate candidate solutions. In each iteration, members of the current population are selected to be the parents of the next generation. These parents undergo stochastic variations, generating new candidate solutions. The fitness of the new candidate solutions is obtained and the fittest candidate solutions are selected to become the parents of the next generation. This process is repeated until some stopping criterion is met, such as reaching a given number of generations or of evaluations of the fitness function.

Evolution strategies were developed to address the problem of continuous optimization. As other evolutionary algorithms, ES algorithms make no specific assumptions about the fitness function. It is only necessary that the fitness function can be evaluated at each possible candidate solution. According to [64], one iteration of an ES algorithm performs the following general steps:

1. A number of individuals of the current population are selected to be parents.

2. New candidate solutions are generated by duplication and recombination of the parents

3. The new candidate solutions undergo mutation and are introduced in the current population.

4. The population is reduced to its original size by environmental selection.

The environmental selection step is deterministic and is based on the fitness ranking of the individuals. It is carried out by allowing only a fixed number of the highest-fitness individuals to survive, keeping the population size constant. Environmental selection can also eliminate "old" individuals from the population.

5.1 Recombination Operators

In Evolution Srategies (ES) algorithms, the crossover (recombination) operation usually takes information from two or more parents to produce a single offspring. The main recombination operators used in ES algorithms are discrete recombination, intermediate recombination and weighted recombination. They are described below and their Python implementations are shown in Listing 5.1.

Discrete recombination

Each gene from the offspring is inherited from a parent which is selected uniformly from a population of ρ parents. [64] stresses that the role of recombination is to keep genetic diversity in the population high. Discrete recombination, as stated, depends on the coordinate system of the search space. As a result, it relies on separability to successfully introduce genetic variation in the population. In other words, it can introduce variation only if the variables that comprise the search space are not heavily dependent on each other.

Intermediate recombination

A child is produced by averaging the values of the genes of a population of ρ parents. In other words, each gene of the child is the average of the same genes of all ρ parents.

Weighted recombination

A child is produced by a weighted average of the values of the genes of a population of ρ parents. The weights are directly proportional to the fitness rankings of the parents. If all weights are equal, then weighted recombination becomes intermediate recombination.

```
1 # ------------------------------------------------------------
2 #              es_select_recombine
3 # Produces a single child through selection and
4 # recombination of two parents from the population
5 # ------------------------------------------------------------
6 # Inputs:
7 #    pop_chrom  - individuals that form the population
8 #    pop_std    - standard deviations of the individuals
9 #    popSize    - number of individuals in the population
10 #    numVar     - number of dimensions of an individual
11 #    cType      - type of recombination desired
12 # Outputs:
13 #    child_chrom - resulting offspring
14 #    child_std   - std of the resulting offspring
15 # ------------------------------------------------------------
16 # file: select_recombine.py
17 # ------------------------------------------------------------
18 import numpy as np
19 # ------------------------------------------------------------
20 def es_select_recombine(pop_chrom, pop_std, popsize,
21                         numVar, cType):
```

```python
child_chrom = np.zeros(numVar)
child_std = np.zeros(numVar)

p = np.zeros(2, dtype = int)
if cType == 1:
    # Randomly select two parents from the entire population
    p[0] = np.random.randint(popsize)
    p[1] = np.random.randint(popsize)

    # "Discrete Sexual Crossover"
    # Each solution feature and standard
    # deviation in the child is randomly
    # selected from one of two parents
    for i in range(numVar):
        ind_p1 = np.random.randint(1)
        ind_p2 = np.random.randint(1)
        child_chrom[i] = pop_chrom[p[ind_p1]][i]
        child_std[i] = pop_std[p[ind_p2]][i]

elif cType == 2:
    # Randomly select two parents from
    # the entire population
    p[0] = np.random.randint(popsize)
    p[1] = np.random.randint(popsize)

    # Intermediate Sexual Crossover
    # Each solution feature and
    # standard deviation is the mean
    # of the corresponding feature/standard
    # deviation of the two parents
    for i in range(numVar):
        child_chrom[i] = np.mean([pop_chrom[p[0]][i],
                                  pop_chrom[p[1]][i]])
        child_std[i] = np.mean([pop_std[p[0]][i],
                                pop_std[p[1]][i]])

elif cType == 3:
    # Discrete Global Crossover
    # Each solution feature and standard
    # deviation in the child is randomly
    # selected from the entire population
    for i in range(numVar):
        # Randomly select two parents from t
        # he entire population
        p[0] = np.random.randint(popsize)
        p[1] = np.random.randint(popsize)

        # Produce one child by randomly picking
        # genes and std from one
        # of the selected parents
        child_chrom[i] = \
            pop_chrom[p[np.random.randint(1)]][i]
        child_std[i] = \
            pop_std[p[np.random.randint(1)]][i]

elif cType == 4:
    # Intermediate Global Crossover
```

```
79      # Each solution feature and standard
80      # deviation in the child is the mean
81      # of the corresponding feature
82      # and standard deviation of parents
83      # that are randomly selected
84      # from the entire population
85      for i in range(numVar):
86          # Randomly select two parents from the entire
    population
87          p[0] = np.random.randint(popsize)
88          p[1] = np.random.randint(popsize)
89          # Produce child by averaging the i-th gene from both
    parents
90          child_chrom[i] = np.mean([pop_chrom[p[0]][i],
91                                    pop_chrom[p[1]][i]])
92          child_std[i] = np.mean([pop_std[p[0]][i],
93                                  pop_std[p[1]][i]])
94
95  else:
96      print('crossover type not implemented')
97      exit()
98
99  return child_chrom, child_std
```

Listing 5.1: Recombination operators for ES algorithms.

Before proceeding, it is important to note that other recombination operators, such as those described in Section 3.6.2, can also be used in ES algorithms.

5.2 Mutation Operators

Mutation introduces variations by adding to the individuals perturbations which are drawn from a multivariate normal distribution $\mathcal{N}(\mathbf{0}, \mathbf{C})$, with covariance matrix $\mathbf{C} \in \mathbb{R}^{n \times n}$. The form of the covariance matrix determines the form of the perturbation.

Isotropic Mutation

If the covariance matrix is proportional to the identity matrix, the perturbation is said to be isotropic or spherical, and the mutation operation is given by $\sigma \mathcal{N}(\mathbf{0}, \mathbf{I})$, where $\sigma > 0$. The resulting distribution is spherical, as seen in Figure 5.1, and thus invariant to rotations around its mean.

Diagonal Mutation

If the covariance matrix is diagonal, the mutation distribution is given by $\mathcal{N}(\mathbf{0}, \text{diag}(\boldsymbol{\sigma})^2)$, where $\boldsymbol{\sigma}$ is a vector of coordinate-wise standard deviations and $\text{diag}(\boldsymbol{\sigma})$ is a diagonal matrix. Samples from a diagonal mutation are shown in Figure 5.2.

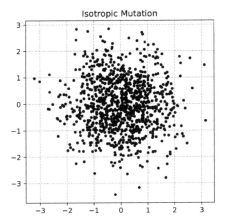

Figure 5.1: Isotropic mutation.

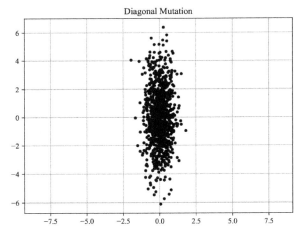

Figure 5.2: Diagonal mutation.

General Mutation

In this case the covariance matrix is symmetric and positive definite. The isotropic and the diagonal mutations are thus particular cases of the general mutation. A Python implementation of the general mutation operator is shown in Listing 5.2. Samples from a general mutation are shown in Figure 5.3.

```
1 # ----------------------------------------------------------
2 #              general_mutation
3 # Perform a general mutation on an individual
4 # ----------------------------------------------------------
5 # Inputs:
6 #   theta  - individual
7 #   cov    - covariance matrix of the mutation
8 # Outputs:
```

```
 9 #   theta  - mutated individual
10 #   ------------------------------------------------------------
11 # file: mutation_general.py
12 #   ------------------------------------------------------------
13 import numpy as np
14 #   ------------------------------------------------------------
15 def general_mutation(theta, cov):
16     # dimensionality
17     nVar = np.shape(theta)[0]
18     # perform mutation
19     theta = theta + np.random.multivariate_normal(np.zeros(nVar),
       cov)
20     # return mutated individual
21     return theta
```

Listing 5.2: Mutation operator for ES algorithms.

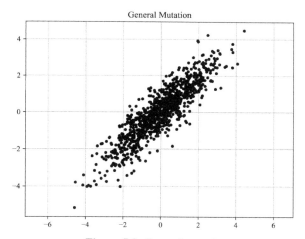

Figure 5.3: General mutation.

The following sections describe a number of ES algorithms, in increasing order of complexity. They all feature a group of important parameters that mark differences between them. These parameters are μ, ρ and λ, where

- μ is the number of individuals in the parent population,

- ρ is the number of individuals of the parent population that are selected for recombination,

- λ is the number of offspring generated in each iteration.

5.3 The $(1+1)$ ES

The first ES algorithm for continuous search spaces [8] consisted of just one parent and one child. Is was a simple random search powered by isotropic perturbations (the mutation of each element of $\mathbf{x}_p$ has the same variance), as seen in Algorithm 5.1. Variance σ^2 is the tuning parameter of the algorithm. Higher values of σ^2 increase the chances of creating individuals that span more areas of the search space, while lower values of σ^2 allow the algorithm to concentrate the search near a promising individual.

Algorithm 5.1. $(1+1)$ ES

1: **procedure** $(1+1)$ ES
2:     Initialize the non-negative mutation standard deviation σ
3:     Randomly generate individual $\mathbf{x}_p \in \mathbb{R}^n$
4:     $f_p \leftarrow$ fitness value of $\mathbf{x}_p$
5:     **while** termination criterion not satisfied **do**
6:         Generate a random perturbation $\mathbf{r} \sim \sigma \mathcal{N}(\mathbf{0}, \mathbf{I})$, with $\mathbf{r} \in \mathbb{R}^n$
7:         $\mathbf{x}_c = \mathbf{x}_p + \mathbf{r}$
8:         $f_c \leftarrow$ fitness value of $\mathbf{x}_c$
9:         **if** $f_c < f_p$ **then**
10:             $\mathbf{x}_p \leftarrow \mathbf{x}_c$
11:             $\mathbf{f}_p \leftarrow \mathbf{f}_c$
12:         **end if**
13:     **end while**
14:     return $\mathbf{x}_p$
15: **end procedure**

Algorithm 5.1 is implemented in Listing 5.3.

```
1
2 # ------------------------------------------------------------------
3 # (1 + 1)  ES
4 # ------------------------------------------------------------------
5 #  Implemented as a minimization algorithm
6 # ------------------------------------------------------------------
7 # Inputs:
8 #    loss      - function to be minimized
9 #    theta     - initial guess for the mean of the search
10 #                distribution
11 #    maxIters - maximum number of optimization iterations
12 #    lb        - n-dimensional vector lower bound on solutions
13 #    ub        - n-dimensional vector upper bound on solutions
14 # Outputs:
15 #    best_theta  - best solution found
16 #    best_scores - history of best scores
17 # ------------------------------------------------------------------
18 # file: one_plus_one_es.py
19 # ------------------------------------------------------------------
20 import numpy as np
21 from es_rep.utils.adjust_to_range import es_adjust_to_range
22 # ------------------------------------------------------------------
23 def one_plus_one_es(loss,theta,maxIterations,lb,ub):
24     ## Settings
```

```
25    numVar   = np.shape(theta)[0]   # problem dimension
26    minDomain = lb
27    maxDomain = ub
28    ## Population
29    pop_chrom = theta
30    ## Compute the cost of each member in Population
31    pop_cost = loss(pop_chrom)
32    ## Initialize the standard deviation
33    pop_std = np.random.rand(numVar)
34
35    ## Optimization
36    # Begin the optimization loop:
37    for id_iter in range(maxIterations):
38        # Generate an isotropic perturbation
39        r = pop_std * np.random.randn(numVar)
40        # Perform mutation
41        child_chrom = pop_chrom + r
42        # Keep child within the search region
43        child_chrom = es_adjust_to_range(child_chrom,
44                                         minDomain, maxDomain)
45        # Calculate the cost of the child
46        child_cost = loss(child_chrom)
47        # Check for improvements
48        if child_cost < pop_cost:
49            # Update the best individual found
50            pop_chrom = child_chrom
51            pop_cost = child_cost
52
53        # Store minimum cost and best solution
54        if id_iter == 0:
55            minCost = np.array([pop_cost])
56            bestSol = np.array([pop_chrom])
57        else:
58            minCost = np.vstack((minCost,pop_cost))
59            bestSol = np.vstack((bestSol,pop_chrom))
60
61    ind_best = np.argmin(minCost)
62    best_theta = bestSol[ind_best]
63    best_scores = minCost
64    return best_theta, best_scores
```

Listing 5.3: $(1+1)$ ES.

1/5th Rule

The performance of the above algorithm can be improved by the 1/5th rule, proposed by ([70],[4]), which states that if the ratio of successful mutations to total mutations is less than 1/5, then the standard deviation σ should be decreased according to $\sigma \leftarrow c\sigma$. Otherwise, it should be increased according to $\sigma \leftarrow \sigma/c$. In both cases, $c = 0.817$. The $(1+1)$ ES with 1/5th rule can be seen in Algorithm 5.2, where G is a user-defined parameter that defines the length of a moving window that stores the result (success of failure) of the last G mutations.

Algorithm 5.2. $(1+1)$ ES with 1/5th Rule

1: **procedure** $(1+1)$ ES WITH 1/5TH RULE
2:     Initialize the non-negative standard deviation σ
3:     Initialize the ratio of successful mutations on the last G generations $\phi = 0$
4:     Randomly generate individual $\mathbf{x}_p \in \mathbb{R}^n$
5:     $f_p \leftarrow$ fitness value of $\mathbf{x}_p$
6:     **while** termination criterion not satisfied **do**
7:         Generate a random perturbation $\mathbf{r} \sim \sigma \mathcal{N}(\mathbf{0}, \mathbf{I})$, with $\mathbf{r} \in \mathbb{R}^n$
8:         $\mathbf{x}_c = \mathbf{x}_p + \mathbf{r}$
9:         $f_c \leftarrow$ fitness value of $\mathbf{x}_c$
10:         **if** $f_c < f_p$ **then**
11:             $\mathbf{x}_p \leftarrow \mathbf{x}_c$
12:             $\mathbf{f}_p \leftarrow \mathbf{f}_c$
13:             Increase ϕ
14:         **else**
15:             Decrease ϕ
16:         **end if**
17:         **if** $\phi < 1/5$ **then**
18:             $\sigma \leftarrow c\sigma$
19:         **else**
20:             $\sigma \leftarrow \sigma/c$
21:         **end if**
22:     **end while**
23:     return $\mathbf{x}_p$
24: **end procedure**

Algorithm 5.2 is implemented in Listing 5.4.

```
1 # -------------------------------------------------------------
2 # (1 + 1) with 1/5th Rule ES
3 # -------------------------------------------------------------
4 # Implemented as a minimization algorithm
5 # -------------------------------------------------------------
6 # Inputs:
7 #   loss      - function to be minimized
8 #   theta     - initial guess for the mean of the search
9 #                 distribution
10 #   maxIters  - maximum number of optimization iterations
11 #   lb        - n-dimensional vector lower bound on solutions
12 #   ub        - n-dimensional vector upper bound on solutions
13 # Outputs:
14 #   best_theta  - best solution found
15 #   best_scores - history of best scores
16 # -------------------------------------------------------------
17 import numpy as np
18 from es_rep.utils.adjust_to_range import es_adjust_to_range
19 # -------------------------------------------------------------
20 def one_plus_one_es_1_5th(loss, theta, maxIters, lb, ub):
21     ## Settings
22     numVar  = np.shape(theta)[0]   # problem dimension
23     minDomain = lb
```

```
maxDomain = ub
## Population
pop_chrom = theta
## Compute the cost of each member in Population
pop_cost = loss(pop_chrom)
## Initialize the standard deviation
pop_std = np.random.rand(numVar)

## Optimization
# Moving window used in the 1/5 rule
mw_index = 0
mw_length = np.minimum(numVar,30)
successful_mutation = np.zeros(mw_length)

# Begin the optimization loop:
for id_iter in range(maxIters):
    # Generate an isotropic perturbation
    r = pop_std * np.random.randn(numVar)
    # Perform mutation
    child_chrom = pop_chrom + r
    # Keep child within the search region
    child_chrom = es_adjust_to_range(child_chrom,
                                    minDomain, maxDomain)
    # Calculate the cost of the child
    child_cost = loss(child_chrom)
    # Check for improvements
    if child_cost < pop_cost:
        # Update the best individual found
        pop_chrom = child_chrom
        pop_cost = child_cost
        # Count as improvement
        successful_mutation[mw_index] = 1
    else:
        # Count as no improvement
        successful_mutation[mw_index] = 0
    # Update the index used in the moving window
    mw_index = mw_index + 1
    if mw_index >= mw_length:
        mw_index = 0
    # 1/5 rule
    if id_iter >= mw_length:
        successRate = sum(successful_mutation)/mw_length
        if successRate < 1./5.:
            pop_std = 0.817*pop_std
        if successRate > 1./5.:
            pop_std = pop_std/0.817

    # Store minimum cost and best solution
    if id_iter == 0:
        minCost = np.array([pop_cost])
        bestSol = np.array([pop_chrom])
    else:
        minCost = np.vstack((minCost,pop_cost))
        bestSol = np.vstack((bestSol,pop_chrom))

ind_best = np.argmin(minCost)
best_theta = bestSol[ind_best]
```

```
81   best_scores = minCost
82   return best_theta, best_scores
```

Listing 5.4: $(1+1)$ ES with 1/5th rule.

Example 7 *This example compares the* $(1+1)$ *ES with the* $(1+1)$ *ES 1/5th rule ES in the minimization of real-valued 20-dimensional sphere. As the ES algorithms were implemented for minimization, the loss function is given by Equation (3.2), that defines the sphere function. Its Python implementation is already given in Listing 3.4.*

The code that implements the comparison is shown in Listing 5.5. Ten Monte Carlo runs are performed by each algorithm, with each run having a different starting point. The convergence curves of both algorithms are shown in Figures 5.4 and 5.5 .

```
1  # -----------------------------------------------------------
2  #       1 + 1 ES Algorithms Minimizing a Sphere
3  # -----------------------------------------------------------
4  # file: fig_one_plus_one_es_sphere.py
5  # -----------------------------------------------------------
6  # Import the necessary libraries and functions
7  import numpy as np
8  from es_rep.algs.one_plus_one_es import one_plus_one_es
9  from es_rep.algs.one_plus_one_es_1_5th_es import
       one_plus_one_es_1_5th
10 from test_functions_rep.so.sphere import sphere
11 # -----------------------------------------------------------
12 # 0 - For repeatability
13 np.random.seed(123)
14
15 # 1 - Define the upper and lower bounds of the search space
16 ndim = 20                # Number of dimensions of the problem
17 lb = -5*np.ones(ndim)    # Bounds of the search space
18 ub = 5*np.ones(ndim)
19
20 # 2 - Define the parameters for the optimization
21 maxIterations = 300      # maximum number of iterations
22 nMC = 10                 # number of MC runs
23
24 # 3 - Parameters for the algorithm
25 theta_0 = np.random.rand(ndim,nMC)    # random initial solution
26
27 # 4 - Define the cost function
28 loss = sphere
29
30 # 5 - Run the (1+1) ES algorithm
31 best_theta  = np.zeros((ndim,nMC))
32 best_scores = np.zeros((maxIterations,nMC))
33 for id_run in range(nMC):
34     np.random.seed(123)
35     [a, b] = one_plus_one_es(loss, theta_0[:,id_run],
       maxIterations, lb, ub)
36     best_theta[:, id_run] = a
37     best_scores[:, id_run] = np.squeeze(b) # remove an unsed
       dimension in b
38
```

```
39
40 # 6 - Plot the convergence curve
41 from auxiliary.plot_convergence_curve import
      plot_convergence_curve
42 fig_file = \
43   '../../../text/chapters/part_ii/es/figs/
      one_plus_one_es_solve_sphere_rv.eps'
44 title_str = \
45   "(1+1)-ES Minimizing a " + str(ndim) + "-dimensional Sphere"
46 plot_convergence_curve(fig_file,title_str,best_scores)
47
48 # 7 - Run the (1+1) 1/5th rule ES algorithm
49 best_theta   = np.zeros((ndim,nMC))
50 best_scores  = np.zeros((maxIterations,nMC))
51 for id_run in range(nMC):
52     np.random.seed(123)
53     [a, b] = one_plus_one_es_1_5th(loss, theta_0[:,id_run],
      maxIterations, lb, ub)
54     best_theta[:, id_run] = a
55     # remove an unused dimension in b
56     best_scores[:, id_run] = np.squeeze(b)
57
58
59 # 8 - Plot the convergence curve
60 from auxiliary.plot_convergence_curve import
      plot_convergence_curve
61 fig_file = \
62   '../../../text/chapters/part_ii/es/figs/
      one_plus_one_1_5th_es_solve_sphere_rv.eps'
63 title_str = \
64   "(1+1)-ES with 1/5th Rule Minimizing a " + str(ndim) + "-
      dimensional Sphere"
65 plot_convergence_curve(fig_file,title_str,best_scores)
```

Listing 5.5: Comparing algorithms $(1+1)$ ES and $(1+1)$ ES with 1/5th rule.

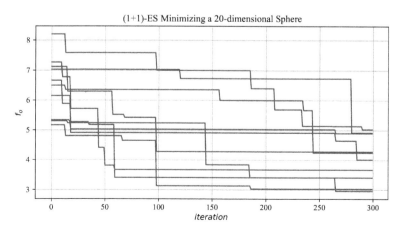

Figure 5.4: Convergence curves of $(1+1)$ ES algorithm solving the real-valued sphere function.

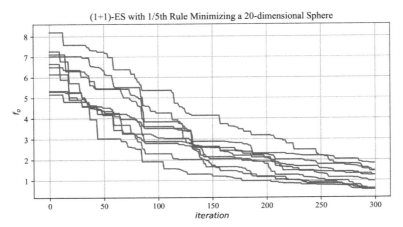

Figure 5.5: Convergence curves of $(1+1)$ ES with 1/5th rule algorithm solving the real-valued sphere function.

Clearly, adapting the standard deviation of the mutations with the 1/5th rule improved the performance of the $(1+1)$ ES algorithm. This is usually the case.

5.4   The $(\mu + \lambda)$ ES

The $(\mu + \lambda)$ ES is a generalization of the $(1+1)$ ES where the population size is μ and λ children are generated at each iteration. From the combined population of μ parents and λ children only the best performing μ individuals are allowed to survive to the next generation. Increasing the population size tends to improve the results found by the algorithm. The pseudocode for $(\mu + \lambda)$ ES is given in Algorithm 5.3.

Algorithm 5.3. $(\mu + \lambda)$ ES

1: **procedure** $(\mu + \lambda)$ ES
2:    $\{(\mathbf{x}, \boldsymbol{\sigma})\} \leftarrow$ randomly generate μ individuals $\mathbf{x}$ and their standard deviations $\boldsymbol{\sigma}$.
3:    **while** termination criterion not satisfied **do**
4:       **for** $k = 1, \ldots, \lambda$ **do**
5:          Randomly select two parents from $\{(\mathbf{x}, \boldsymbol{\sigma})\}$
6:          $(\mathbf{x}'_k, \boldsymbol{\sigma}'_k) \leftarrow$ Generate a single child by recombining the parents
7:          $\Sigma'_k \leftarrow \mathrm{diag}((\sigma'_{k1})^2, \ldots, (\sigma'_{kn})^2) \in \mathbb{R}^{n \times n}$
8:          Generate a random vector $\mathbf{r} \sim \mathcal{N}(\mathbf{0}, \Sigma'_k)$
9:          Mutate the child according to $\mathbf{x}'_k \leftarrow \mathbf{x}'_k + \mathbf{r}$
10:       **end for**
11:       $\mathbf{P} \leftarrow \{(\mathbf{x}, \boldsymbol{\sigma})\} \cup \{(\mathbf{x}', \boldsymbol{\sigma}')\}$
12:       $\{(\mathbf{x}, \boldsymbol{\sigma})\} \leftarrow$ best μ individuals from $\mathbf{P}$
13:    **end while**
14:    return the individual with the best fitness value
15: **end procedure**

Self-Adaptation

The performance of $(\mu + \lambda)$ ES can be improved by adapting the standard deviation of the mutations. There is no clear way to adapt the 1/5th adaptation strategy described in Section 5.3 to the $(\mu + \lambda)$ ES, but there is another adaptation strategy, called *self-adaptation* [75], that can be used. In self-adaptation, the standard deviation of the mutation is generated by recombination and mutation. After a child $(\mathbf{x}', \boldsymbol{\sigma}')$ is created, both n-dimensional vectors $\mathbf{x}'$ and $\boldsymbol{\sigma}'$ are mutated as follows:

$$
\begin{aligned}
\sigma_i' &\leftarrow \sigma_i' \exp(\tau' \rho_0 + \tau \rho_i) \\
\mathbf{x}_i' &\leftarrow \mathbf{x}_i' + \sigma_i' r_i
\end{aligned}
\tag{5.1}
$$

for $i \in [1, n]$, where ρ_0, ρ_i and r_i are random scalars sampled from $\mathcal{N}(0, 1)$. Parameters τ' and τ are user-defined, but the authors suggest the following setting:

$$
\tau = \frac{1}{\sqrt{2\sqrt{n}}}
\tag{5.2}
$$

$$
\tau' = \frac{1}{\sqrt{2n}}
\tag{5.3}
$$

The pseudocode for $(\mu + \lambda)$ ES enhanced with self-adaptation is shown in Algorithm 5.4.

Algorithm 5.4. $(\mu + \lambda)$ ES with Self-Adaptation

1: **procedure** $(\mu + \lambda)$ ES WITH SELF-ADAPTATION
2:      $\{(\mathbf{x}, \boldsymbol{\sigma})\} \leftarrow$ randomly generate μ individuals $\mathbf{x}$ and their standard deviations $\boldsymbol{\sigma}$.
3:      **while** termination criterion not satisfied **do**
4:          **for** $k = 1, \ldots, \lambda$ **do**
5:              Randomly select two parents from $\{(\mathbf{x}, \boldsymbol{\sigma})\}$
6:              $(\mathbf{x}_k', \boldsymbol{\sigma}_k') \leftarrow$ Generate a single child by recombining the parents
7:              Sample a random scalar ρ_0 from $\mathcal{N}(0, 1)$
8:              Sample a random vector $[\rho_1, \ldots, \rho_n]$ from $\mathcal{N}(0, 1)$
9:              $\sigma_{ki}' \leftarrow \sigma_{ki}' \exp(\tau' \rho_0 + \tau \rho_i)$ for $i \in [1, n]$
10:            $\Sigma_k' \leftarrow \mathrm{diag}((\sigma_{k1}')^2, \ldots, (\sigma_{kn}')^2) \in \mathbb{R}^{n \times n}$
11:            Generate a random vector $\mathbf{r} \sim \mathcal{N}(\mathbf{0}, \Sigma_k')$
12:            Mutate the child according to $\mathbf{x}_k' \leftarrow \mathbf{x}_k' + \mathbf{r}$
13:          **end for**
14:          $\mathbf{P} \leftarrow \{(\mathbf{x}, \boldsymbol{\sigma})\} \cup \{(\mathbf{x}', \boldsymbol{\sigma}')\}$
15:          $\{(\mathbf{x}, \boldsymbol{\sigma})\} \leftarrow$ best μ individuals from $\mathbf{P}$
16:      **end while**
17:      return the individual with the best fitness value
18: **end procedure**

A Python implementation of Algorithm 5.4 is shown in Listing 5.6.

```
1  # ------------------------------------------------------------
2  # (Mu + lambda) ES with Self-Adaptation
3  # ------------------------------------------------------------
4  #  Implemented as a minimization algorithm
5  # ------------------------------------------------------------
6  # Inputs:
7  #    loss      - function to be minimized
8  #    theta     - initial guess for the mean of the search
9  #                  distribution
10 #    maxIters  - maximum number of optimization iterations
11 #    lb        - n-dimensional vector lower bound on solutions
12 #    ub        - n-dimensional vector upper bound on solutions
13 #    popSize   - number of individuals in the population
14 #    lambd     - number of children generated at each iteration
15 # Outputs:
16 #    best_theta  - best solution found
17 #    best_scores - history of best scores
18 # ------------------------------------------------------------
19 # file: mu_plus_lambda_self_adapt_es.py
20 # ------------------------------------------------------------
21 import numpy as np
22 from auxiliary.init_rv import init_rv
23 from es_rep.utils.adjust_to_range import es_adjust_to_range
24 from es_rep.utils.select_recombine import es_select_recombine
25 # ------------------------------------------------------------
26 def mu_plus_lambda_self_adapt_es(loss, theta, maxIterations, lb,
       ub, popsize, lambd):
27     ## Settings
28     numVar   = np.shape(theta)[0]    # problem dimension
29     minDomain = lb
30     maxDomain = ub
31
32     crossoverType = 2    # 1 - discrete sexual crossover"
33                          # 2 - intermediate sexual crossover"
34                          # 3 - discrete global crossover"
35                          # 4 - intermediate global crossover"
36
37     ## Population
38     pop_chrom = np.zeros((popsize,numVar))
39     pop_cost = np.zeros(popsize)
40     pop_std = np.zeros((popsize,numVar))
41     for popindex in range(popsize):
42         # generate individual
43         if popindex == 0:
44             # the initial solution is part of
45             # the first population
46             pop_chrom[popindex] = theta
47         else:
48             pop_chrom[popindex] = init_rv(1, numVar, lb, ub)
49         # Standard deviation of the individual
50         pop_std[popindex] = np.random.rand(numVar)
51         # Cost
52         pop_cost[popindex] = loss(pop_chrom[popindex])
53
54     ## Children
```

```python
child_chrom = np.zeros((lambd,numVar))
child_cost = np.zeros(lambd)
child_std = np.zeros((lambd,numVar))

## Optimization
# Constants for self - adaptation
tau = 1 / np.sqrt(2 * np.sqrt(numVar))
tauprime = 1 / np.sqrt(2 * numVar)

# Begin the optimization loop
for id_iter in range(maxIterations):
    # Produce the children
    for childIndex in range(lambd):
        # Generate child
        child_chrom[childIndex], child_std[childIndex]  = \
            es_select_recombine(pop_chrom, pop_std,
                                popsize, numVar,
                                crossoverType)

        # Adaptation
        rho_0 = np.random.randn(1)
        rho = np.random.randn(numVar)
        child_std[childIndex] = \
            np.multiply(child_std[childIndex],
                        np.exp(tauprime * rho_0 + tau * rho))

        # Perform mutation on the child
        r = np.random.randn(numVar)
        child_chrom[childIndex] = \
            child_chrom[childIndex] + \
            np.multiply(child_std[childIndex],r)

        # Keep Children within the search region
        child_chrom[childIndex] = \
            es_adjust_to_range(child_chrom[childIndex],
                               minDomain, maxDomain);

        # Calculate the cost of the child
        child_cost[childIndex] = \
            loss(child_chrom[childIndex])

    # Children and parents form the total population
    totalPop_chrom = np.concatenate((pop_chrom, child_chrom))
    totalPop_cost = np.concatenate((pop_cost, child_cost))
    totalPop_std = np.concatenate((pop_std, child_std))

    # Sort the population members from best (lower cost) to
    # worst(higher cost)
    inds = np.argsort(totalPop_cost)
    totalPop_chrom = totalPop_chrom[inds]
    totalPop_cost  = totalPop_cost[inds]
    totalPop_std   = totalPop_std[inds]

    # Select the popSize best individuals
    pop_chrom = totalPop_chrom[0:popsize]
    pop_cost  = totalPop_cost[0:popsize]
```

```
112         pop_std    = totalPop_std[0:popsize]
113
114         # Store minimum and average costs
115         if id_iter == 0:
116             MinCost = np.array([pop_cost[0]])
117             AvgCost = np.array([np.mean(pop_cost)])
118             BestSol = np.array([pop_chrom[0]])
119         else:
120             MinCost = np.vstack((MinCost,pop_cost[0]))
121             AvgCost = np.vstack((AvgCost, np.mean(pop_cost)))
122             BestSol = np.vstack((BestSol,pop_chrom[0]))
123
124     ind_best = np.argmin(MinCost)
125     best_theta = BestSol[ind_best]
126     best_scores = MinCost
127     return best_theta, best_scores
```

Listing 5.6: $(\mu + \lambda)$ with Self-Adaptation ES.

Example 8 *This example uses the $(\mu + \lambda)$ with self-adaptation ES to minimize the real-valued 20-dimensional sphere. As the algorithm is implemented for minimization, the loss function is given by Equation (3.2), that defines the sphere function. The code that implements the optimization is given in Listing 5.7. The convergence curves for 10 Monte Carlo runs, each with a different starting point, are shown in Figure 5.6.*

```
1  # -----------------------------------------------------
2  #       Mu + Lambda ES Algorithm Minimizing a Sphere
3  # -----------------------------------------------------
4  # file: fig_mu_plus_lambda_es_sphere.py
5  # -----------------------------------------------------
6  # Import the necessary libraries and functions
7  import numpy as np
8  from es_rep.algs.mu_plus_lambda_self_adapt_es \
9      import mu_plus_lambda_self_adapt_es
10 from test_functions_rep.so.sphere import sphere
11
12 # 0 - Repeatability
13 np.random.seed(123)
14
15 # 1 - Define the upper and lower bounds of the search space
16 ndim = 20                # Number of dimensions of the problem
17 lb = -5*np.ones(ndim)    # Bounds of the search space
18 ub = 5*np.ones(ndim)
19
20 # 2 - Define the parameters for the optimization
21 maxIterations = 300  # maximum number of iterations
22 nMC = 10             # number of MC runs
23
24 # 3 - Parameters for the algorithm
25 popsize = 25    # number of individuals in the population
26 lambd   = 5     # number of children generated at each iteration
27 theta_0 = np.random.rand(ndim,nMC)  # random initial solution
28
29 # 4 - Define the cost function
```

```
30 loss = sphere
31
32 # 5 - Run the (mu + lambda) algorithm
33 best_theta   = np.zeros((ndim,nMC))
34 best_scores  = np.zeros((maxIterations,nMC))
35 for id_run in range(nMC):
36     np.random.seed(123)
37     [a, b] = mu_plus_lambda_self_adapt_es(loss,
38                                 theta_0[:, id_run],
39                                 maxIterations,
40                                 lb, ub, popsize, lambd)
41     best_theta[:, id_run] = a
42     # remove an unused dimension in b
43     best_scores[:, id_run] = np.squeeze(b)
44
45 # 6 - Plot the convergence curve
46 from auxiliary.plot_convergence_curve import
       plot_convergence_curve
47 fig_file = \
48     '../../../text/chapters/part_ii/es/figs/
       mu_plus_lambda_es_solve_sphere_rv.eps'
49 title_str = \
50     "$(\mu+\lambda)$-ES with Self-adaptation Minimizing a " + str(
       ndim) + "-dimensional Sphere"
51 plot_convergence_curve(fig_file,title_str,best_scores)
```

Listing 5.7: Minimization of a 20-d sphere function with $(\mu + \lambda)$ ES.

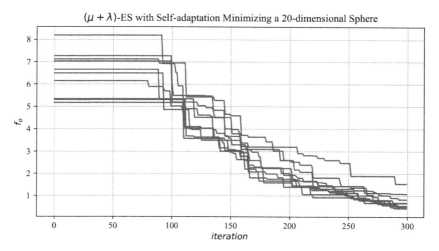

Figure 5.6: Convergence curve of $(\mu + \lambda)$ with self-adaptation ES solving the real-valued sphere function.

5.5 Natural Evolution Strategies

NES algorithms ([89], [21]) are evolution-inspired black-box optimization algorithms. NES algorithms represent the population with a probability distribution $p_\psi(\mathbf{x})$, where ψ are the parameters of the distribution. The algorithm aims at minimizing the average cost $\mathbb{E}_{\mathbf{x} \sim p_\psi} f_c(\mathbf{x})$, where $f_c(\cdot)$ is the cost function being minimized. The minimization is performed by searching for the best ψ with stochastic gradient descent. The natural gradient of the expected cost with relation to ψ is estimated according to

$$\nabla_\psi \mathbb{E}_{\mathbf{x} \sim p_\psi} f_c(\mathbf{x}) = \mathbb{E}_{\mathbf{x} \sim p_\psi} \{ f_c(\mathbf{x}) \nabla_\psi \log p_\psi(\mathbf{x}) \}. \tag{5.4}$$

NES algorithms work as follows. The search distribution is used to sample new search points. From the cost values of the samples the algorithm estimates the natural gradient of the expected cost. The distribution parameters are then updated by performing gradient descent and a new iteration starts. The natural gradient is a second-order method which normalizes the update with respect to uncertainty. The normalization helps prevent undesirable effects such as oscillations and premature convergence.

The authors stress that all members of the NES family operate based on the same principles. NES algorithms essentially differ in the type of distribution they use. This is justifiable if you think that different search spaces require different search distributions. For instance, in a low dimensionality problem with highly correlated variables, it is interesting to model the full covariance matrix. Modeling the full covariance matrix, though, may not be possible in problems with higher dimensionality due to computer memory limitations. In such cases, it may be interesting to use a diagonal covariance and thus assume separability between the variables of the search domain. Also, highly multi-modal search spaces may benefit from heavy-tailed distributions.

Another difference between NES algorithms is the gradient approximation method they use. For some distributions it is possible to analytically compute the natural gradient, while for other distributions the natural gradient must be estimate from samples.

OpenAI NES

A NES algorithm that recently gained attention in the academic community was proposed in [72]. The authors show that their simple NES can perform on par with sophisticated Deep Reinforcement Learning algorithms in a set of complex control problems, such as training neural networks to play Atari games based solely on image frames of the game and teaching legged robots to walk. One of the main points in favor on their proposed ES is that it can be easily parallelized, decreasing the time needed to obtain a result, a crucial feature when dealing with real-world problems. This algorithm is usually called OpenAI NES, because the authors of the paper worked at OpenAI at the time the paper was published.

In OpenAI NES, the population is sampled from an isotropic multivariate Gaussian with covariance $\sigma^2\mathbf{I}$. This representation allows writing

$$\mathbb{E}_{\mathbf{x}\sim p_\psi} f_c(\mathbf{x}) = \mathbb{E}_{\varepsilon\sim\mathcal{N}(0,I)}\{f_c(\mathbf{x}+\sigma\varepsilon)\}. \tag{5.5}$$

The gradient of the cost function is thus written as

$$\nabla_{\mathbf{x}}\mathbb{E}_{\varepsilon\sim\mathcal{N}(0,I)} f_c(\mathbf{x}+\sigma\varepsilon) = \frac{1}{\sigma}\mathbb{E}_{\varepsilon\sim\mathcal{N}(0,I)}\{f_c(\mathbf{x}+\sigma\varepsilon)\varepsilon\} \tag{5.6}$$

which is approximately calculated using the cost of the candidate solutions. The pseudocode of OpenAI NES algorithm is shown in Algorithm 5.5. The implementation of OpenAI NES is shown in Listing 5.8.

Algorithm 5.5. OpenAI Natural Evolution Strategies

1: **procedure** OPENAI NES
2:     Inputs: $\alpha \in \mathbb{R}$, $\sigma \in \mathbb{R}$, $\lambda \in \mathbb{R}$ and $\mathbf{x}_0 \in \mathbb{R}^n$.
3:     $\mathbf{w} \leftarrow \mathbf{x}_0$ ▷ Initial solution
4:     **while** termination criterion not satisfied **do**
5:         **for** $k = 1,\ldots,\lambda$ **do**
6:             Sample random vector $\varepsilon_k = (\varepsilon_{k_1},\ldots,\varepsilon_{k_n})$ from $\mathcal{N}(0,\mathbf{I})$▷ Generate perturbation
7:             $\mathbf{w}^{try} \leftarrow \mathbf{w} + \sigma\varepsilon_k$ ▷ Generate candidate solution $\mathbf{w}^{try}$
8:             $F_k \leftarrow f_c(\mathbf{w}^{try})$ ▷ Compute the cost of $\mathbf{w}^{try}$
9:         **end for**
10:        $F \leftarrow \{F_1,\ldots,F_\lambda\} \in \mathbb{R}^{\lambda\times 1}$ ▷ Cost vector of all candidate solutions
11:        $P \leftarrow \{\varepsilon_1,\ldots,\varepsilon_\lambda\} \in \mathbb{R}^{n\times\lambda}$ ▷ Matrix of all perturbations
12:        $F_n \leftarrow \left(\frac{F-mean(F)}{std(F)}\right) \in \mathbb{R}^{\lambda\times 1}$ ▷ Normalize the cost vector
13:        $\mathbf{w} = \mathbf{w} - \frac{\alpha}{\lambda\sigma}PF_n$ ▷ Minimization update
14:    **end while**
15:    return $\mathbf{w}$
16: **end procedure**

```
 1 # ------------------------------------------------------------------
 2 # OpenAI Natural Evolution Strategies
 3 # ------------------------------------------------------------------
 4 # Implemented as a minimization algorithm
 5 # ------------------------------------------------------------------
 6 # Inputs:
 7 #    loss      - function to be minimized
 8 #    theta     - initial guess for the mean of the search
 9 #                distribution
10 #    maxIters  - maximum number of optimization iterations
11 #    lb        - n-dimensional vector lower bound on solutions
12 #    ub        - n-dimensional vector upper bound on solutions
13 #    lambd     - number of individuals in the population
14 #    alpha     - learning rate of the gradient descent
15 #    sigma     - standard deviation of the isotropic mutation
16 # Outputs:
```

```
17 #    x_best   - best solution found
18 #    bestval_h - history of best scores
19 # ---------------------------------------------------------------
20 import numpy as np
21 # ---------------------------------------------------------------
22 def openai_es(loss, theta, maxIters, lb, ub, lambd, alpha, sigma)
   :
23    # best value found
24    x_best = theta
25    v_best = loss(theta)
26    # stores the global best at each iteration
27    bestval_h = []
28    # number of dimensions of the problem
29    nVar = np.shape(theta)[0]
30    w = theta # our initial guess
31    for id_iter in range(maxIters):
32       # npop samples from a normal distribution N(0,I)
33       P = np.random.randn(nVar,lambd)
34       # cost of each sample
35       costs = np.zeros(lambd)
36       for j in range(lambd):
37          w_try = w + sigma*P[:,j] # jitter w using gaussian noise
38          costs[j] = loss(w_try) # evaluate the jittered version
39          if costs[j]<v_best: # updating the best individual found
40             x_best = w_try
41             v_best = costs[j]
42       # normalize the costs
43       F = (costs - np.mean(costs)) / (np.std(costs) + 1e-08)
44       # perform the parameter update.
45       w = w - alpha / (lambd * sigma) * np.matmul(P, F)
46       # This extra evaluation of the goal function for
47       # updating the best individual found
48       wscore = loss(w)
49       # updating the best individual found
50       if wscore < v_best:
51          x_best = w
52          v_best = wscore
53          # stores the global best at each iteration
54       bestval_h.append(v_best)
55
56    # Returns
57    return x_best, bestval_h
```

Listing 5.8: Natural ES implementation.

Example 9 *This example applies OpenAI NES to the minimization of the real-valued 20-dimensional sphere given by Equation (3.2). The code that implements the optimization is given in Listing 5.9, and the convergence curves for 10 MC runs are shown in Figure 5.7.*

```
1 # ---------------------------------------------------------------
2 #     OpenAi NES Algorithm Minimizing a Sphere
3 # ---------------------------------------------------------------
4 # file: fig_openai_nes_sphere.py
5 # ---------------------------------------------------------------
```

```
 6 # Import the necessary libraries and functions
 7 import numpy as np
 8 from es_rep.algs.openai_nes import openai_es
 9 from test_functions_rep.so.sphere import sphere
10
11 # 0 - Repeatability
12 np.random.seed(123)
13
14 # 1 - Define the upper and lower bounds of the search space
15 ndim = 20                    # Number of dimensions of the problem
16 lb = -5*np.ones(ndim)     # Bounds of the search space
17 ub = 5*np.ones(ndim)
18
19 # 2 - Define the parameters for the optimization
20 maxIterations = 300   # maximum number of iterations
21 nMC = 10               # number of MC runs
22 # 3 - Parameters for the algorithm
23 npop = 25           # population size
24 sigma = 0.1         # noise standard deviation
25 alpha = 0.01        # learning rate
26 theta_0 = np.random.rand(ndim,nMC)   # random initial solution
27
28 # 4 - Define the cost function
29 fcost = sphere
30
31 # 5 - Run the NES algorithm
32 best_theta  = np.zeros((ndim,nMC))
33 best_scores = np.zeros((maxIterations,nMC))
34 for id_run in range(nMC):
35     np.random.seed(123)
36     [a, b] = openai_es(fcost, theta_0[:, id_run], maxIterations,
        lb, ub, npop, alpha, sigma)
37     best_theta[:, id_run] = a
38     best_scores[:, id_run] = np.squeeze(b) # remove an unsed
        dimension in b
39
40
41 # 6 - Plot the convergence curves
42 from auxiliary.plot_convergence_curve import
        plot_convergence_curve
43 fig_file = \
44     '../../../text/chapters/part_ii/es/figs/
        openai_nes_solve_sphere_rv.eps'
45 title_str = \
46     "OpenAI NES Minimizing a " + str(ndim) + "-dimensional Sphere"
47 plot_convergence_curve(fig_file,title_str,best_scores)
```

Listing 5.9: Minimization of a 20-d sphere function with OpenAI NES.

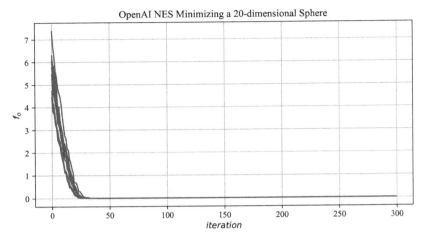

Figure 5.7: Convergence curve of the OpenAI NES solving the real-valued sphere function.

5.6 Covariance Matrix Adaptation Evolution Strategies

One of the best known members of the ES class of algorithms is the covariance matrix adaptation evolution strategy (CMA-ES) ([42], [41]). CMA-ES is a stochastic search method for the optimization of functions with continuous domains. It can handle nonlinear and non-convex functions, and has been very successful in solving optimization problems with low and medium dimensions. Adapting the full covariance matrix also allows CMA-ES to be effective on non-separable problems. Just for the record, an *n*-dimensional optimization problem is said to be separable when it can be solved by solving *n* "1-dimensional" problems independently, something much easier than solving the original *n*-dimensional problem.

Broadly speaking, the main idea behind CMA-ES is to build an approximation of the contour lines of the objective function *f* and use this approximation to guide the search for candidate solutions in the domain of the objective function. This is done by iteratively refining the values of the parameters of a multivariate normal distribution, such that the distribution becomes increasingly more likely to yield samples in regions of lower values of the objective function (remember that we want to minimize the objective function).

Properly adapting the covariance matrix of the normal distribution, as shown in Figure 5.8, is at the center of this strategy. It is easy to see by the shape of the confidence ellipses that, given the same mean value, a normal distribution with covariance matrix in plot (b) is more likely to yield samples in regions of lower values of the objective function than a normal distribution with covariance matrix of plot (a).

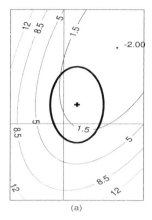 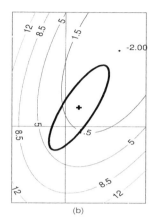

(a)   (b)

Figure 5.8: Covariance matrix adaptation can be used to guide the search for a better solution. Plots (a) and (b) respectively display the 95% confidence ellipses of the identity covariance matrix and of a properly tuned covariance matrix. Thinner lines are the contour lines of the objective function.

The CMA-ES Algorithm

CMA-ES works with two main parameters, the mean and the covariance matrix of a multivariate normal distribution, which acts as the search distribution. At any iteration, CMA-ES performs the following steps. First, a population of candidate solutions is sampled from the current search distribution. The fitness of each candidate solution is calculated and the candidate solutions with better fitness values (lower cost values) are selected. The selected candidate solutions are then used to calculate a new mean and a new covariance matrix for the search distribution, and a new iteration begins.

Generating Candidate Solutions

Generating new candidate solutions is done by sampling from multivariate normal distribution $\mathcal{N}(\mathbf{m}^{(g)}, \mathbf{C}^{(g)})$, where $\mathbf{m}^{(g)}$ and $\mathbf{C}^{(g)}$ are respectively the mean and covariance parameters at generation (iteration) g. The k-th individual of a population of $\lambda > 2$ candidate solutions is generated according to

$$\mathbf{x}_{\mathbf{s}_k}^{(g+1)} \sim \mathcal{N}(\mathbf{0}, \mathbf{C}^{(g)})$$
$$\mathbf{x}_k^{(g+1)} = \mathbf{m}^{(g)} + \sigma^{(g)} \mathbf{x}_{\mathbf{s}_k}^{(g+1)} \tag{5.7}$$

where

$\mathbf{x}_{\mathbf{s}_k}^{(g+1)} \in \mathbb{R}^n$ is the step used in the generation of $\mathbf{x}_k^{(g+1)} \in \mathbb{R}^n$

$\mathcal{N}(\mathbf{0}, \mathbf{C}^{(g)})$ is a normal distribution with zero mean and covariance matrix $\mathbf{C}^{(g)}$.

$\mathbf{x}_k^{(g+1)} \in \mathbb{R}^n$ is the kth candidate solution at generation $g+1$.

$\mathbf{m}^{(g)} \in \mathbb{R}^n$ is the mean value of the search distribution at generation g.

$\sigma^{(g)} \in \mathbb{R}^+$ is the global step-size at generation g.

$\mathbf{C}^{(g)} \in \mathbb{R}^{n \times n}$ is the covariance matrix of the search distribution at generation g.

Updating the Mean of the Search Distribution

The new mean $\mathbf{m}^{(g+1)}$ is calculated by adding to the current mean $\mathbf{m}^{(g)}$ the weighted average of the steps (see Equation (5.7)) that generated the μ best candidate solutions in terms of cost value:

$$\mathbf{m}_{\mathbf{s}_i}^{(g+1)} = \sum_{i=1}^{\mu} w_i \mathbf{x}_{\mathbf{s}_i}^{(g+1)} \tag{5.8}$$

$$\mathbf{m}^{(g+1)} = \mathbf{m}^{(g)} + c_m \mathbf{m}_{\mathbf{s}_i}^{(g+1)} \tag{5.9}$$

where $\mathbf{m}_{\mathbf{s}_i}^{(g+1)}$ is the step that generates the new mean $\mathbf{m}^{(g+1)}$ and $\mathbf{x}_{\mathbf{s}_i}^{(g+1)}$ is the step that gave rise to the ith lowest cost candidate solution $\mathbf{x}_i^{(g+1)}$. The weights w_i are restricted by

$$\sum_{i=1}^{\mu} w_i = 1, \quad w_1 \geq w_2 \geq \cdots \geq w_\mu > 0. \tag{5.10}$$

Note that Equation (5.10) assumes that $f(\mathbf{x}_1^{(g+1)}) \leq f(\mathbf{x}_2^{(g+1)}) \leq \cdots \leq f(\mathbf{x}_\lambda^{(g+1)})$, where f is the objective function to be minimized. Equation (5.8) thus tells us that more importance is given to candidate solutions with lower costs, a strategy that has an intuitive appeal.

How the Covariance Matrix is Adapted

The adaptation of the covariance matrix is guided by the following strategy. First, create a number of candidate solutions according to Equation (5.7). Take the steps that yielded the lowest-cost candidate solutions. Use these steps to update the covariance matrix of the search distribution in a way that the resulting covariance matrix will be more likely to generate samples that lead to low-cost candidate solutions than the original covariance matrix. This adaptation can be properly done by means of the mathematical fact described in what follows.

Consider the K n-dimensional vectors $\mathbf{s}_1, \ldots, \mathbf{s}_K$. The singular distribution $\mathcal{N}(0,1)\mathbf{s}_i \sim \mathcal{N}(\mathbf{0}, \mathbf{s}_i \mathbf{s}_i^T)$ is the distribution that generates $\mathbf{s}_i$ with maximum likelihood among all zero-mean normal distributions. Thus, if $\mathbf{x}_{\mathbf{s}_i}$ is a step that led to a low-cost candidate solution, the covariance matrix of the search distribution can be adapted according to the following cumulative sum

$$C^{(g+1)} = (1 - c_1)C^{(g)} + c_1 x_{s_i}^{(g+1)} (x_{s_i}^{(g+1)})^T, \tag{5.11}$$

where $C^{(g+1)}$ is the covariance matrix of the search distribution at generation $g + 1$ and c_1 is a user-defined scalar number that works as learning rate. Covariance matrix $C^{(g+1)}$ has a higher probability of generating step $x_{s_i}^{(g+1)}$ again as compared to covariance matrix $C^{(g)}$.

Evolution Paths

If the covariance matrix is updated according to Equation (5.11), the signal information of the step x_{s_i} is lost, since $x_{s_i} x_{s_i}^T = (-x_{s_i})(-x_{s_i}^T)$. To preserve the signal information, steps are used to construct the *evolution path* ([40],[42]) $p_c \in \mathbb{R}^n$ given by

$$p_c^{(g+1)} = (1 - c_c)p_c^{(g)} + \sqrt{c_c(2 - c_c)\mu_{eff}} m_{s_i}^{(g+1)} \tag{5.12}$$

where $c_c \leq 1$ is a user-defined scalar that acts as time constant, since Equation (5.12) assumes the form of an exponential smoothing. The term $\sqrt{c_c(2 - c_c)\mu_{eff}}$ is a normalization factor, where $\mu_{eff} = \frac{1}{\sum_{i=1}^{\mu} w_i^2}$.

Using p_c and the λ steps that yielded the best λ candidate solutions, the covariance matrix should be updated according to

$$C^{(g+1)} = \left(1 - c_1 - c_\mu\right) C^{(g)} + c_1 p_c^{(g+1)} p_c^{(g+1)^T} + c_\mu \sum_{i=1}^{\lambda} w_i x_{s_i}^{(g+1)} x_{s_i}^{(g+1)^T}$$

$$c_1 \approx 2/n^2$$

$$c_\mu \approx min(\mu_{eff}/n^2, 1 - c_1).$$

Updating the Global Step Size

Using the same strategy adopted in the construction of Equation (5.12), the evolution path p_σ is

$$p_\sigma^{(g+1)} = (1 - c_\sigma)p_\sigma^{(g)} + \sqrt{c_\sigma(2 - c_c)\mu_{eff}} \left(C^{(g)}\right)^{-\frac{1}{2}} m_{s_i}^{(g+1)}, \tag{5.13}$$

where $c_\sigma < 1$ is the time constant. The new step-size $\sigma^{(g+1)}$ is given by

$$\sigma^{(g+1)} = \sigma^{(g)} + \exp\left(\frac{c_\sigma}{d_\sigma}\left(\frac{\|p_\sigma^{(g+1)}\|}{E\|\mathcal{N}(0, I)\|} - 1\right)\right). \tag{5.14}$$

Python Implementation

Listing 5.10 brings a Python implementation of CMA-ES. It implements the basic features of the algorithm, and it is intended to be readable instead of computationally efficient, that is why the code uses loops instead of vectorization. As seen in the equations that comprise the algorithm, there are many parameters other than the mean and covariance of the search distribution whose values have to be defined by the user. This is no easy task. Fortunately, the authors of CMA-ES make available default settings for these parameters in ([42],[39]). Listing 5.10 brings these default parameter settings.

```python
# ---------------------------------------------------------------
# CMA-ES: Evolution Strategies with Covariance Matrix Adaptation
# ---------------------------------------------------------------
# implemented as a minimization algorithm
# ---------------------------------------------------------------
# Inputs:
#   loss      - function to be minimized
#   theta_0   - initial guess for the mean of the search
#               distribution
#   sigma_0   - initial standard deviation for generating
#               solutions
#   maxIters  - maximum number of optimization iterations
# Outputs:
#   best_theta   - best solution found
#   best_scores  - history of best scores
# ---------------------------------------------------------------
# file: cmaes.py
# ---------------------------------------------------------------
import numpy as np
import scipy
import scipy.linalg
# ---------------------------------------------------------------
def cmaes(loss, theta_0, sigma_0, maxIters):
    # --------- Strategy Parameters
    numVar = np.shape(theta_0)[0]  # problem dimension
    # population size
    lambd = (4 + np.int(np.ceil(3 * np.log(numVar))))*10
    # number of parents for recombination
    mu = np.int(lambd / 2.0)
    # recombination weights
    w = np.zeros(mu)
    for ii in range(mu):
        w[ii] = np.log(mu + 0.5) - np.log(ii + 1.0)
    w = w / sum(w)  # normalize recombination weights array
    # variance effective selection mass
    mueff = sum(w) ** 2 / sum(w ** 2)
    # learning rate for updating the mean (cm < 1 for noisy
    # functions)
    cm = 1
    # time constant for cumulation for the covariance matrix
    cc = (4 + mueff / numVar) / (numVar + 4 + 2 * mueff / numVar)
    # const for cumulation for sigma control
    cs = (mueff + 2) / (numVar + mueff + 5)
    # learning rate for rank-one update of the covariance matrix
    c1 = 2 / ((numVar + 1.3) ** 2 + mueff)
    # learning rate for rank-mu update
    cmu = min(1 - c1, 2 * (mueff - 2 + 1 / mueff) / ((numVar + 2)
        ** 2 + mueff))
    # damping for sigma
```

```
ds = 1 + 2 * max(0, np.sqrt((mueff - 1) / (numVar + 1)) - 1) \
    + cs
# ---------- Initial search distribution
sigma = sigma_0 # step size (standard deviation)
Cov = np.eye(numVar) # initial covariance matrix
# -------------------- Cumulative paths
pc = np.zeros((1,numVar))
ps = np.zeros((1,numVar))
chiN = numVar ** 0.5 * (1 - 1 / (4 * numVar) +\
        1 / (21 * numVar ** 2))  # expectation of ||N(0,I)||
# -------------------- Optimization
## Population
pop_step = np.zeros((lambd,numVar))
pop_cost = np.zeros(lambd)
pop_position = np.zeros((lambd,numVar))

M_step = np.zeros((maxIters+1,numVar))
M_cost = np.zeros(maxIters+1)
M_position = np.zeros((maxIters+1, numVar))

M_position[0] = theta_0
M_cost[0] = loss(M_position[0])
# Generations
for id_run in range(maxIters):
    # Generate the population
    for i in range(lambd):
        pop_step[i] = \
            np.random.multivariate_normal(np.zeros(numVar),
                                            Cov)
        # Equation (5.7)
        pop_position[i] = M_position[id_run] + \
                        sigma*pop_step[i]
        # Compute the cost of the ith individual
        pop_cost[i] = loss(pop_position[i])

    # Sort the population members from
    # best (lower cost) to worst(higher cost)
    inds = np.argsort(pop_cost)
    pop_step = pop_step[inds]
    pop_cost = pop_cost[inds]
    pop_position = pop_position[inds]

    # Store best candidate solution
    if id_run == 0:
        MinCost = np.array([pop_cost[0]])
        BestSol = np.array([pop_position[0]])
    else:
        MinCost = np.vstack((MinCost,pop_cost[0]))
        BestSol = np.vstack((BestSol,pop_position[0]))

    # Update the mean
    M_step[id_run + 1] = np.zeros((1,numVar))
    for j in range(mu):
        # Equation (5.8)
        M_step[id_run + 1] = M_step[id_run + 1] + \
                            w[j]*pop_step[j]
    # Equation (5.9)
```

```
102    M_position[id_run+1] = M_position[id_run] + \
103                        cm*M_step[id_run + 1]
104    # Compute the cost of M_position[id_run+1]
105    M_cost[id_run+1] = loss(M_position[id_run+1])
106
107    # Update evolution paths
108    U = scipy.linalg.sqrtm(Cov)
109    # Equation (5.12)
110    pc=(1-cc)*pc+np.sqrt(cc*(2-cc)*mueff)*M_step[id_run + 1]
111    # Equation (5.14)
112    ps = (1 - cs) * ps + \
113        np.sqrt(cs * (2 - cs) * mueff) * \
114        M_step[id_run + 1] * np.linalg.inv(U.T)
115
116
117    # Update the covariance matrix
118    # Equation (5.13)
119    Cov=(1-c1-cmu)*Cov+c1*(pc.T*pc)
120    for j in range(mu):
121        temp = np.expand_dims(pop_step[j], axis=0)
122        Cov=Cov+cmu*w[j]*(temp.T*temp)
123
124    # Update the step-size sigma
125    # Equation (5.15)
126    sigma = sigma * np.exp((cs / ds) *
127                        (np.linalg.norm(ps) / chiN - 1))
128
129    # Return values
130    ind_best_theta = np.argmin(MinCost)
131    best_theta = BestSol[ind_best_theta]
132    best_scores = MinCost
133    return best_theta, best_scores
```

Listing 5.10: CMA-ES implementation.

Example 10 *This example applies CMA-ES to the minimization of the real-valued 20-dimensional sphere given by Equation (3.2). The code that implements the optimization is given in Listing 5.11, and the convergence curves for 10 MC runs are shown in Figure 5.9.*

```
1  # --------------------------------------------------
2  #      CMA-ES Algorithm Minimizing a Sphere
3  #             fig_cma_es_sphere.py
4  # --------------------------------------------------
5  # Import the necessary libraries and functions
6  import numpy as np
7  import matplotlib.pyplot as plt
8  from es_rep.algs.cmaes import cmaes
9  from test_functions_rep.so.sphere import sphere
10 # --------------------------------------------------
11 # Plot the convergence curve
12 # --------------------------------------------------
13 def plot_convergence_curve(fig_name,title_str,fbest_h,
14                         fig_size_x = 8,fig_size_y = 4,
15                         dpi=1000):
16     num_vals = len(fbest_h)
```

```
17    t = np.linspace(0, num_vals-1, num_vals)
18    fig, ax = plt.subplots(figsize=(fig_size_x,fig_size_y),
19                            dpi=dpi) # figura 800x600 pixels
20    ax.plot(t, fbest_h,c='0.35')
21    #ax.set_xlabel(r'$\mathit{iteration}$', fontsize=18)
22    #ax.set_ylabel(r'$f_o$', fontsize=18)
23    ax.set_xlabel(r'$\mathit{iteration}$')
24    ax.set_ylabel(r'$f_o$')
25    ax.set_title(title_str)
26    ax.grid(True)
27    plt.savefig(fig_name, format="eps",dpi=dpi)
28 # -----------------------------------------------------
29 # Minimization
30 # -----------------------------------------------------
31 # Repeatability
32 np.random.seed(123)
33
34 # 1 - Define the upper and lower bounds of the search space
35 ndim = 20                  # Number of dimensions of the problem
36 ubc = 5
37 lbc = -5
38 lb = lbc*np.ones(ndim)      # lower bound for the search space
39 ub = ubc*np.ones(ndim)      # upper bound for the search space
40
41 # 2 - Define the parameters for the optimization
42 maxIterations = 300   # maximum number of iterations
43 nMC = 10              # number of MC runs
44 # 3 - Parameters for the algorithm
45 sigma_0 = 0.3*(ubc - lbc)
46 theta_0 = np.random.rand(ndim,nMC)   # random initial solution
47
48 # 4 - Define the cost function
49 fcost = sphere
50
51 # 5 - Run the CMAES algorithm
52 best_theta  = np.zeros((ndim,nMC))
53 best_scores = np.zeros((maxIterations,nMC))
54 for id_run in range(nMC):
55     np.random.seed(123)
56     [a, b] = cmaes(fcost, theta_0[:, id_run], sigma_0,
57        maxIterations)
58     best_theta[:, id_run] = a
59     best_scores[:, id_run] = np.squeeze(b) # remove an unused
60        dimension in b
61
62 # Plot the convergence curves-----------------------------
63 fig_file = 'figure_5_9.eps'
64 title_str = "CMA-ES Minimizing a " + str(ndim) + "-dimensional
65    Sphere"
66 plot_convergence_curve(fig_file,title_str,best_scores)
```

Listing 5.11: Minimization of a 20-d sphere function with CMA-ES.

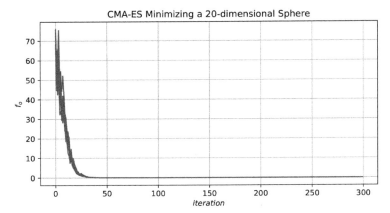

Figure 5.9: Convergence curve of the CMA-ES solving the real-valued sphere function.

Chapter 6

Genetic Algorithms

The concept of genetic algorithms was originally proposed by John Holland and his colleagues in [44]. A GA is an evolutionary algorithm that seeks to mimic elements of the theory of evolution of species by Charles Darwin. The idea that underpins genetic algorithms is the survival of the fittest individuals. This means that the fittest individuals have more chances of mating and passing their genes to the next generation. Despite being one of the first classes of evolutionary algorithms devised, GAs have been extensively applied to difficult optimization problems. The basic Genetic Algorithm (GA) discussed in this chapter has been found capable of succeeding in the very complex task of training deep convolutional neural networks in a variety of application domains by [84].

Genetic algorithms make extensive use of the genetic operators described in Chapter 3. At each generation (iteration of the algorithm), individuals are selected for mating according to one of the operations described in Section 3.5. The selected individuals pass their genes to their offspring by means of recombination operators, as discussed in Section 3.6. New genetic information is brought to the population by means of mutation operations, as described in Section 3.7. To allow the fittest individuals to survive throughout generations, GAs make use of elitism operators, as in Section 3.8. The pseudo-code for a GA that follows this description is given in Listing 6.1, where p_c, p_m and e_r are respectively the crossover probability, the mutation probability and the elitism rate.

Algorithm 6.1. Genetic Algorithm

1: $p_c \leftarrow$ receive the crossover probability
2: $p_m \leftarrow$ receive the mutation probability
3: $e_r \leftarrow$ receive the elitism rate
4: $f(\cdot) \leftarrow$ receive the fitness function
5: $f_s(\cdot) \leftarrow$ receive the selection function
6: $f_c(\cdot) \leftarrow$ receive the crossover function
7: $f_m(\cdot) \leftarrow$ receive the mutation function
8: $X \leftarrow$ randomly generate N individuals
9: $F = f(X) \leftarrow$ compute the fitness values of X
10: **while** termination criterion not satisfied **do**
11:     **for** $k = 1, \ldots, N$ **do**
12:         $\mathbf{p}_1, \mathbf{p}_2 = f_s(X)$ $\triangleright$ select two parents from X
13:         $\mathbf{c}_k \leftarrow f_c(\mathbf{p}_1, \mathbf{p}_2, p_c)$ $\triangleright$ Generate one child
14:         $\mathbf{c}_k \leftarrow f_m(\mathbf{c}_k, p_m)$ $\triangleright$ Mutate the child
15:     **end for**
16:     $F_c = f(C) \leftarrow$ compute the fitness values of $C = \{\mathbf{c}_1, \ldots, \mathbf{c}_N\}$
17:     $X, F = f_e(X, F, C, F_c, e_r)$ $\triangleright$ keep N individuals while preserving elite chromosomes
18: **end while**
19: Return the individual of X with the best fitness value

As discussed in Section 3.1, evolutionary algorithms work with candidate solutions that are encodings of the decision variables. The the two main kinds of encodings are discrete encodings (binary, Gray and integer) and real-valued encodings. The next two sections present genetic algorithms respectively capable of handling real-valued representations and binary representations.

6.1 Real-Valued Genetic Algorithm

A real-value GA is a GA where the candidate solutions are strings of real-value variables. The implementation follows the pseudocode given in Algorithm 6.1. All that needs to be done is to use the genetic operators capable of handling real-valued chromosomes. The resulting continuous genetic algorithm is show in Listing 6.1.

```
 1 # ----------------------------------------------------------------
 2 #                           GAc
 3 # Genetic algorithm for real-valued chromosomes
 4 # ----------------------------------------------------------------
 5 # implemented as a maximization algorithm
 6 # ----------------------------------------------------------------
 7 # Inputs:
 8 #    N         - number of individuals in the population
 9 #    maxIters  - maximum number of generations
10 #    pc        - crossover probability
11 #    pm        - mutation probability
12 #    er        - elitism rate
13 #    ffitness  - function to be maximized
14 #    fsel      - function that selects parents
```

```
15 #    fcross   - function that performs crossover
16 #    fmutation- function that performs mutation
17 #    lb        - n-dimensional vector lower bound on solutions
18 #    ub        - n-dimensional vector upper bound on solutions
19 # Outputs:
20 #    best_chrom          - best solution found
21 #    best_fits_history   - best fitness found in each generation
22 # ------------------------------------------------------------
23 # file: gac.py
24 # ------------------------------------------------------------
25 import numpy as np
26 from auxiliary.init_rv import init_rv
27 from operators_rep.elitism.elitism import elitism
28 # ------------------------------------------------------------
29 def gac(N, maxIters, pc, pm, er, ffitness, fsel, fcross,
30         fmutation, lb, ub):
31     ## Initialization
32     numVar = np.shape(lb)[0]  # problem dimension
33     ## Generate population
34     pop_chrom = init_rv(N, numVar, lb, ub)
35     # Compute the fitness values of the population
36     pop_fit = np.zeros(N)
37     for i in range(N):
38         pop_fit[i] = ffitness(pop_chrom[i])
39     ## Main loop
40     for id_iter in range(maxIters):
41         # Produces N offspring per generation, two at a time
42         children_chrom = np.zeros((N, numVar))
43         children_fit = np.zeros(N)
44         # produces one child
45         for k in range(0, N):
46             # Selection
47             parent1_chrom, parent2_chrom = fsel(pop_chrom,
48                                                 pop_fit)
49             # Crossover
50             child_chrom,_ = fcross(parent1_chrom,
51                                    parent2_chrom,pc)
52             # Mutation
53             child_chrom = fmutation(child_chrom, pm, lb, ub)
54             # New children
55             children_chrom[k]   = child_chrom
56         # Compute the fitness values of the N children
57         for j in range(N):
58             children_fit[j] = ffitness(children_chrom[j])
59         # Elitism - preserve the best M individuals
60         new_pop_chrom, new_pop_fit = elitism(pop_chrom,
61                                              pop_fit,
62                                              children_chrom,
63                                              children_fit, er)
64
65         # Population for the next generation
66         pop_chrom = np.copy(new_pop_chrom)
67         pop_fit   = np.copy(new_pop_fit)
68
69         ## Just for the purpose of storing data for the
70         # convergence curve
71         # Sort in descending fitness order for finding the best
```

```
72        # individual in the population
73        ids_sorted = np.argsort(-pop_fit)
74        ind_best = ids_sorted[0]
75        # Store best individual
76        if id_iter == 0:
77            best_fits_history = np.array([pop_fit[ind_best]])
78            bestSol = np.array([pop_chrom[ind_best]])
79        else:
80            best_fits_history = np.vstack((best_fits_history,
81                                            pop_fit[ind_best]))
82            bestSol = np.vstack((bestSol, pop_chrom[ind_best]))
83
84    # Returns
85    ind_best = np.argmax(pop_fit)
86    best_chrom = pop_chrom[ind_best]
87    return best_chrom, best_fits_history
```

Listing 6.1: Real-valued genetic algorithm.

Example 11 *This example uses the continuous GA to minimize the real-valued 20-dimensional sphere. To perform the minimization using a GA, it is necessary to define the fitness function and the proper genetic operators.*

Fitness function. As the sphere function is a continuous function with real-valued domain, it is natural to use a real-valued representation for the candidate solutions. The real-valued representation means that no coding or decoding is actually required. The code that implements the fitness function is given in Listing 6.2.

```
1  # --------------------------------------------------
2  #   Fitness for the real-valued sphere function
3  # --------------------------------------------------
4  # Input:
5  #    X    - real-valued chromosome
6  # Output:
7  #    F    - f(X)
8  # --------------------------------------------------
9  # file: fitness_sphere_rv.py
10 # --------------------------------------------------
11 from test_functions_rep.so.sphere import sphere
12 # --------------------------------------------------
13 def fitness_sphere_rv(X):
14     fitness = -sphere(X)
15     return fitness
```

Listing 6.2: Fitness function for a 20-d sphere function.

Selection function. The selection function is the tournament selection shown in Listing 3.17.
Crossover function. The crossover function chosen for this example is the SBX function shown in Listing 3.23.
Mutation function. The mutation function chosen for this example is the polynomial shown in Listing 3.27.

The code that implements the optimization process is given in Listing 6.3. The resulting convergence curve is shown in Figure 6.1.

```
1 # -----------------------------------------------------
2 #      GAc Algorithm Minimizing a Sphere
3 # -----------------------------------------------------
4 # file: fig_gab_sphere.py
5 # -----------------------------------------------------
6 # Import the necessary libraries and functions
7 import numpy as np
8 from fitnessf_max.fitnessf_sphere_rv import \
9     fitness_sphere_rv
10 from operators_rep.selection.selection_tournament import \
11     selection_tournament
12 from operators_rep.crossover.crossover_rv_sbx import \
13     sbx_crossover
14 from operators_rep.mutation.mutation_polynomial_rv import \
15     mutation_polynomial_rv
16 from ga_rep.algs.gac import gac
17 # -----------------------------------------------------
18 # 1 - Define the upper and lower bounds of the search space
19 ndim = 20             # Number of dimensions of the problem
20 lb = 5*np.ones(ndim)  # lower bound for the search space
21 ub = -5*np.ones(ndim) # upper bound for the search space
22
23 # 2 - Define the parameters for the optimization
24 npop = 30                # number of individuals in the population
25 maxIterations = 300   # maximum number of iterations
26
27 # 3 - Parameters for the algorithm
28 pc = 0.5            # crossover probability
29 pm = 0.8            # mutation probability
30 er = 0.1            # elitism rate
31 crossoverf  = sbx_crossover             # implements crossover
32 mutationf   = mutation_polynomial_rv    # implements mutation
33 selectionf  = selection_tournament      # implements selection
34 ffitness    = fitness_sphere_rv         # fitness function
35
36 # 4 - Run the GA algorithm
37 best_theta, best_scores = gac(npop, maxIterations, pc, pm,
38                               er, ffitness,
39                               selectionf, crossoverf,
40                               mutationf, lb, ub)
41 # remove an unsed dimension in best_scores
42 best_scores= np.squeeze(best_scores)
43
44 # 5 - Plot the convergence curve
45 # Not necessary for solving the problem
46 from auxiliary.plot_convergence_curve \
47     import plot_convergence_curve
48 fig_file = \
49     '../../../text/chapters/part_ii/ga/figs/gac_solve_sphere_rv.
     eps'
50 title_str = \
51     "Continuous GA Minimizing a " + str(ndim) + "-dimensional
     Sphere"
52 plot_convergence_curve(fig_file,title_str,-best_scores)
```

Listing 6.3: Minimization of a 20-d sphere function with a continuous GA.

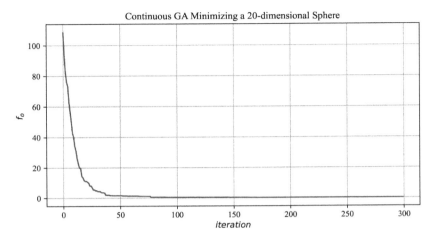

Figure 6.1: Convergence curve of GAc solving the real-valued sphere function.

6.2   Binary Genetic Algorithm

The binary genetic algorithm also follows the pseudocode shown in Algorithm 6.1. The difference between the real-valued and the binary algorithms are the genetic operators used in each of them. Listing 6.4 brings a Python implementation of the GA that works with binary/gray coded candidate solutions. The last input parameter (nbits_word) is necessary to inform the algorithm the dimensionality of the binary chromosomes used to represent a candidate solution.

```
 1 # ----------------------------------------------------------------
 2 #                       GAb
 3 # Genetic algorithm to solve continuous problems
 4 # with discrete coded chromosomes
 5 # ----------------------------------------------------------------
 6 # implemented as a maximization algorithm
 7 # ----------------------------------------------------------------
 8 # Inputs:
 9 #    N         - number of individuals in the population
10 #    maxIters  - maximum number of generations
11 #    pc        - crossover probability
12 #    pm        - mutation probability
13 #    er        - elitism rate
14 #    ffitness  - function to be maximized
15 #    fsel      - function that selects parents
16 #    fcross    - function that performs crossover
17 #    fmutation - function that performs mutation
18 #    lb        - n-dimensional vector lower bound on solutions
19 #    ub        - n-dimensional vector upper bound on solutions
20 #    nbits_word- number of bits thar represents a chromosome
21 # Outputs:
22 #    best_chrom        - best solution found
23 #    best_fits_history - best fitness found in each generation
24 # ----------------------------------------------------------------
```

```python
25 # file: gab.py
26 # ---------------------------------------------------------------
27 import numpy as np
28 from auxiliary.init_bin import init_bin
29 from operators_rep.elitism.elitism import elitism
30 # ---------------------------------------------------------------
31 def gab(N, maxIters, pc, pm, er, ffitness, fsel, fcross,
32        fmutation, lb, ub, nbits_word):
33     ## Initialization
34     numVar = np.shape(lb)[0]  # problem dimension
35     ## Generate population
36     pop_chrom = init_bin(N, numVar, nbits_word)
37     pop_fit   = np.zeros(N)
38     # Compute the fitness values of the population
39     for i in range(N):
40         pop_fit[i] = ffitness(pop_chrom[i], numVar,
41                               lb, ub, nbits_word)
42     ## Main loop
43     # for id_gen in range(maxGen):
44     for id_iter in range(maxIters):
45         # Produces N offspring per generation, two at a time
46         children_chrom = np.zeros((N, nbits_word), dtype=int)
47         children_fit = np.zeros(N)
48         for k in range(0, N):
49             # Selection
50             parent1_chrom, parent2_chrom = fsel(pop_chrom,
51                                                 pop_fit)
52             # Crossover
53             child_chrom, _ = fcross(parent1_chrom,
54                                     parent2_chrom, pc)
55             # Mutation
56             child_chrom = fmutation(child_chrom, pm)
57             # New children
58             children_chrom[k]   = child_chrom
59         # Compute the fitness values of the N children
60         for j in range(N):
61             children_fit[j] = ffitness(children_chrom[j], numVar,
62                                        lb, ub, nbits_word)
63         # Elitism - preserve the best M individuals
64         new_pop_chrom, new_pop_fit = elitism(pop_chrom, pop_fit,
65                                              children_chrom,
66                                              children_fit, er)
67         # Population for the next generation
68         pop_chrom = np.copy(new_pop_chrom)
69         pop_fit   = np.copy(new_pop_fit)
70
71         ## Just for the purpose of storing data for the
72         # convergence curve
73         # Sort in descending fitness order for finding the best
74         # individual in the population
75         ids_sorted = np.argsort(-pop_fit)
76         ind_best = ids_sorted[0]
77         # Store best individual
78         if id_iter == 0:
79             best_fits_history = np.array([pop_fit[ind_best]])
80             bestSol = np.array([pop_chrom[ind_best]])
81         else:
```

```
82        best_fits_history = np.vstack((best_fits_history,
83                                        pop_fit[ind_best]))
84        bestSol = np.vstack((bestSol, pop_chrom[ind_best]))
85
86    # Returns
87    ind_best = np.argmax(pop_fit)
88    best_chrom = pop_chrom[ind_best]
89    return best_chrom, best_fits_history
```

Listing 6.4: Python code for a binary genetic algorithm.

Example 12 *This example uses a binary GA to minimize the real-valued 20-dimensional sphere. Each decision variable is represented by 4 bits, resulting in 80-bit chromosomes.*

Fitness function. The chromosomes use gray coding, with fitness value as in Listing 6.5.

```
1 # ------------------------------------------------------------
2 #                   fitness_sphere_gray
3 # Computes the fitness value of search point X
4 # ------------------------------------------------------------
5 # Inputs:
6 #    X           - string containing the gray code representation of
7 #                  the search point
8 #    N           - number of decision variables
9 #    a and b     - [a, b] interval for the decision variables
10 #    nbits_word - how many bits are used in the representation of X
11 # Output:
12 #    fitness     - fitness value of X
13 # ------------------------------------------------------------
14 # file: fitness_sphere_gray.py
15 # ------------------------------------------------------------
16 from test_functions_rep.so.sphere import sphere
17 from encoding_rep.gray2dec import gray2decInterval
18 from encoding_rep.gen2phen import gen2phen
19 # ------------------------------------------------------------
20 def fitness_sphere_gray(X,N,a,b,nbits_word):
21     # converts gray-coded X into a decimal number in the interval
       [a,b]
22     Xru = gen2phen(gray2decInterval, X, N, a, b, nbits_word)
23     # calculate the fitness value of Xdu
24     fitness_value = -sphere(Xru)
25     return fitness_value
```

Listing 6.5: Gray-coded fitness function for a 20-d sphere function.

Selection function. The selection function is the tournament selection shown in Listing 3.17. This selection strategy can be used with both discrete and continuous representations.

Crossover function. The crossover function chosen for this example is the double-point crossover shown in Listing 3.19.

Mutation function. The mutation function chosen for this example is the binary mutation shown in Listing 3.24.

The code that implements the optimization is given in Listing 6.6. The resulting convergence curve is shown Figure 6.2.

```
1  # ------------------------------------------------------------
2  #        GAb Algorithm Minimizing a Sphere
3  # ------------------------------------------------------------
4  # file: fig_gab_sphere.py
5  # ------------------------------------------------------------
6  # Import the necessary libraries and functions
7  import numpy as np
8  from encoding_rep.gray2dec import gray2decInterval
9  from fitnessf_max.fitnessf_sphere_gray import \
10     fitness_sphere_gray
11 from encoding_rep.gen2phen import gen2phen
12 from operators_rep.selection.selection_tournament import \
13     selection_tournament
14 from operators_rep.crossover.crossover_dp import \
15     crossover_dp
16 from operators_rep.mutation.mutation_binary import \
17     mutation_binary
18 from ga_rep.algs.gab import gab
19 # ------------------------------------------------------------
20 # 1 - Define the search space
21 ndim = 20                    # Number of dimensions of the problem
22 lb = -5*np.ones(ndim)        # lower bound for the search space
23 ub = 5*np.ones(ndim)         # upper bound for the search space
24 nbits_var = 4                # number of bits to represent a single
25                              # decision variable
26 nbits_word = ndim*nbits_var  # number of genes used to represent
27                              # the vector of decision variables
28
29 # 2 - Define the parameters for the optimization
30 npop = 30               # number of individuals in the population
31 maxIterations = 300     # maximum number of iterations
32
33
34 # 3 - Parameters for the algorithm
35 pc = 0.8           # crossover probability
36 pm = 0.1           # mutation probability
37 er = 0.1           # elitism rate
38 crossoverf  = crossover_dp           # implements crossover
39 mutationf   = mutation_binary        # implements mutation
40 selectionf  = \
41     selection_tournament             # implements selection
42 fitnessf = fitness_sphere_gray       # fitness function
43
44 # 4 - Run the binary GA
45 best_theta, best_scores = gab(npop, maxIterations, pc, pm,
46                               er, fitnessf, selectionf, crossoverf,
47                               mutationf, lb, ub, nbits_word)
48
49 # 5 - Convert binary coded "best_theta" into a real-value
50 # number in [lb, ub]
51 best_theta = gen2phen(gray2decInterval, best_theta, ndim, lb, ub,
52     nbits_word)
52 # remove an unused dimension in best_scores
53 best_scores = np.squeeze(best_scores)
```

```
54
55 # 6 - Plot the convergence curves
56 from auxiliary.plot_convergence_curve \
57     import plot_convergence_curve
58 fig_file = \
59     '../../../text/chapters/part_ii/ga/figs/gab_solve_sphere_rv.
       eps'
60 title_str = \
61     "Binary GA Minimizing a " + str(ndim) + "-dimensional Sphere"
62 plot_convergence_curve(fig_file, title_str, -best_scores)
```

Listing 6.6: Minimization of a 20-d sphere function with a binary GA.

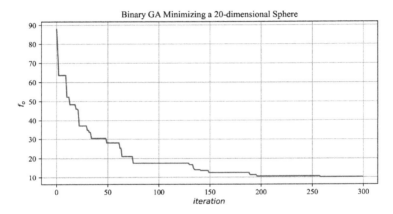

Figure 6.2: Convergence curve of GAb solving the real-valued sphere function.

Chapter 7

Differential Evolution

The DE ([80],[81],[83]) is a simple yet powerful evolutionary algorithm designed to optimize single-objective functions with continuous domains. It was motivated by the need to solve the Chebychev Polynomial fitting problem proposed by Rainer Storn. DE algorithms are simple to program and demand low computational resources, something that makes them very interesting for practitioners.

The general working of the DE is as follows. The algorithm first randomly creates a population of N n-dimensional real-valued vectors (candidate solutions) positioned in the region of the search space defined by $[\mathbf{b}_L, \mathbf{b}_U]$, which are respectively lower and upper bound vectors that define the search region. Then, for each candidate solution $\mathbf{x}_i$, the algorithm performs mutation and recombination to produce a single temporary candidate solution called *trial vector*. If the cost of the trial vector is lower than the cost of $\mathbf{x}_i$, then the trial vector replaces $\mathbf{x}_i$ in the population and becomes a new candidate solution. This process is repeated until the stopping criterion is met. Let us detail the process of generating candidate solutions.

Generating Candidate Solutions

The process starts by picking one candidate solution $\mathbf{x}_i$ from the population. After picking $\mathbf{x}_i$, the algorithm selects three different candidate solutions $\mathbf{x}_a, \mathbf{x}_b$ and $\mathbf{x}_c$ from the population (all different from $\mathbf{x}_i$). Let us respectively call them V_1, V_2 and V_b, where V_b stand for *base vector*. Then, the algorithm calculates the *difference vector* as

$$V_d = V_1 - V_2 \tag{7.1}$$

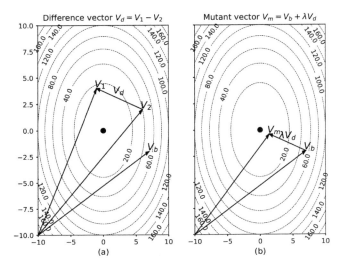

Figure 7.1: Difference and mutant vectors creation. The dashed lines are the contour curves of the two-dimensional real-valued sphere function. The black circle located in coordinates $(0,0)$ is the global minimum.

as seen in plot (a) of Figure 7.1. It then creates *mutant vector* V_m by adding to V_b the difference vector multiplied by the scaling factor λ,

$$V_m = V_b + \lambda V_d \tag{7.2}$$

as seen in plot (b) of Figure 7.1. This process is called *differential mutation*.

After the mutant vector V_m has been created, a trial vector V_t is produced as a crossover between $\mathbf{x}_i$ and mutant vector V_m, according to

$$V_t(j) = \begin{cases} V_m(j) & if\,(r_j < p_c)\ or\ j = J_r \\ \mathbf{x}_i(j) & \text{otherwise} \end{cases} \tag{7.3}$$

for $j \in [1, n]$. r_j is a uniformly distributed random number in the interval $[0, 1]$ and J_r is a uniformly distributed random integer in the interval $[1, n]$. The role of J_r is to ensure that under no circumstances V_t will be a clone of $\mathbf{x}_i$

The trial vector becomes a candidate solution if and only if $f_c(V_t) < f_c(\mathbf{x}_i)$, where f_c is the cost function being minimized. In this case, V_t replaces $\mathbf{x}_i$ in the population. The pseudocode for the DE algorithm is given in Listing 7.1.

Algorithm 7.1. Classic Differential Evolution

1: **procedure** DE/RAND/1/BIN
2:    $\alpha \in (0, 0.9]$ is the step size parameter
3:    $p_c \in [0, 1)$ is the crossover probability parameter
4:    $P \leftarrow$ randomly create the initial population of N individuals $\mathbf{x}_i \in \mathbb{R}^n$
5:    **while** termination criterion is not satisfied **do**
6:        **for** $i \in [1, N]$ **do**
7:            $\mathbf{x}_i \leftarrow$ pick the i-th candidate solution
8:            $\mathbf{x}_a \leftarrow$ Randomly select $\mathbf{x}_a$ where $a \neq i$.
9:            $V_1 \leftarrow \mathbf{x}_a$
10:           $\mathbf{x}_b \leftarrow$ Randomly select $\mathbf{x}_b$ where $b \neq a \neq i$.
11:           $V_2 \leftarrow \mathbf{x}_b$
12:           $\mathbf{x}_c \leftarrow$ Randomly select $\mathbf{x}_c$ where $c \neq b \neq a \neq i$.
13:           $V_b \leftarrow \mathbf{x}_c$
14:           $V_d \leftarrow V_1 - V_2$ ▷ Create the difference vector
15:           $V_m \leftarrow V_b + \alpha V_d$ ▷ Create the mutant vector
16:           $i_r \leftarrow$ random integer $\in [1, n]$
17:           **for** each dimension $j \in [1, n]$ **do**
18:               $r_j \leftarrow$ random number $\in [0, 1]$
19:               **if** $r_j < p_c$ or $j = i_r$ **then**   ▷ Create V_t
20:                   $V_t(j) = V_m(j)$
21:               **else**
22:                   $V_t(j) = \mathbf{x}_i(j)$
23:               **end if**
24:           **end for**
25:           **if** $f_c(V_t) < f_c(\mathbf{x}_i)$ **then**
26:               $\mathbf{x}_i \leftarrow V_t$ ▷ Replace $\mathbf{x}_i$ with V_t
27:           **end if**
28:        **end for**
29:    **end while**
30:    Return P
31: **end procedure**

Why DE works

The authors of the algorithm give some intuitive clues about why the algorithm works. The first clue is that as the optimization proceeds, the strength of perturbations of the form $V_1 - V_2$ tend to decrease, since the trial vectors should all concentrate around at least a local minimum. The second clue is that perturbation steps are correlated between dimensions, allowing DE to tackle highly nonseparable problems, which are common in real-world situations. The authors show that the result of these and other DE features is *contour matching*, which means that the DE population distributes itself along the contours of the objective function, which is a very desirable feature.

Python Implementation

```python
# ----------------------------------------------------------
#                          DE
#          Classic Differential Evolution
# ----------------------------------------------------------
#  Implemented as a minimization algorithm
# ----------------------------------------------------------
# Inputs:
#   f_cost      - function to be minimized
#                 distribution
#   pop_size  - number of individuals in the population
#   max_iters - maximum number of optimization iterations
#   pc          - crossover probability
#   lb          - n-dimensional vector lower bound on solutions
#   ub          - n-dimensional vector upper bound on solutions
#   step_size - strength of perturbation
#   theta_0    - initial guess (optional)
# Outputs:
#   best_theta  - best solution found
#   best_scores - history of best scores
# ----------------------------------------------------------
# file: de.py
# ----------------------------------------------------------
import numpy as np
# ----------------------------------------------------------
def de(f_cost,pop_size, max_iters, pc,
        lb, ub, step_size = 0.4, theta_0 = None):
    # problem dimension
    n_dim = np.shape(lb)[0]
    # randomly initialize the population
    pop_chrom = (ub-lb)*np.random.random_sample(size=(pop_size,
                                          n_dim)) + lb


    if theta_0 is not None:
        pop_chrom[0] = theta_0

    # obtain the cost of each solution
    pop_cost = np.zeros(pop_size)
    for id_p in range(pop_size):
        pop_cost[id_p] = f_cost(pop_chrom[id_p])
    # optimization
    for id_iter in range(max_iters):
        for id_pop in range(pop_size):
            # pick candidate solution
            xi = pop_chrom[id_pop]
            # ids_cs - vector containing the indexes of
            # the all other candidate solutions but xi
            ids_cs = np.linspace(0, pop_size - 1,
                                pop_size, dtype=int)
            # remove id_pop from ids_cs
            ids_cs = np.where(ids_cs != id_pop)
            # convert tuple to ndarray
            ids_cs = np.asarray(ids_cs)[0]
            # randomly pick 3 candidate solutions using
            # indexes ids_cs
            xa, xb, xc = pop_chrom[np.random.choice(ids_cs, 3,
```

```
                                          replace = False)]
            V1 = xa
            V2 = xb
            Vb = xc
            # create the difference vector
            Vd = V1 - V2
            # create the mutant vector
            Vm = Vb + step_size*Vd
            # make sure the mutant vector is in [lb, ub]
            Vm = np.clip(Vm, lb, ub)
            # create a trial vector by recombination
            Vt = np.zeros(n_dim)
            jr = np.random.rand() # index of the dimension
                                  # that will undergo crossover
                                  # iregardlessly of pc
            for id_dim in range(n_dim):
                rc = np.random.rand()
                if rc < pc or id_dim == jr:
                    # perform recombination
                    Vt[id_dim] = Vm[id_dim]
                else:
                    # copy from Vb
                    Vt[id_dim] = xi[id_dim]
            # obtain the cost of the trial vector
            vt_cost = f_cost(Vt)
            # select the id_pop individual for the next iteration
            if vt_cost < pop_cost[id_pop]:
                pop_chrom[id_pop] = Vt
                pop_cost[id_pop] = vt_cost

        # Store minimum cost and best solution
        ind_best = np.argmin(pop_cost)
        if id_iter == 0:
            minCost = [pop_cost[ind_best]]
            bestSol = [pop_chrom[ind_best]]
        else:
            minCost = np.vstack((minCost,pop_cost[ind_best]))
            bestSol = np.vstack((bestSol,pop_chrom[ind_best]))

    # Return values
    ind_best_cost = np.argmin(minCost)
    best_theta = bestSol[ind_best_cost]
    best_scores = minCost
    return best_theta, best_scores
```

Listing 7.1: Differential Evolution algorithm.

Parameter setting

As with any other EA, the performance of DE is dependent on the settings of its parameters. The parameters of the classic DE are the population size N, the scaling factor λ and the crossover rate p_c. Practical advice on how to set those parameters can be found in [67]. All advice is summarized below. It is worthwhile to note that the authors also stress that there is no parameter setting that works well for all problems.

Setting N**.** Set the number of parents N to 10 times the number of dimensions of the objective function, but making N much higher, such as $N > 40$, does not increase the convergence properties significantly.

Setting λ**.** Set $\lambda = 0.8$. For noisy objective functions, a technique called *dither* has been found to improve convergence behaviour significantly. The technique consists of selecting λ from the interval $[0.5, 1.0]$ randomly for each iteration of the algorithm or for each difference vector.

Setting p_c**.** Set, $p_c = 0.9$. If the objective function is separable (something uncommon for real-world optimization problems), the setting should be $p_c = 0.2$, since this low value improves search along coordinate axes.

DE Variations

Many DE variations were proposed as results of variations in the mutation and selection schemas used in the classic DE shown in Algorithm 7.1. DE variations also arise when different scheduling schemas for the scale factor λ are used. Different variations have different names, but those names share the same structure used to name the classic DE shown in Algorithm 7.1. The components of the name of the classic DE have the following meanings:

rand - vectors V_1, V_2 and V_b are chosen randomly

1 - only one difference vector is used in the process of creating mutation vector V_m

bin - the algorithm uses binary crossover to create trial vector V_t.

Two well known variations are DE/rand/2/bin and DE/best/1/bin Variation *DE/rand/2/bin* ([81], [82]) uses two difference vectors $V_{d1} = V_1 - V_2$ and $V_{d2} = V_3 - V_4$ to create the mutant vector $V_m = V_b + \lambda(V_{d1} + V_{d2})$. This can increase exploration in relation to the classic *DE/rand/1/bin* because the total difference vector is not constrained to lie in the direction of the differences between pairs of vectors. This is the only difference in relation to the classic *DE/rand/1/bin*, which creates V_m according to Equation (7.2).

The variation called *DE/best/1/bin* ([81], [82]) always chooses V_b as the best individual in the population. This strategy has the effect of increasing exploitation and reducing exploration in relation to the classic *DE/rand/1/bin*, which chooses V_b randomly in each iteration of the algorithm.

Those were only a few possible DE variants. Different combinations of crossover, mutation schemas can give rise to other variants. The point is that so far there is no DE variant that is better than the other variants in all possible optimization problems. The best DE variant as well as the best parameter setting are problem dependent.

Example 13 *This example uses the DE algorithm to minimize the real-valued 20-dimensional sphere. As the algorithm is implemented for minimization, the loss func-*

tion is given by Equation (3.2), that defines the sphere function. The code that imple-ments the optimization is given in Listing 7.2. The convergence curves for 10 Monte Carlo runs, each with a different starting point, are shown in Figure 7.2. The parameter setting is $N = 20$, $p_c = 0.9$ and $\lambda = 0.8$.

```
1 # -----------------------------------------------------
2 #       DE Algorithm Minimizing a Sphere
3 # -----------------------------------------------------
4 # Import the necessary libraries and functions
5 import numpy as np
6 from de_rep.algs.de import de
7 from test_functions_rep.so.sphere import sphere
8 # Repeatability
9 np.random.seed(123)
10
11 # 1 - Define the upper and lower bounds of the search space
12 n_dim = 20              # Number of dimensions of the problem
13 ubc = 5
14 lbc = -5
15 lb = lbc*np.ones(n_dim)  # lower bound for the search space
16 ub = ubc*np.ones(n_dim)  # upper bound for the search space
17
18 # 2 - Define the parameters for the optimization
19 max_iters = 300  # maximum number of iterations
20 nMC = 10         # number of MC runs
21
22 # 3 - Parameters for the algorithm
23 pc = 0.9 # crossover probability
24 theta_0 = np.random.rand(n_dim, nMC)  # random initial solution
25 pop_size = 20   # number of individuals in the population
26
27 # 4 - Define the cost function
28 f_cost = sphere
29
30 # 5 - Run the DE algorithm
31 best_theta  = np.zeros((n_dim, nMC))
32 best_scores = np.zeros((max_iters,nMC))
33 np.random.seed(123) # for repeatability
34 for id_run in range(nMC):
35     # call DE
36     [a, b] = de(f_cost,pop_size, max_iters,
37                 pc, lb, ub, step_size = 0.8)
38     # store the best solution found
39     best_theta[:, id_run] = a
40     # Store the vector on minimum values found in
41     # each iteration of the algorithm
42     # Squeeze - remove an unsed dimension in b
43     best_scores[:, id_run] = np.squeeze(b)
44
45 # 6 - Plot the convergence curves-------------------------
46 # Not necessary for solving the problem
47 from auxiliary.plot_convergence_curve import
        plot_convergence_curve
48 fig_file = '../../../text/chapters/part_ii/de/figs/
        de_solve_sphere_rv.eps'
```

```
49 title_str = "DE Minimizing a " + str(n_dim) + "-dimensional Sphere
      "
50 plot_convergence_curve(fig_file,title_str,best_scores)
```

Listing 7.2: Minimization of the 20d sphere function with DE.

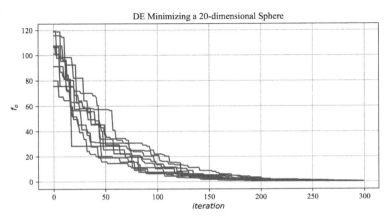

Figure 7.2: Convergence curve of DE solving the real-valued sphere function.

MULTI-OBJECTIVE EVOLUTIONARY ALGORITHMS

Multi-objective optimization problems have already been addressed in Section 2.8. At that time the distinction between multi-objective and many-objective optimization was not stressed, but now is the time to highlight this difference. The two main focuses of multi-objective and many-objective optimization are *convergence* and *diversity*. Convergence is the ability to find a good approximation of the Pareto front, while diversity is related to how well the solutions found by the algorithm spread along the Pareto front.

Achieving good convergence and good coverage becomes increasingly difficult as the number of optimization goals rise. According to ([43], [15]), when the optimization problem involves four or more objectives, a number of problems arise.

As the number of objectives increases, the portion of a randomly generated population that is non-dominated also increases. The rise in the number of non-dominated solutions makes it harder for Multi-Objective Evolutionary Algorithms (MOEA) which use the concept of Pareto dominance to create new solutions in every generation, negatively impacting the convergence of the optimization process. Also there is an exponential increase in the number of solutions on the Pareto front, implying that MOEAs may need to find thousands of non-dominated solutions to approximate the Pareto front. The sheer size of the search space would also make it harder to maintain diversity and thus properly cover the Pareto front.

Another important issue in high-dimensional search spaces (high number of optimization goals) is that it becomes more difficult to generate solutions that are near their parents. This need gave rise to special recombination operators, such as SBX, which focus on generating solutions near the parents.

According to [31], two of the main classes of MOEAs are Pareto-based MOEAs and decomposition-based MOEAs. Pareto-based MOEAs use the concept of Pareto ranking [36] to order the population at different fronts. The idea that underpins Pareto ranking is to rank the population of the MOEA according to Pareto optimality, such that the nondominated solutions obtain the best possible rank and have the same probability of survival. Decomposition-based MOEAs work by decomposing the optimization problem into several subproblems, each one of them targeting different parts of the Pareto front.

In the following chapters, Non-dominated Sorting Genetic Algorithm II (NSGA-II) and Multi-Objective Evolutionary Algorithm Based on Decomposition (MOEA/D) are described. The first algorithm is one of the most prominent representatives of Pareto-based MOEAs, while the second is an important representative of the decomposition-based approach.

Chapter 8

Non-Dominated Sorted Genetic Algorithm II

NSGA-II [23] is an elitist multi-objective Pareto-based genetic algorithm. It emerged as an answer to the problem of poor coverage of the Pareto front that the first Non-dominated Sorting Genetic Algorithm (NSGA) [79] suffered.

In order to increase the coverage of the Pareto-optimal front, NSGA-II relies on a computationally efficient mechanism to find non-dominated solutions, called *fast Non-Dominated Sorting*, and on a measure of the spread of the solutions over the Pareto front called *crowding distance*.

Pareto Ranking

Pareto-ranking uses the concept of Pareto dominance to assign selection probabilities to candidate solutions. The rank of a given candidate solution is calculated according to its dominance in relation to the other members of the population. The higher the number of members that it dominates, the lower is its ranking. A lower rank thus corresponds to a better candidate solution. Goldberg in [36] proposed the first Pareto ranking procedure, which in essence is:

Algorithm 8.1. Goldberg's Pareto ranking

1: **procedure** PARETO RANKING
2:     $P \leftarrow$ initial population
3:     $i \leftarrow 0$
4:     **while** P is not empty **do**
5:         $F_i \leftarrow$ all non-dominated solutions in P
6:         $P \leftarrow P - F_i$ ▷ Remove solutions in F_i from P
7:         $i \leftarrow i + 1$
8:     **end while**
9: **end procedure**

In Algorithm 8.1, F_i, $i = 0, 1, \ldots$ are called *non-dominated fronts*. Solutions belonging to front F_i receive rank i, so solutions in F_0 receive rank 0.

The set of non-dominated fronts of a population could be found by Algorithm 8.1, but the approach is computationally intensive. That is why NSGA-II uses a more sophisticated and computationally efficient procedure to find the non-dominated fronts in a given population, known as fast non-dominated sorting.

Fast Non-Dominated Sorting

In essence, the non-dominated sorting works by first creating for each candidate solution p in population P the following variables:

■ n_p : the number of solutions that dominate solution **p**

■ S_p : the set of solutions that solution **p** dominates.

Then, for each candidate solution, the algorithm counts the number of solutions that dominate it and also finds all solutions that are dominated by it, updating the above variables. After that, all solutions that have $n_p = 0$ are non-dominated and are attributed to $\mathcal{F}_0$. For each solution **p** with $n_p = 0$, the algorithm visits each member $\mathbf{q} \in S_p$ and decreases the number of solutions that dominate **q** by one, that is, it makes $n_q = n_q - 1$. If n_q reaches zero, then it is safe to conclude that the only solutions that dominate **q** are solutions that belong to $\mathcal{F}_0$, thus **q** is attributed to $\mathcal{F}_1$. The procedure continues until all non-dominated fronts have been identified. The reader interested in a detailed description of the fast non-dominated sorting procedure is referred to [23]. Algorithm 8.2 is a pseudocode for the fast non-dominated sorting which is based on the pseudocode given in [23]. The Python code for fast non-dominated sorting is shown in Listing 8.1.

Algorithm 8.2. Fast Non-Dominated Sort

1: **procedure** FAST SORTING
2:     $\mathcal{F}_0 \leftarrow \emptyset$
3:     $\mathcal{P}$ is the population
4:     **for** each $\mathbf{p} \in \mathcal{P}$ **do**
5:         $S_p \leftarrow \emptyset$ and $n_p = 0$
6:         **for** $\mathbf{q} \in \mathcal{P}$ **do**
7:             **if** $\mathbf{p}$ dominates $\mathbf{q}$ **then**
8:                 $S_p = S_p \cup \{\mathbf{q}\}$
9:             **else if** $\mathbf{q}$ dominates $\mathbf{p}$ **then**
10:                 $n_p = n_p + 1$
11:             **end if**
12:         **end for**
13:         **if** $n_p == 0$ **then**   ▷ $\mathbf{p}$ belongs to the first non-dominated front.
14:             $\mathcal{F}_0 = \mathcal{F}_0 \cup \{\mathbf{p}\}$
15:         **end if**
16:     **end for**
17:     $i = 0$
18:     **while** $\mathcal{F}_i \neq \emptyset$ **do**
19:         $\mathcal{Q} \leftarrow \emptyset$ ▷ storage for members of the next non-dominated front.
20:         **for** each $\mathbf{p} \in \mathcal{F}_i$ **do**
21:             **for** $\mathbf{q} \in S_p$ **do**
22:                 $n_q = n_q - 1$
23:                 **if** $n_q == 0$ **then**   ▷ $\mathbf{q}$ belongs to the next non-dominated front.
24:                     $\mathcal{Q} = \mathcal{Q} \cup \{\mathbf{q}\}$
25:                 **end if**
26:             **end for**
27:         **end for**
28:     **end while**
29:     $i = i + 1$
30:     $\mathcal{F}_i \leftarrow \mathcal{Q}$
31: **end procedure**

```
 1 #  ------------------------------------------------------------
 2 #              Fast Non-Dominated Sorting
 3 #  ------------------------------------------------------------
 4 # Inputs:
 5 #    pop_chrom      - population of candidate solutions
 6 #    pop_cost       - cost of each individual in pop_chrom
 7 # Outputs:
 8 #    F              - Pareto fronts
 9 #    pop_rank       - rank of each solution
10 # ------------------------------------------------------------
11 # file: non_dominated_sort.py
12 # ------------------------------------------------------------
13 import numpy as np
14 # ------------------------------------------------------------
15 def fast_non_dominated_sort(pop_chrom, pop_cost):
16     n_pop = len(pop_cost)
```

```
17    # Rank of each candidate solution
18    pop_rank = np.zeros(n_pop, dtype=int)
19    # Set of solutions that solution p dominates
20    S = [[] for _ in range(n_pop)]
21    # Number of solutions that dominate solution p
22    n = np.zeros(n_pop, dtype=int)
23    # Pareto fronts
24    F = [[]]
25    # For each candidate solution p_idx
26    for p_idx in range(n_pop):
27        # for each candidate solution q_idx
28        for q_idx in range(n_pop):
29            if p_idx == q_idx:
30                continue
31            # if solution p_idx dominates solution q_idx
32            if dominates(pop_cost[p_idx], pop_cost[q_idx]):
33                # add solution q_idx to S_{p_idx}
34                S[p_idx].append(q_idx)
35            elif dominates(pop_cost[q_idx], pop_cost[p_idx]):
36                # increase the number of solutions that dominate
37                # solution p_idx
38                n[p_idx] = n[p_idx] + 1
39        # If no solution dominates solution p_idx
40        if n[p_idx] == 0:
41            # add solution p_idx to the first Pareto front
42            pop_rank[p_idx] = 0
43            F[0].append(p_idx)
44    # Build the other Pareto fronts
45    i = 0  # initialize the front counter
46    while (F[i] != []):
47        # used to store the members of the next front
48        Q = []
49        # for each solution p_idx in the ith front
50        for p_idx in F[i]:
51            # for each solution q_idx dominated by
52            # solution p_idx
53            for q_idx in S[p_idx]:
54                # decrease the number of solutions that
55                # dominate solution q_idx
56                n[q_idx] = n[q_idx] - 1
57                # if the number of solutions that dominate
58                # solution q_idx has reached zero
59                if (n[q_idx] == 0):
60                    # then all solutions that dominate
61                    # solution q_idx are from fronts
62                    # numbered i or bellow, this means
63                    # that solution q_idx belongs to
64                    # front i + 1
65                    pop_rank[q_idx] = i + 1
66                    if q_idx not in Q:
67                        Q.append(q_idx)
68        i = i + 1
69        F.append(Q)
70    del F[len(F) - 1]
71
72    return F, pop_rank
73  # ------------------------------------------------------------
```

```
74 # Returns 1 if x dominates y, otherwise returns 0
75 # ----------------------------------------------------------------
76 def dominates(x, y):
77     if all(x <= y) and any(x < y):
78         return 1
79     else:
80         return 0
```

Listing 8.1: Fast non-dominated sorting.

Crowding Distance

To improve the coverage of the Pareto front, it is interesting to have solutions that are well spread over the front. This means that there should be no wide gaps around any given solution, because that would mean a poor coverage of the Pareto front.

The authors of NSGA-II proposed the crowding distance as a metric of the density of solutions around a given solution. If a given solution has a high crowding distance, then there is a wide gap around it, meaning that the solution is in a poorly covered part of the Pareto front. NSGA-II should thus try to generate more solutions around it, in order to improve the coverage of the Pareto front. The crowding distance of solution x_i is defined as the average length of the sides of the cuboid formed by solutions x_{i-1} and x_{i+1}.

When choosing solutions from the population, NSGA-II takes into consideration both the rank and the crowding distance of the solution. The operator that automatizes this comparison is called *Crowded-Comparison Operator* (CCO). CCO is given in Algorithm 8.3 and the corresponding code is given in Listing 8.2. The Python implementation of the crowding distance computation is shown in Listing 8.4.

Algorithm 8.3. Crowded-Comparison Operator

1: **procedure** CCO
2:     $(\mathbf{p}, \mathbf{q}) \leftarrow$ solutions to be compared
3:     **if** rank($\mathbf{p}$) < rank($\mathbf{q}$) **then**
4:         return $\mathbf{p}$
5:     **else if** rank($\mathbf{q}$) < rank($\mathbf{p}$) **then**
6:         return $\mathbf{q}$
7:     **else if** cdist($\mathbf{p}$) > cdist($\mathbf{q}$) **then**   ▷ cdist($\mathbf{q}$) stands for the crowding distance of $\mathbf{q}$
8:         return $\mathbf{p}$
9:     **else if** cdist($\mathbf{q}$) > cdist($\mathbf{p}$) **then**
10:        return $\mathbf{q}$
11:    **end if**
12: **end procedure**

```
1 # ----------------------------------------------------------------
2 #                     CCO for NSGA-II
3 # ----------------------------------------------------------------
4 # p0_rank         - rank of the first candidate
```

```
 5 # p0_cdist        - crowding distance of the first candidate
 6 # p1_rank         - rank of the second candidate
 7 # p1_cdist        - crowding distance of the econd candidate
 8 # ------------------------------------------------------------
 9 # file: crowded_comparison.py
10 # ------------------------------------------------------------
11 def crowded_comparison_operator(p0_rank,p0_cdist, p1_rank,
      p1_cdist):
12     if p0_rank < p1_rank:
13         return 0
14     if p1_rank < p0_rank:
15         return 1
16     if (p0_rank == p1_rank) and (p0_cdist > p1_cdist):
17         return 0
18     if (p0_rank == p1_rank) and (p1_cdist > p0_cdist):
19         return 1
20     return 0
```

Listing 8.2: Python code for the Crowded Compared Operator.

Binary Tournament

In NSGA-II, parents are selected for mating according to a binary tournament that works similarly to tournament selection seen in Section 3.5.3. The main difference is that instead of using the fitness values of the solutions to make the selection, CCO results are used. The Python code for the NSGA-II binary tournament is shown in Listing 8.3.

```
 1 # ------------------------------------------------------------
 2 #          Binary Tournament for NSGA-II
 3 # ------------------------------------------------------------
 4 # Inputs:
 5 #    pop_chrom      - population of candidate solutions
 6 #    pop_rank       - rank of each individual in pop_chrom
 7 #    pop_cdist      - crowding distance of each individual in
 8 #                     pop-chrom
 9 # Outputs:
10 # parent1           - first selected parent
11 # parent2           - second selected parent
12 # ------------------------------------------------------------
13 # file: binary_tournament_nsga2.py
14 # ------------------------------------------------------------
15 import random
16 import numpy as np
17 from nsga_rep.utils.crowded_comparison import \
18     crowded_comparison_operator
19 # ------------------------------------------------------------
20 def binary_tournament(pop_chrom, pop_rank, pop_cdist):
21     # number of chromosomes
22     M = np.shape(pop_chrom)[0]
23     # randomly select num_indvs individuals without replacement
24     num_indvs = 3 # this number could be a formal parameter
25     inds = random.sample(range(1, M), num_indvs)
26     # selected individuals
27     selected_chroms = pop_chrom[inds]
```

```
28    selected_ranks = pop_rank[inds]
29    selected_cdists = pop_cdist[inds]
30
31    # select two parents using the crowded comparison operator
32    # nc - counts victories in the comparison
33    nc = np.zeros(num_indvs, dtype=int)
34    for i in range(num_indvs):
35        p0_rank = selected_ranks[i]
36        p0_cdist = selected_cdists[i]
37        for j in range(i+1,num_indvs):
38            p1_rank  = selected_ranks[j]
39            p1_cdist =  selected_cdists[j]
40            # calculate the cco
41            cco = crowded_comparison_operator(p0_rank, p0_cdist,
42                                              p1_rank, p1_cdist)
43            # counts the victory in the comparison
44            if cco == 0:
45                nc[i] = nc[i] + 1
46            else:
47                nc[j] = nc[j] + 1
48
49    # sort in descending order of victories
50    inds_nc = np.argsort(-nc)
51    # return the first two in number of victories
52    ind_p1 = inds_nc[0]
53    parent1 = selected_chroms[ind_p1]
54    ind_p2 = inds_nc[1]
55    parent2 = selected_chroms[ind_p2]
56
57    return parent1, parent2
```

Listing 8.3: Binary Tournament for NSGA-II.

The NSGA-II Algorithm

At iteration k, NSGA-II starts with population P_k of N n-dimensional candidate solutions. It then enters the loop where it generates N children. To create a child, a pair of parents is selected by binary tournament where the selection criterion is the CCO operator. The selected parents are recombined, producing an offspring that then undergoes mutation. All children are stored in matrix Q_k.

A combined population $R_k = P_k \cup Q_k$ is formed. Using fast non-dominated sorting, the Pareto fronts $\mathcal{F}_0, \mathcal{F}_1, \ldots$ of R_k are found. Then, the population for the next generation, P_{k+1}, is created.

P_{k+1} is created as en empty set. Then the algorithm makes $P_{k+1} = P_{k+1} \cup \mathcal{F}_0$. If the number of elements of P_{k+1}, $|P_{k+1}|$, is equal to N, the creation of P_{k+1} is completed, and the algorithm starts a new iteration. If, though, we have $|P_{k+1}| < N$, the creation procedure continues, with fronts being added to P_{k+1}, in the order of their ranking, until $|P_{k+1}| = N$.

During the process of adding fronts to P_{k+1}, one of the fronts will not fit entirely in P_{k+1}. Let us call this front $\mathcal{F}_{last}$. When this happens, the solutions of $\mathcal{F}_{last}$ will be ordered in descending order of the CCO, and the ordered solutions will be sequentially inserted in P_{k+1} until $|P_{k+1}| = N$.

The pseudocode of NSGA-II and the corresponding Python code are respectively shown in Algorithm 8.4 and Listing 8.4.

Algorithm 8.4. Non-Dominated Sorted Genetic Algorithm II

1: **procedure** NSGA-II
2:    $k \leftarrow 0$ ▷ index of the current iteration
3:    $P_k \leftarrow$ initial population of N candidate solutions
4:    $Q_k \leftarrow \emptyset$ ▷ population of children
5:    **while** termination criterion not satisfied **do**
6:       **for** $i \in \{0, \ldots, N-1\}$ **do**
7:          $(\mathbf{p}_1, \mathbf{p}_2) \leftarrow$ select two parents from P_k
8:          $\mathbf{r} \leftarrow$ recombine$(\mathbf{p}_1, \mathbf{p}_2)$ ▷ create a child by crossover
9:          $\mathbf{q} \leftarrow$ mutate$(\mathbf{r})$ ▷ mutate the child
10:          $Q_k \leftarrow Q_k \cup \{\mathbf{q}\}$ ▷ update the population of children
11:       **end for**
12:       $R_k \leftarrow P_k \cup Q_k$ ▷ create a combined population
13:       $\mathcal{F} \leftarrow$ all non-dominated fronts in R_k ▷ $\mathcal{F} = (\mathcal{F}_0, \mathcal{F}_1, \ldots)$
14:       $P_{k+1} \leftarrow \{\}$ ▷ new population
15:       **while** P_{k+1} does not have N individuals **do**
16:          $i \leftarrow 0$
17:          **if** P_{k+1} has room for all elements of $\mathcal{F}_i$ **then**
18:             $P_{k+1} \leftarrow P_{k+1} \cup \mathcal{F}_i$ ▷ add i-th front to the parent population
19:          **else**
20:             $P_{k+1} \leftarrow P_{k+1} \cup$ the first $(N - |P_{k+1}|)$ points of $\mathcal{F}_i$
21:          **end if**
22:          $i \leftarrow i + 1$
23:       **end while**
24:       Delete the fronts that could not be inserted in P_{k+1}
25:       $k \leftarrow k + 1$
26:    **end while**
27: **end procedure**

```
 1 # ---------------------------------------------------------------
 2 #                           NSGA-II
 3 # Non-Dominated Sorting Genetic algorithm for Continuous
 4 #                         Optimization
 5 # ---------------------------------------------------------------
 6 # implemented as a minimization algorithm
 7 # ---------------------------------------------------------------
 8 # Inputs:
 9 #    pop_size    - number of individuals in the population
10 #    max_iters   - maximum number of optimization iterations
11 #    pc          - crossover probability
12 #    pm          - mutation probability
13 #    f_init      - function that creates the initial population
14 #    f_cost      - function to be minimized
15 #    f_cross     - function that performs crossover
16 #    f_mut       - function that performs mutation
```

```
17 #    lb        - n-dimensional vector lower bound on solutions
18 #    ub        - n-dimensional vector upper bound on solutions
19 #    n_dim     - dimensionality of the candidate solutions
20 #    n_goals   - number of goals of f_cost
21 # Outpus:
22 #    pop_chrom - Approximate Pareto front
23 #    pop_fit   - Approximate Pareto set
24 # -------------------------------------------------------------
25 # file: nsga2.py
26 # -------------------------------------------------------------
27 from nsga_rep.utils.binary_tournament_nsga2 import \
28     binary_tournament
29 from nsga_rep.utils.non_dominated_sort import \
30     fast_non_dominated_sort
31 # -------------------------------------------------------------
32 def nsga2(pop_size, max_iters, pc, pm, f_init, f_cost,
33          f_cross, f_mut, lb, ub, n_dim, n_goals):
34     ## Generate population
35     # This implementation of NSGA-2 requires the population
36     # size to be an even number greater than 2
37     if pop_size % 2 != 0 or pop_size <= 2:
38         raise ValueError("The population size must be an \
39         even number greater than 2")
40     # Generating
41     pop_chrom = f_init(pop_size, n_dim, lb, ub)
42     # Calculate the fitness values of the individuals
43     pop_cost = np.zeros((pop_size, n_goals))
44     for pop_index in range(pop_size):
45         pop_cost[pop_index] = f_cost(pop_chrom[pop_index])
46     # Calculate population ranks and non-dominated fronts
47     F, pop_rank = fast_non_dominated_sort(pop_chrom, pop_cost)
48     # calculate crowding distance for all population
49     pop_cdist = crowding_distance(pop_cost, F, n_goals)
50     ## Main loop
51     for id_iter in range(max_iters):
52         # Generate children
53         # children
54         children_chrom = np.zeros((pop_size, n_dim))
55         children_fit = np.zeros((pop_size, n_goals))
56         # generating loop
57         for k in range(0, pop_size - 1, 2):
58             # selection according to rank and crowding distance
59             [parent1_chrom, parent2_chrom] = \
60                 binary_tournament(pop_chrom,
61                                   pop_rank,
62                                   pop_cdist)
63             # crossover
64             [child1_chrom, child2_chrom] = \
65                 f_cross(parent1_chrom, parent2_chrom, pc)
66             # make sure the offspring is in [lb, ub]
67             child1_chrom = np.clip(child1_chrom, lb, ub)
68             child2_chrom = np.clip(child2_chrom, lb, ub)
69             # mutation
70             child1_chrom = f_mut(child1_chrom, pm, lb, ub)
71             child2_chrom = f_mut(child2_chrom, pm, lb, ub)
72             # new children
73             children_chrom[k] = child1_chrom
```

```
74          children_chrom[k + 1] = child2_chrom
75          # calculate the fitness values of the children
76          children_fit[k] = f_cost(children_chrom[k])
77          children_fit[ k +1] = f_cost(children_chrom[k + 1])
78
79      # Combined population
80      pop_comb_chrom = np.vstack((pop_chrom, children_chrom))
81      pop_comb_fit = np.vstack((pop_cost, children_fit))
82      # Non-Dominated Sorting
83      [F, _] = \
84          fast_non_dominated_sort(pop_comb_chrom,
85                                  pop_comb_fit)
86      # Crowding distance
87      pop_comb_cdist = \
88          crowding_distance(pop_comb_fit,
89                            F,
90                            n_goals)
91      # Gonna create a new population inserting the
92      # fronts one by one
93      inds_F = F[0]
94      # sort the first front in descending cdist order
95      sorted_ids = np.argsort(-pop_comb_cdist[inds_F])
96      sorted_ids = np.array(inds_F)[sorted_ids]
97      # sorted front and corresponding fitness values
98      sorted_front = pop_comb_chrom[sorted_ids]
99      sorted_fit = pop_comb_fit[sorted_ids]
100     # add the first front, creating the new population
101     new_pop_chrom = sorted_front
102     new_pop_fit = sorted_fit
103     # Update the new population
104     n_fronts = len(F)
105     for id_front in range(1, n_fronts):
106         inds_F = F[id_front]
107         # If there is room, add another front
108         if len(new_pop_chrom)  <= pop_size:
109             # sort the front according to descending crowding
110             # distance
111             sorted_ids = np.argsort(-pop_comb_cdist[inds_F])
112             sorted_ids = np.array(inds_F)[sorted_ids]
113             sorted_front = pop_comb_chrom[sorted_ids]
114             sorted_fit = pop_comb_fit[sorted_ids]
115             # update the new population
116             new_pop_chrom = np.vstack((new_pop_chrom,
117                                        sorted_front))
118             new_pop_fit = np.vstack((new_pop_fit,
119                                      sorted_fit))
120         else:
121             break
122     # Select only the best first pop_size individuals
123     new_pop_chrom = new_pop_chrom[:pop_size]
124     new_pop_fit = new_pop_fit[:pop_size]
125     # Population for the next iteration
126     pop_chrom = np.copy(new_pop_chrom)
127     pop_cost = np.copy(new_pop_fit)
128     # Compute population ranks and non-dominated fronts
129     F, pop_rank = fast_non_dominated_sort(pop_chrom, pop_cost
    )
```

```
130        # Compute crowding distance for all population
131        pop_cdist = crowding_distance(pop_cost, F, n_goals)
132    ## Returns
133    return pop_cost, pop_chrom
134
135 # -----------------------------------------------------------
136 #              Compute the Crowding Distance
137 # -----------------------------------------------------------
138 # Inputs:
139 #   pop_cost  - vector containing the cost of each candidate
140 #               solution in the current population
141 #   F         - Pareto fronts of the current population
142 #   n_goals   - number of goals of f_cost
143 # Outpus:
144 #   pop_chrom - Approximate Pareto front
145 #   pop_fit   - Approximate Pareto set
146 # -----------------------------------------------------------
147 # file: crowding_distance.py
148 # -----------------------------------------------------------
149 import math
150 import numpy as np
151 # -----------------------------------------------------------
152 def crowding_distance(pop_cost, F, n_goals):
153     # Number of fronts
154     n_fronts = len(F)
155     # Crowding distance for each solution in the
156     # population
157     # pop_cdist = np.zeros((len(pop_cost),1))
158     pop_cdist = np.zeros(len(pop_cost))
159     # For each front
160     for idf in range(n_fronts):
161         # Solutions indexes in this front
162         sol_indexes = F[idf]
163         # Fitness values for each solution in the front
164         front_costs = pop_cost[sol_indexes]
165         # Number of solutions in this front
166         n_solutions = len(sol_indexes)
167         # Distances for each dimension of each solution
168         # dist = np.zeros((n_solutions, n_goals))
169         dist = np.zeros(n_solutions)
170         # For each dimension of the solutions
171         for idg in range(n_goals):
172             # Sort in ascending order of cost value
173             # in dimension idg
174             sorted_idx = np.argsort(front_costs[:, idg])
175             # Vector of cost values in dimension idg
176             # sorted in ascending order
177             cj = front_costs[sorted_idx, idg]
178             # Both the smallest and largest costs in this front
179             # have infinite crowding distance
180             # pop_cdist[sol_indexes[0]] = math.inf
181             # pop_cdist[sol_indexes[-1]] = math.inf
182             dist[sorted_idx[0]] = math.inf
183             dist[sorted_idx[-1]] = math.inf
184             # For each intermediate solution in this front
185             for ii in range(1, n_solutions - 1):
186                 # Obtain the smallest and the largest
```

```
187    # cost values in dimension idg
188    c_ini = cj[0]
189    c_end = cj[-1]
190    # Normalizing factor
191    den = n_goals * np.abs(c_end - c_ini)
192    # Difference in the function values of
193    # two adjacent solutions
194    num = np.abs(cj[ii + 1] - cj[ii - 1])
195    if den == 0:
196        # print('crowding error')
197        # dist[sorted_idx[ii], idg] = math.inf
198        continue
199    # else:
200    # Absolute normalized difference in the
201    #   function values of two adjacent
202    # solutions
203    dist[sorted_idx[ii]] += num / den
204    # The crowding distance of solution ii is the sum
   of the
205    # distances of each of its dimensions
206    # pop_cdist[sol_indexes[ii]] = pop_cdist[
   sol_indexes[ii]] + dist[sorted_idx[ii], idg]
207    for idpop in range(n_solutions):
208        pop_cdist[sol_indexes[idpop]] = dist[idpop]
209    # return the crowding distance of each candidate solution
210    return pop_cdist
```

Listing 8.4: NSGA-II.

Chapter 9

Multiobjective Evolutionary Algorithm Based on Decomposition

Consider the continuous multi-objective optimization problem

$$\underset{\mathbf{x}}{\text{minimize}} \quad F(\mathbf{x}) = \{f_{o_1}(\mathbf{x}), \dots, f_{o_{n_g}}(\mathbf{x})\}$$
$$\text{subject to} \quad \mathbf{x} \in \Omega \tag{9.1}$$

where $\mathbf{x} \in \mathbb{R}^{n_x}$, Ω is the feasible region of the decision space, $F : \Omega \to \mathbb{R}^{n_g}$ consists of n_g real-valued objective functions.

In order to solve problem (9.1), MOEA/D [92] decomposes it into a number of single-objective subproblems. The single-objective subproblems are constructed by aggregating the different optimization objectives $f_{o_i}(\cdot)$, $i \in \{1, \dots, n_g\}$, in a single function. A commonly used aggregation approach is the Tchebycheff method (see Section 10.5), which yields the following scalarized objective function

$$f_s(\mathbf{x}|\lambda^j) = \max_{i \in \{1, \dots, n_g\}} \lambda_i^j |f_{oi}(\mathbf{x}) - z_i^\star| \tag{9.2}$$

where $\mathbf{x} \in \mathbb{R}^{n_x}$, $\mathbf{z}^\star \in \mathbb{R}^{n_g}$ is the reference point, i.e., $z_i^\star = \min\{f_i(\mathbf{x}) | \mathbf{x} \in \Omega\}$, and $\lambda_i^j \geq 0$ is the ith component of the weight vector $\lambda^j = \{\lambda_1^j, \dots, \lambda_{n_g}^j\} \in \mathbb{R}^{n_g}$.

In MOEA/D, a subproblem is defined as the minimization of a given scalarized function such as (9.2). A subproblem thus is defined by its weight vector. The jth subproblem that results from applying the Tchebycheff approach to decompose problem (9.1) is written as

$$\underset{\mathbf{x}}{\text{minimize}} \quad f_s(\mathbf{x}|\lambda^j)$$
$$\text{subject to} \quad \mathbf{x} \in \Omega \tag{9.3}$$

where Ω is the feasible region of the search space.

The motivation behind using the Tchebycheff approach to scalarization is that for each Pareto point $\mathbf{x}^{\star}$ there is a weight vector λ such that $\mathbf{x}^{\star}$ is the optimal solution of (9.3), and each optimal solution of (9.3) is a Pareto optimal solution of (9.1). It is thus possible to obtain different Pareto solutions by *altering the weight vector* λ.

A central idea in MOEA/D is that the optimal solutions to two neighboring subproblems should be similar. The neighborhood of a subproblem is defined as the set of its T closest subproblems. The distance between two subproblems is computed as the distance between their weight vectors. Each individual in the population of MOEA/D represents the best solution found so far for one of the subproblems. To solve a given subproblem, MOEA/D exploits information from the solutions in the neighborhood of the subproblem.

Initialization

MOEA/D first initializes a population of N individuals $P = \{\mathbf{x}_1,\ldots,\mathbf{x}_N\}$, computes the multi-objective costs of those individuals, obtaining the cost vector $\{F(\mathbf{x}_1),\ldots,F(\mathbf{x}_N)\}$, and then initializes the reference point $\mathbf{z} = \{z_1,\ldots,z_{n_g}\}$, where z_i is the lowest cost for the ith optimization goal in the entire population. An external population, EP, will be used to store all non-dominated solutions found by the algorithm. It is initialized as an empty set.

Evenly distributed weight vectors λ^j, $j = \{1,\ldots,N\}$, are then created, thus defining N subproblems. The Euclidean distances between the weight vectors are used to compute the neighborhood B of each subproblem.

Update

For each subproblem i, $i = \{1,\ldots,N\}$, repeat the following steps.

Reproduce. Randomly select two parents from the neighborhood of the ith subproblem. Then generate a new child y using genetic operators.

Repair / improvement. Apply any necessary repair or improvement heuristic on y. The result is y'. An example of repair heuristic can be simply to maintain y' within the limits of the search space.

Update z. If $z_i > f_i(y')$, then make $z_i = f_i(y')$.

Update the neighboring solutions. For each subproblem j in the neighborhood of the ith subproblem, do the following. If y' produces a lower value of the jth subproblem than the jth individual of the population, then replace the jth individual of the population with y'.

Update EP. Remove all solutions that are dominated by y' from the EP. Add y' to the EP if none of the remaining solutions in EP dominates y'.

Stopping

If the stopping criteria has not been satisfied, restart the update steps, otherwise the EP is returned as the approximate Pareto front. The pseudocode of MOEA/D is given in Algorithm 9.1.

Algorithm 9.1. Multi-Objective Evolutionary Algorithm Based on Decomposition

---

1: $N \leftarrow$ population size
2: $N_e \leftarrow$ maximum size of the external population
3: $M \leftarrow$ maximum number of iterations
4: $T \leftarrow$ number of neighbors
5: $F \leftarrow$ multi-objective goal function
6: $lb \leftarrow$ lower limits of the search space
7: $ub \leftarrow$ upper limits of the search space
8: $nGoals \leftarrow$ number of optimization goals of F
9: $p_c \leftarrow$ crossover probability
10: $p_m \leftarrow$ mutation probability
11: **procedure** MOEA/D
12:     EP $\leftarrow$ empty external population
13:     $\lambda \leftarrow$ initialize N evenly spread weight vectors
14:     $B_i \leftarrow$ compute the T nearest neighbors of weight vector λ_i, $i \in \{1,\dots,N\}$
15:     $P \leftarrow$ initialize the population with N individuals
16:     $F_P \leftarrow$ compute the multi-objective cost of the individuals in P
17:     $z \leftarrow$ create the reference point according to F_P
18:     **for** $id\_i \in \{1,\dots M\}$ **do**
19:         **for** $id\_p \in \{1,\dots,N\}$ **do**
20:             $\mathbf{p}_1, \mathbf{p}_2 \leftarrow$ with probability p_c, randomly select two individuals from B_{id_p} or from P
21:             $\mathbf{y} = \text{crossover}(\mathbf{p}_1, \mathbf{p}_2)$ ▷ produce a child by recombing $\mathbf{p}_1$ and $\mathbf{p}_2$
22:             $\mathbf{y} = \text{mutation}(\mathbf{y}, p_m)$ ▷ with probability p_m mutate the child
23:             $\mathbf{y}' = \text{repair}(\mathbf{y})$ ▷ Repair and/or improve $\mathbf{y}$
24:             $z = \text{update}(z, F(\mathbf{y}'))$ ▷ Update z
25:             $P, F_P = \text{update\_neighborhood}(id\_p, B_{id\_p}, P, F_P, z, \mathbf{y}', F(\mathbf{y}'))$ ▷ update neighbors of P_{id_p}
26:             $EP = \text{update\_EP}(EP, \mathbf{y}', F(\mathbf{y}'), N_e)$ ▷ Update the external population
27:         **end for**
28:     **end for** return EP
29: **end procedure**

```
1 # ------------------------------------------------------------
2 # MOEA/D - Implemented for minimization
3 # ------------------------------------------------------------
4 # Inputs
5 #    popSize    - population size
6 #    epMaxSize  - maximum size of the external population
```

```python
7 #    maxIters    - maximum number of iterations
8 #    T           - number of the weight vectors in a
9 #                     neighborhood of each weight vector
10 #   F           - multi-objective cost function
11 #   lb          - lower limit of the search space
12 #   ub          - upper limit of the search space
13 #   nGoals      - number of goals of F
14 #   pc          - probability of neighbors crossing over
15 #   pm          - mutation probability
16 # Outputs:
17 #   EP_f        - Approximate Pareto front
18 #   EP_x        - Approximate Pareto set
19 # -----------------------------------------------------
20 # file: moead.py
21 # -----------------------------------------------------
22 import numpy as np
23 from moead_rep.utils.cross import cross
24 from moead_rep.utils.init_pop import init_rv
25 from moead_rep.utils.z_update import z_update
26 from moead_rep.utils.update_EP import update_EP
27 from moead_rep.utils.repair_child import f_repair
28 from moead_rep.utils.update_neighborhood import \
       update_solutions_in_B
29 from moead_rep.utils.initialize_L_B import \
       initialize_lambda_neighbors
30 from operators_rep.mutation.mutation_gaussian_rv import \
       mutation_gaussian_rv as mut
31 # -----------------------------------------------------
32 def moead(popSize, epMaxSize, maxIters, T, F, lb, ub, nGoals, pc,
       pm):
33     ## Initialization
34     numVar = np.shape(lb)[0]  # problem dimension
35     # initialize neighborhoods and weight vectors
36     lambd, B = initialize_lambda_neighbors(popSize, T, nGoals)
37     # Randomly generate a population respecting upper
38     # and lower bounds
39     pop_chrom = init_rv(popSize, numVar, lb, ub)
40     # create the reference point
41     z = np.infty*np.ones(nGoals)
42     # Compute the cost values of the
43     # population
44     pop_cost = np.zeros((popSize, nGoals))
45     for i in range(popSize):
46         # compute the cost
47         pop_cost[i] = F(pop_chrom[i])
48         # update the reference point
49         z = z_update(z,pop_cost[i])
50     # Indicate if the external population has been created
51     EP_created = False
52     ## Optimization loop
53     for id_i in range(maxIters):
54         # For each candidate solution
55         for id_p in range(popSize):
56             # Reproduction --------------------------
57             if np.random.rand() < pc:
58                 # Randomly select two parents from the
59                 # neighborhood of sub-problem id_p
```

```
60          ids_n = B[id_p]
61          id_parents = np.random.choice(ids_n, 2,\
62                                  replace=False)
63          p1_chrom = pop_chrom[id_parents[0]]
64          p2_chrom = pop_chrom[id_parents[1]]
65      else:
66          # Randomly select two parents from the
67          # entire population
68          id_parents = np.random.choice(range(popSize),\
69                              2, replace=False)
70          p1_chrom = pop_chrom[id_parents[0]]
71          p2_chrom = pop_chrom[id_parents[1]]
72      # produce a child by crossover
73      y_prime_chrom = cross(p1_chrom, p2_chrom, lb, ub)
74      # mutate the child
75      y_prime_chrom = mut(y_prime_chrom, pm, lb, ub)
76      # Improvement and/or repair --------------
77      y_prime_chrom = f_repair(y_prime_chrom,lb,ub)
78      # child's cost
79      y_prime_cost = F(y_prime_chrom)
80      # Update z ---------------------------------
81      z = z_update(z,y_prime_cost)
82      # Update of neighboring solutions --------
83      pop_chrom, pop_cost = update_solutions_in_B(id_p,
84                                  B,
85                                  pop_chrom,
86                                  pop_cost,
87                                  y_prime_chrom,
88                                  y_prime_cost,
89                                  z,lambd)
90      # Updating EP ----------------------------------
91      if EP_created == False:
92          EP_created = True
93          # create external population
94          EP_x = np.array([y_prime_chrom])
95          EP_f = np.array([y_prime_cost])
96      else:
97          # update external population
98          EP_x, EP_f = update_EP(y_prime_chrom,
99                              y_prime_cost,
100                             EP_x,
101                             EP_f)
102     # Limit the size of the EP. This is just to
103     # prevent the EP from growing too much and
104     # thus demanding too much memory
105     if len(EP_f)>epMaxSize:
106         # random selection of the survivors
107         ids = np.random.choice(len(EP_f),
108                             epMaxSize,
109                             replace=False)
110         # keep just the selected survivors
111         EP_f = EP_f[ids]
112         EP_x = EP_x[ids]
113 # Final results
114 return EP_f, EP_x
```

Listing 9.1: MOEAD algorithm.

All functions used in Listing 9.1 are given below.

■ Scalarized cost function - implemented in Listing 9.2.

■ Compute weight vectors and their neighborhoods - implemented in Listing 9.3.

■ Initialize the population - implemented in Listing 9.4.

■ Produce offspring by crossover - implemented in Listing 9.5.

■ Repair offspring - implemented in Listing 9.6.

■ Updating **z** - implemented in Listing 9.7.

■ Updating neighboring solutions - implemented in Listing 9.8.

■ Check domination - implemented in Listing 9.9.

■ Updating external population - implemented in Listing 9.10.

```
1  # -------------------------------------------------
2  # Tchebycheff scalarized cost function
3  # -------------------------------------------------
4  # fc    - value of the multi-objective cost function for
5  #         a given individual
6  # z     - reference point
7  # lambd - weight vector
8  # -------------------------------------------------
9  # file: scalarized_cost.py
10 # -------------------------------------------------
11 import numpy as np
12 # -------------------------------------------------
13 def scalarized_cost(fc, z, lambd):
14     g = np.max(lambd * np.abs(fc - z))
15     return g
```

Listing 9.2: Scalarized cost functions.

```
1  # -------------------------------------------------
2  # Initialize weight vectors and the corresponding
3  # neighborhoods
4  # -------------------------------------------------
5  # nGoals        - number of goals
6  # popSize       - population size
7  # T             - number of neighbors
8  # -------------------------------------------------
9  # initialize_L_B.py
10 # -------------------------------------------------
11 import numpy as np
12 from scipy.spatial.distance import cdist
13 # -------------------------------------------------
14 def initialize_lambda_neighbors(popSize, T, nGoals):
15     # 1 - Compute the lambda vectors
16     # # There are popSize lambda vectors
```

```
17    # # each lambda vector has nGoals elements
18    lambdas = np.zeros((popSize, nGoals))
19    for il in range(popSize):
20        lambdas[il] = np.random.rand(nGoals)
21    # 2 - Compute neighborhoods
22    subProblem_ids_neighbors = np.zeros((popSize, T), dtype=int)
23    # Compute distances between weight vectors
24    D = cdist(lambdas,lambdas)
25    # Compute the T nearest neighbors of each weight vector
26    for i in range(popSize):
27        inds = np.argsort(D[i,:])
28        # Start at 1 in order to prevent the ith element from
29        # being its own neighbor
30        subProblem_ids_neighbors[i] = inds[1:T+1]
31    return lambdas, subProblem_ids_neighbors
```

Listing 9.3: Initialization of the λ weight vectors and their neighborhoods.

```
1  # ----------------------------------------------------
2  # Initiates a real-valued population of M individuals
3  # and N decision variables in the interval [lb,ub]
4  # ----------------------------------------------------
5  # M      - number of individuals
6  # N      - dimensionality of the individuals
7  # lb     - lower limit of the search space
8  # ub     - upper limit of the search space
9  # ----------------------------------------------------
10 import numpy as np
11 # ----------------------------------------------------
12 def init_rv(M, N, lb, ub):
13     pop_chrom = np.random.uniform(lb, ub, (M, N))
14     pop_chrom[0] = lb
15     pop_chrom[-1] = ub
16     return pop_chrom
```

Listing 9.4: Initializing the population.

```
1  # ------------------------------------------------------------
2  # Produces a single child by crossover
3  # ------------------------------------------------------------
4  # p1     - first parent
5  # p2     - second parent
6  # lb     - lower bound
7  # ub     - upper bound
8  # ------------------------------------------------------------
9  import numpy as np
10 # ------------------------------------------------------------
11 def cross(p1, p2, lb, ub):
12     gamma = 0.5
13     # draw a vector of len(p1) uniformly distributed
14     # samples from [-gamma, 1 + gamma]
15     alpha = np.random.uniform(-gamma, 1 + gamma, len(p1))
16     # blend the two parents, using as weights vector alpha
17     y = alpha * p1 + (1 - alpha) * p2
18     # enforce the boundaries of the search space
19     y = np.minimum(np.maximum(y, lb), ub)
```

```
20    # return the result of the crossover
21    return y
```

Listing 9.5: Producing offspring.

```
1 # ----------------------------------------------------------
2 # Function that repairs a child in case of constraint
3 # violation. This example only enforces the limits of
4 # the search space.
5 # ----------------------------------------------------------
6 # file: repair_child.py
7 # ----------------------------------------------------------
8 import numpy as np
9 # ----------------------------------------------------------
10 def f_repair(x,lb,ub):
11     # Bound x
12     x = np.minimum(x,ub)
13     x = np.maximum(x,lb)
14
15     return x
```

Listing 9.6: Repairing the offspring.

```
1 # ----------------------------------------------------------
2 #  Update z for minimization
3 # ----------------------------------------------------------
4 # z      - reference point
5 # fc     - multi-objective cost of y'
6 # ----------------------------------------------------------
7 # file: z_update.py
8 # ----------------------------------------------------------
9 import numpy as np
10 # ----------------------------------------------------------
11 def z_update(z, fc):
12     z = np.minimum(z, fc)
13     return z
```

Listing 9.7: Updating z.

```
1 # ----------------------------------------------------------
2 # Update of neighboring solutions
3 # ----------------------------------------------------------
4 # id_p        - index of the solution whose neighbors are
5 #               being updadted
6 # B           - matrix where each ith row is the vector
7 #               of indexes of the ith solution
8 # pop_chrom - individuals of the population
9 # pop_cost  - costs of the individuals of the population
10 # y_chrom   - new child
11 # y_cost    - cost of the new child
12 # z         - reference point
13 # lambd     - weight vectors
14 # ----------------------------------------------------------
15 # file: update_neighborhood.py
16 # ----------------------------------------------------------
17 from moead_rep.utils.scalarized_cost import scalarized_cost
```

```
18 # ---------------------------------------------------------
19 def update_solutions_in_B(id_p, B, pop_chrom, pop_cost,
20                           y_chrom, y_cost, z, lambd):
21     # Get the ids of the subproblems in the vicinity of
22     # subproblem id_p
23     ids_n = B[id_p]
24     # For each subproblem id_n in the neighborhood
25     for id_n in ids_n:
26         # Compute the scalarized cost of the new
27         # candidate solution
28         y_prime_g = scalarized_cost(y_cost,
29                                     z, lambd[id_n])
30         # Compute the scalarized cost of the
31         # current candidate solution
32         pop_g = scalarized_cost(pop_cost[id_n],
33                                 z, lambd[id_n])
34         # If the new candidate solution produces a
35         # smaller scalarized cost than the current
36         # candidate solution, replace the current
37         # candidate solution with the new candidate
38         # solution
39         if y_prime_g < pop_g:
40             pop_chrom[id_n] = y_chrom
41             pop_cost[id_n] = y_cost
42     return pop_chrom, pop_cost
```

Listing 9.8: Updating neighboring solutions.

```
1 # ---------------------------------------------------------
2 # Returns 1 if x dominates y, otherwise returns 0
3 # ---------------------------------------------------------
4 def dominates(x, y):
5     if all(x <= y) and any(x < y):
6         return 1
7     else:
8         return 0
```

Listing 9.9: Checking domination.

```
1 # ---------------------------------------------------------
2 # Update the external population
3 # ---------------------------------------------------------
4 # y_chrom   - new child
5 # y_cost    - cost of the new child
6 # EP_x      - individuals in the external population
7 # EP_f      - multi-objective costs of individuals in the
8 #             external population
9 # ---------------------------------------------------------
10 # file: update_EP.py
11 # ---------------------------------------------------------
12 import numpy as np
13 from moead_rep.utils.dominates import dominates
14 # ---------------------------------------------------------
15 def update_EP(y_chrom, y_cost, EP_x, EP_f):
16     # Find solutions in EP_f that are not dominated
17     # by y_cost
```

```
18  ids_to_keep = list()
19  for id_ep in range(len(EP_f)):
20      if not dominates(y_cost, EP_f[id_ep]):
21          ids_to_keep.append(id_ep)
22  # Remove from EP all solutions dominated by
23  # y_cost
24  EP_f = EP_f[ids_to_keep]
25  EP_x = EP_x[ids_to_keep]
26
27  # Check if y_cost is dominated by any solution
28  # in EP_f
29  y_cost_dominated = False
30  for id_f in range(len(EP_f)):
31      # check domination
32      if dominates(EP_f[id_f], y_cost):
33          y_cost_dominated = True
34          break
35  # add y_chrom/y_cost to EP if no solutions in EP_f
36  # dominate y_cost
37  if y_cost_dominated == False:
38      EP_f = np.vstack((EP_f, y_cost))
39      EP_x = np.vstack((EP_x, y_chrom))
40  return EP_x, EP_f
```

Listing 9.10: Updating external population.

APPLYING EVOLUTIONARY ALGORITHMS

Chapter 10

Solving Optimization Problems with Evolutionary Algorithms

This chapter discusses how to use evolutionary algorithms to solve optimization problems. It describes how to solve both single-objective and multi-objective optimization problems, with greater emphasis on the last class of problems, for it is not uncommon for real-world problems to have more than one objective. Each topic discussed will be illustrated with examples.

10.1   Benchmark Problems

Three benchmark problems are used in this chapter, a constrained single-objective optimization problem, a noisy unconstrained single-objective optimization problem and an unconstrained multi-objective optimization problem. They are widely used benchmarks.

10.1.1   Single-Objective

G08 is a single-objective multimodal constrained function given by

$$f(\mathbf{x}) \quad = \quad -\frac{sin^3(2\pi x_1)sin(2\pi x_2)}{x_1^3(x_1 + x_2)} \tag{10.1}$$

$$g_1(\mathbf{x}) \quad = \quad x_1^2 - x_2 + 1 \leq 0 \tag{10.2}$$

$$g_2(\mathbf{x}) \quad = \quad 1 - x_1 + (x_2 - 4)^2 \leq 0 \tag{10.3}$$

where $0 <= x_1 \leq 10$ and $0 \leq x_2 \leq 10$.

Figure 10.1 shows that G08 is a multimodal optimization problem, with multiple local minima close to the optimal solution, which is $f(\mathbf{x}^\star) = -0.0958250414180359$.

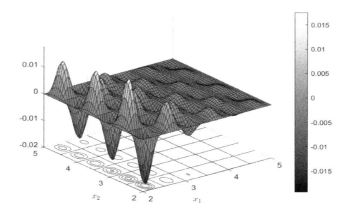

Figure 10.1: G08 is a multimodal function.

Figure 10.2 shows that the feasible region is relatively small. This makes it harder for an optimization algorithm to find the global optimal solution.

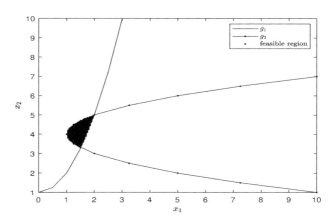

Figure 10.2: Feasible region for G08.

The Python code for the G08 function is

```
1 # --------------------------------------------------------
2 #                        G08
3 # Implements the 2-dimensional G08 function
4 # --------------------------------------------------------
5 # file: g08.py
6 # --------------------------------------------------------
```

```
7 import math as m
8 # --------------------------------------------------------
9 def g08(x):
10     f = -(m.sin(2 * m.pi * x[0]) ** 3) * \
11         (m.sin(2 * m.pi * x[1])) / ((x[0] ** 3) * (x[0] + x[1]))
12     g1 = x[0] ** 2 - x[1] + 1 # g1 <= 0
13     g2 = 1 - x[0] + (x[1] - 4) ** 2 # g2 <= 0
14     return f, g1, g2
```

Listing 10.1: G08 function.

10.1.2 Multi-Objective

ZDT1 is a two-objective n-dimensional unconstrained optimization problem given by

$$f_1(\mathbf{x}) = x_1 \tag{10.4}$$

$$f_2(\mathbf{x}) = g\left(1 - \sqrt{\frac{x_1}{g}}\right) \tag{10.5}$$

where

$$g = 1 + \frac{9}{n-1}\sum_{j=2}^{n} x_j$$

with n equal to the number of decision variables (dimensions) and $x_j \in [0,1]$. The Pareto front of ZDT1 is shown in Figure 10.3.

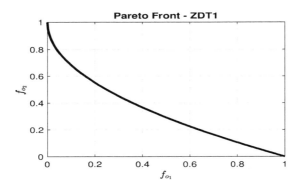

Figure 10.3: Pareto Front of ZDT1.

The Python code for the ZDT1 function is

```
1 # --------------------------------------------------------
2 #   ZDT1 Benchmark Function
3 # The Pareto-optimal front is formed with g(x) = 1
4 # --------------------------------------------------------
5 import numpy as np
```

```
6 # ---------------------------------------------------------
7 def zdt1(x):
8     n_dim = len(x)
9     f1 = x[0]    # objective 1
10    g = 1 + 9 * np.sum(x[1:n_dim]) / (n_dim-1)
11    h = 1 - np.sqrt(f1 / g)
12    f2 = g * h    # objective 2
13    return np.array([f1, f2])
```

Listing 10.2: ZDT1 function.

10.1.3 Noisy

To illustrate the effects of noise in the optimization process the Griewank function (see Section 2.7) corrupted with log normal Gaussian noise will be used. The noisy cost function that will be seen by the optimization algorithms is given by

$$f(\mathbf{x}, \beta) = f(\mathbf{x}) \times \exp(\beta \mathcal{N}(0, 1)) \tag{10.6}$$

where β is the strength of the log-normal Gaussian noise. $\beta = 0.01$ is a moderate noise level, while $\beta = 0.05$ means a high noise level.

The global minimum of Griewank is $f(\mathbf{x}^\star) = 0$ at $\mathbf{x}^\star = (0, \ldots, 0)$. The Griewank was chosen due to its multimodality, a common feature on real-world optimization problems. Figure 10.4 shows the effect of noise on the Griewank function contour curves. As the noise level increases, the contour curves become blurry, indicating that the information received by the optimization algorithm is more misleading.

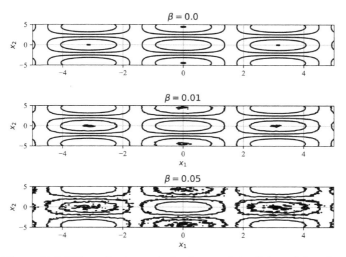

Figure 10.4: Effect of noise on the landscape of the Griewank function.

The Python code for the Griewank function is

```
1 # ---------------------------------------------------------
2 #                      Griewank
```

```
3 # Implements the n-dimensional griewank function
4 # -----------------------------------------------------
5 # file: griewank.py
6 # -----------------------------------------------------
7 import numpy as np
8 # -----------------------------------------------------
9 def griewank(xx):
10     d = len(xx)
11     sum = 0
12     prod = 1
13
14     for ii in range(d):
15         xi = xx[ii]
16         sum = sum + xi**2/4000
17         prod = prod * np.cos(xi/np.sqrt(ii + 1))
18     y = sum - prod + 1
19     return y
```

Listing 10.3: Griewank function.

10.2 Dealing With Constraints

The concept of constrained optimization has already been introduced in Section 2.5, but here it will be seen how to use evolutionary algorithms to solve constrained optimization problems. Assume the following minimization problem

$$
\begin{aligned}
\underset{\mathbf{x}}{\text{minimize}} \quad & f_o(\mathbf{x}) \\
\text{subject to} \quad & g_i \geq 0, \quad i = 1, \dots, m, \\
& h_j = 0, \quad j = 1, \dots, p,
\end{aligned}
\tag{10.7}
$$

where $\mathbf{x}$ is the candidate solution, f_o is the function to be minimized, and g_i and h_j are respectively inequality and equality constraints.

Penalty Functions

One widely used mechanism for dealing with constraints is by applying the concept of *penalty functions*. Penalty functions were originally proposed by Richard Courant in the 1940s. The idea is to transform the constrained optimization problem given in Equation (10.7) into the unconstrained problem given in Equation (10.8) by adding a certain value to the objective function, based on the amount of constraint violation present in a certain solution.

$$
\underset{\mathbf{x}}{\text{minimize}} \quad f_{oc}(\mathbf{x})
\tag{10.8}
$$

A general mathematical formulation for an objective function modified with a penalty function can be written as

$$
f_{oc}(\mathbf{x}) = f_o(\mathbf{x}) + \left[\sum_{i=1}^{m} r_i G_i + \sum_{j=1}^{p} c_j H_j \right]
\tag{10.9}
$$

where $f_{oc}(\mathbf{x})$ is the new objective function, G_i and H_j are respectively functions of the constraints g_i and h_j, and r_i and c_j are positive scalars called *penalty factors*. The common forms of G_i and H_j are

$$G_i(\mathbf{x}) = \max[0, g_i(\mathbf{x})]^\alpha \qquad (10.10)$$
$$L_j(\mathbf{x}) = \|h_j(\mathbf{x})\|^\beta \qquad (10.11)$$

where $\alpha \geq 1$ and $\beta \geq 1$ are scalar values .

Penalty functions make it possible to tackle constrained optimization problems with a regular EA. The main problem with penalty functions is that it is not possible to know a priori how strong should be the penalization for a given optimization problem. On the one hand, too high penalty values can prevent the algorithm from finding good solutions that may be located at the boundary of the feasible region. On the other hand, too low penalty values can make the optimization algorithm waste effort exploring infeasible regions of the search space.

Barrier Functions

If the value of the penalization increases to infinity (a very high value when compared to the maximum value of the unconstrained objective function) as the candidate solution approaches the boundary of the feasible region, the penalty function is called a *barrier function*. The mathematical formulation for the unconstrained optimization problem that results from using a barrier function to handle constraints is

$$\underset{\mathbf{x}}{\text{minimize}} \quad f_o(\mathbf{x}) + p(\mathbf{x}) \qquad (10.12)$$

where

$$p(\mathbf{x}) = \begin{cases} 0, & x \in S \\ \infty, & x \notin S \end{cases}$$

with S being the set of feasible solutions.

Example 14 *To illustrate the effect of using a barrier function to handle constraints, let us solve the following minimization problem*

$$\underset{\mathbf{x}}{\text{minimize}} \quad x_1^2 + x_2^2$$
$$\text{subject to} \quad (x_2 \leq 3) \text{ or } (x_2 \geq 6) \qquad (10.13)$$

To turn this constrained optimization problem into an unconstrained optimization problem a barrier function is applied. The resulting unconstrained problem is

$$f_o(x_1, x_2) = x_1^2 + x_2^2 + p(\mathbf{x}) \qquad (10.14)$$
$$p(\mathbf{x}) = \begin{cases} 0, & (x_2 \leq 3) \text{ or } (x_2 \geq 6) \\ 400, & 3 < x_2 < 6 \end{cases} \qquad (10.15)$$

where 400 can be considered a very high value when compared to the values of the unconstrained objective function.

The effect on the search landscape of using the barrier function to enforce the constraints is seen in Figure 10.5. The top figure shows the search landscape if the objective function were unconstrained, while the lower figure displays the search landscape that results from using the barrier function to enforce the constraints. Clearly the region where $3 < x_2 < 6$ has much higher values of the objective function than the regions where $(x_2 \leq 3)$ or $(x_2 \geq 6)$, making the region $3 < x_2 < 6$ infeasible.

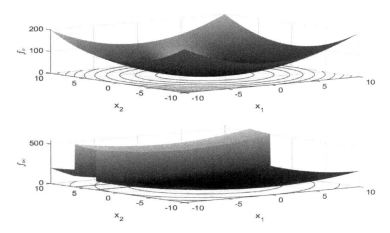

Figure 10.5: The effect of using a barrier function to enforce constraints.

There are more modern approaches to constraint handling, but despite their shortcomings, penalty functions are still one of the most common approaches to handle constraints in the evolutionary algorithms community. Evolutionary algorithms are unconstrained search techniques and thus incorporating constraints into the fitness function is an open research area. Those interested in delving into the subject are referred to [18].

Example 15 *To illustrate the process of solving a single-objective optimization problem with an evolutionary algorithm, let us use a continuous genetic algorithm to solve the G08 function.*

Fitness Function

As the G08 function is a real-valued function, a real-valued representation would be natural. Penalty functions will be used to enforce both the search limits and the inequality constraints of G08.

The Python code for the fitness function is given in Listing 10.4. Note that the fitness function imports the function that implements function G08. Also note the signal change in the line before the return. This is necessary because this function is to be used for minimization by algorithms that were written for maximization.

```
1 # -----------------------------------------------------
2 #  Minimization of the G08 Function
3 # For Maximization Algorithms, like the GA
4 # -----------------------------------------------------
5 from test_functions_rep.so.g08 import g08
6 # -----------------------------------------------------
7 def fitness_g08(x):
8     # barrier functions to enforce the search domain limits
9     if x[0]<=0 or x[0]>10:
10        f = 100
11        return -f
12    if x[1]<0 or x[1]>10:
13        f = 100
14        return -f
15    # goal function
16    f,g1,g2 = g08(x)
17    # barrier function to enforce inequality constraints
18    if g1>0 or g2>0:
19        f = 100
20    # for minimization by algorithms that perform
21    # maximization
22    f = -f
23    return f
```

Listing 10.4: Python code for the fitness function G08.

Selecting the EA

A continuous genetic algorithm (see Section 6.1) is a proper choice for handling real-valued fitness functions. Any other EA capable of handling continuous optimization problems could have been used. The Python code for the continuous GA is shown in Listing 6.1.

Solving the Problem

Listing 10.5 shows how to set values for the configuration parameters and how to call the genetic algorithm to minimize the G08 function.

```
1 # -----------------------------------------------------
2 #       Solving G08 with a Continuous GA
3 # -----------------------------------------------------
4 # file: solve_g08_gac.py
5 # -----------------------------------------------------
6 import numpy as np
7 # function that creates a random population
8 from auxiliary.init_rv import init_rv
9 # fitness function for minimizing G08
10 from fitnessf_max.fitnessf_g08 import fitness_g08
11 # function that implements linear ranking selection
12 from operators_rep.selection.selection_linear_ranking_sus \
13     import selection_linear_ranking_sus
14 # function that implements uniform crossover
15 from operators_rep.crossover.crossover_rv_blending \
16     import blending_crossover
17 # function that implements gaussian mutation
```

```
18 from operators_rep.mutation.mutation_gaussian_rv \
19     import mutation_gaussian_rv
20 # function that implements the continuous GA
21 from ga_rep.algs.gac import gac
22 # ------------------------------------------------
23 # 1 - Define the upper and lower bounds of the search space
24 ndim = 2              # Number of dimensions of the problem
25 ubc = 5
26 lbc = -5
27 lb = lbc*np.ones(ndim)# lower bound for the search space
28 ub = ubc*np.ones(ndim)# upper bound for the search space
29 # ------------------------------------------------
30 # 2 - Define parameters for the optimization
31 npop = 100            # number of individuals in the population
32 maxIterations = 200   # maximum number of iterations
33 # ------------------------------------------------
34 # 3 - Parameters for the GA
35 pc = 0.8             # crossover probability
36 pm = 0.1             # mutation probability
37 er = 0.1             # elitism rate
38
39 initf       = init_rv                 # creates the initial
        population
40 fitnessf    = fitness_g08             # fitness function
41 crossoverf  = blending_crossover      # implements crossover
42 mutationf   = mutation_gaussian_rv    # implements mutation
43 selectionf  = \
44     selection_linear_ranking_sus      # implements selection
45 # ------------------------------------------------
46 # 4 - Call the genetic algorithm
47 best_chrom, _ = gac(npop,
48                     maxIterations,\
49                     pc,pm,er,\
50                     fitnessf, \
51                     selectionf,
52                     crossoverf,\
53                     mutationf,lb,ub)
54 # ------------------------------------------------
55 # 5 - Print the results found
56 from test_functions_rep.so.g08 import g08
57 best_fval,_,_ = g08(best_chrom)
58 print('The minimum value of G08 is %.5f'%(best_fval))
59 print('The minimum is located at ',best_chrom)
60 # ------------------------------------------------
```

Listing 10.5: Python code for the solving G08 with a genetic algorithm.

10.3   Dealing with Costly Objective Functions

In real-world applications, it is very often the case that the evaluation of the objective function is achieved by running costly (in terms of time, money, wear and tear of expensive equipment etc) experiments. Examples of such situations are crash tests of automobiles, wind-tunnel experiments, chemical experiments etc.

The common approach to dealing with such situations is to build a computational surrogate model ([33], [34],[88]) of the objective function, and use this model during the optimization. The surrogate model replaces the objective function in regions of the search space where the surrogate model is capable of simulating the objective function with acceptable accuracy, thus decreasing the number of evaluations of the true objective function. For candidate solutions located in regions of the search space where the model is not accurate enough, the true objective function is evaluated and the resulting data is used to improve the surrogate model. Typical surrogate models are built using regression methods such as Gaussian processes [65] and neural networks ([85], [87]).

It would not be necessary to modify an evolutionary algorithm to use a surrogate model, but the objective function would have to be built around the surrogate model. Building surrogate models is beyond the scope of this book. The interested reader is referred to ([1], [66])

10.4   Dealing with Noise

As described in Section 1.1, one of the most important characteristics of real-world optimization problems is the presence of noise disturbing the objective function. Although evolutionary algorithms tend to be inherently robust to low levels of noise due to their distributed nature and non-reliance on gradient information [12], higher levels of noise can make it harder for the optimizer to find a good solution or can even cause the optimization process to diverge altogether.

Assuming that the noise is additive, the noisy objective function could be written as

$$f_n(\mathbf{x}) = f_o(\mathbf{x}) + \varepsilon \tag{10.16}$$

where $f_n(\mathbf{x})$ is the value of the noise-corrupted objective function at $\mathbf{x} \in \mathbb{R}^n$, $f_o(\mathbf{x})$ is the value of the noise-free objective function at $\mathbf{x}$ and ε is the value of the random noise that perturbs the objective function.

If the probability distribution of ε was known, the effective value of $f_o(\mathbf{x})$ would be given by

$$\bar{f}_o(\mathbf{x}) = \int_{-\infty}^{\infty} (f_o(\mathbf{x}) + \varepsilon) \, p(\varepsilon) d\varepsilon \tag{10.17}$$

where $p(\varepsilon)$ is the probability distribution of ε.

Unfortunately it is almost always the case that the noise term ε follows an unknown probability distribution, preventing the adoption of analytic approaches to calculate the integral in Equation (10.17). In what follows two simple but widely used approaches to handling noise are described. The reader is referred to [69] for a thorough discussion about noise in evolutionary optimization.

Implicit Averaging

Implicit averaging is based on the idea that, as evolutionary algorithms are population-based heuristics, a given candidate solution can be encountered more then once during the optimization process. Every time it is encountered, its fitness value is reevaluated. The result is that a given candidate solution will eventually be evaluated many times [3], as long as the population is big enough [2]. Thus, the inherent multi-population structure of evolutionary algorithms would make them more robust to noise than traditional optimization methods.

Example 16 *This example shows how to use an EA to solve a noisy optimization problem, using implicit averaging. The goal is to visualize the deleterious effects of noise. To this end, a PSO algorithm was used to minimize a noisy Griewank function with different levels of noise. Twenty Monte Carlo runs were performed and the results are shown as box-plots in Figure 10.6.*

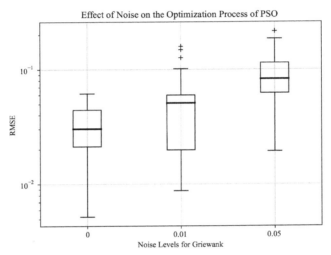

Figure 10.6: Variability of the RMSE of the solutions found by PSO for the 20-d Griewank function with 3 different levels of noise.

The figure depicts the variability of the RMSE between the solution found by the algorithm and the true minimum value of the cost function. The RMSE formulation is

$$\text{RMSE}(\mathbf{y}, \hat{\mathbf{y}}) = \sqrt{\frac{1}{n} \sum_{i=1}^{n} (y_i - \hat{y}_i)^2} \tag{10.18}$$

where y_i is the ith element of the true value $\mathbf{y} \in \mathbb{R}^n$ and $\hat{y}_i$ is the ith element of the estimate $\hat{\mathbf{y}} \in \mathbb{R}^n$.

The lower the RMSE value, the better the estimate is, hence lower values of the RMSE indicate that better solutions were found. The variability is also important. Smaller boxes indicate less variability and hence better results. The line inside each box is the median of the RMSE values. Lower medians also indicate better results. There is thus a negative correlation between noise levels and the quality of the results obtained by PSO. The Python code for this example is in Listing 10.6.

```
 1 # ------------------------------------------------------------
 2 #      Effect of Noise on Optimization
 3 # ------------------------------------------------------------
 4 # file: fig_pso_noise_effect.py
 5 # ------------------------------------------------------------
 6 # Import the necessary libraries and functions
 7 import numpy as np
 8 from pso_rep.pso import pso
 9 from test_functions_rep.so.griewank import griewank
10 from sklearn.metrics import mean_squared_error
11 # ------------------------------------------------------------
12 # 1 - Define the upper and lower bounds of the search
13 #     space
14 # ------------------------------------------------------------
15 ndim = 20                    # Number of dimensions
16 lb = -5*np.ones(ndim)    # Bounds of the search space
17 ub = 5*np.ones(ndim)
18
19 # ------------------------------------------------------------
20 # 2 - Define the parameters for the optimization
21 # ------------------------------------------------------------
22 nMC = 20
23 maxIters = 300   # Number of optimization iterations
24
25 # ------------------------------------------------------------
26 # 3 - Parameters for the PSO
27 # ------------------------------------------------------------
28 noP = 10             # Number of particles
29 c1 = np.ones(ndim)   # Cognitive scaling parameter
30 c2 = np.ones(ndim)   # Social scaling parameter
31 w_min = 0.4*np.ones(ndim) # Minimum inertia
32 w_max = 0.9*np.ones(ndim) # Maximum inertia
33
34 # ------------------------------------------------------------
35 # 4 - Define the cost function
36 # ------------------------------------------------------------
37 # the global minimum of Griewank is
38 # f(xstar) = 0.0 at xstar = [0,0,...,0]
39 cost_fun = griewank
40 x_star = np.zeros(ndim)
41
42 def noisy_cost(xx, beta):
43     # noise-free value
44     y = cost_fun(xx)
45     # incorporate noise
46     y = y*np.exp(beta*np.random.randn())
47     # return the noisy measurement
48     return y
49
50
51 # ------------------------------------------------------------
52 # fitness function for zero noise
53 # ------------------------------------------------------------
54 def fit_zero(x):
55     noise_level = 0
56     fit = -noisy_cost(x, noise_level)
57     return fit
```

```
58
59 # ------------------------------------------------
60 # fitness function for moderate noise
61 # ------------------------------------------------
62 def fit_mod(x):
63     noise_level = 0.01
64     fit = -noisy_cost(x, noise_level)
65     return fit
66
67 # ------------------------------------------------
68 # fitness function for high noise
69 # ------------------------------------------------
70 def fit_high(x):
71     noise_level = 0.05
72     fit = -noisy_cost(x, noise_level)
73     return fit
74
75 # ------------------------------------------------
76 # 5 - Run the PSO algorithm
77 # ------------------------------------------------
78 #   Noiseless Monte Carlo runs
79 np.random.seed(123) # for repeatability
80 rmse_nf   = np.zeros(nMC)
81 for id_run in range(nMC):
82     [a, _, _] = pso(fit_zero, maxIters, lb, ub,
83                     noP, c1, c2, w_min, w_max)
84     rmse_nf[id_run] = mean_squared_error(x_star,a)
85 # ------------------------------------------------
86 #   Monte Carlo runs with moderate noise
87 np.random.seed(123) # for repeatability
88 rmse_mod  = np.zeros(nMC)
89 for id_run in range(nMC):
90     [a, _, _] = pso(fit_mod, maxIters, lb, ub,
91                     noP, c1, c2, w_min, w_max)
92     rmse_mod[id_run] = mean_squared_error(x_star,a)
93 # ------------------------------------------------
94 #   Monte Carlo runs with high noise
95 # ------------------------------------------------
96 np.random.seed(123) # for repeatability
97 rmse_high  = np.zeros(nMC)
98 for id_run in range(nMC):
99     [a, _, _] = pso(fit_high, maxIters, lb, ub,
100                    noP, c1, c2, w_min, w_max)
101     rmse_high[id_run] = mean_squared_error(x_star,a)
102
103 # ------------------------------------------------
104 # 6 - BoxPlots
105 # ------------------------------------------------
106 data_to_plot = [ rmse_nf , rmse_mod , rmse_high ]
107 xticklables = ['0','0.01 ','0.05 ']
108 title = 'Effect of Noise on the Optimization Process of PSO '
109 xlabel = 'Noise Levels for Griewank '
110 ylabel = 'RMSE '
111
112 import matplotlib.pyplot as plt
113 bp = plt.boxplot(data_to_plot, notch=0, sym='+', vert=1, whis=1.5)
114 ticks = np.arange(1,len(xticklables)+1)
```

```
115 plt.xticks(ticks,labels=xticklables)
116 plt.ylabel(ylabel)
117 plt.xlabel(xlabel)
118 plt.yscale('log')
119 plt.grid(True, linestyle='-', which='major', color='lightgrey',
        alpha=0.5)
120 plt.title(title)
121 plt.show()
122
123 # change color and linewidth of the medians
124 for median in bp['medians']:
125     median.set(color='k', linewidth=2)
```

Listing 10.6: PSO solving a noisy Griewank without explicit averaging.

Example 17 *The same minimization of the last example was performed again this time using the DE algorithm. Figure 10.7 shows that the noise seems to have had more intense effects on DE than on PSO. Anyway, the inverse correlation between noise levels and good results was also true for DE. The Python code for this example is in Listing 10.7.*

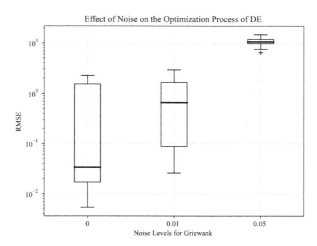

Figure 10.7: Variability of the RMSE of the solutions found by DE for the 20-d Griewank function with 3 different levels of noise.

```
1 # ------------------------------------------------------------
2 #     Effect of Noise on Optimization
3 # ------------------------------------------------------------
4 # file: fig_de_noise_effect.py
5 # ------------------------------------------------------------
6 # Import the necessary libraries and functions
7 import numpy as np
8 from de_rep.algs.de import de
9 from test_functions_rep.so.griewank import griewank
10 from sklearn.metrics import mean_squared_error
11 # ------------------------------------------------------------
```

```python
12 # 1 - Define the upper and lower bounds of the search
13 #       space
14 # ------------------------------------------------------
15 ndim = 20                    # Number of dimensions of the problem
16 lb = -5*np.ones(ndim)        # Bounds of the search space
17 ub = 5*np.ones(ndim)
18
19 # ------------------------------------------------------
20 # 2 - Define the parameters for the optimization
21 # ------------------------------------------------------
22 nMC = 20
23 maxIters = 300   # Number of optimization iterations
24
25 # ------------------------------------------------------
26 # 3 - Parameters for the DE
27 # ------------------------------------------------------
28 pop_size = 20
29 step_size=0.8
30 pc = 0.9
31
32 # ------------------------------------------------------
33 # 4 - Define the cost function
34 # ------------------------------------------------------
35 # the global minimum of Griewank is
36 # f(xstar) = 0.0 at xstar = [0,0,...,0]
37 cost_fun = griewank
38 x_star = np.zeros(ndim)
39
40 def noisy_cost(xx, beta):
41     # noise-free value
42     y = cost_fun(xx)
43     # incorporate noise
44     y = y*np.exp(beta*np.random.randn())
45     # return the noisy measurement
46     return y
47
48 # ------------------------------------------------------
49 # cost function for zero noise
50 # ------------------------------------------------------
51 def cost_zero(x):
52     noise_level = 0
53     fit = noisy_cost(x, noise_level)
54     return fit
55
56 # ------------------------------------------------------
57 # cost function for moderate noise
58 # ------------------------------------------------------
59 def cost_mod(x):
60     noise_level = 0.01
61     fit = noisy_cost(x, noise_level)
62     return fit
63
64 # ------------------------------------------------------
65 # cost function for high noise
66 # ------------------------------------------------------
67 def cost_high(x):
68     noise_level = 0.05
```

```
69      fit = noisy_cost(x, noise_level)
70      return fit
71
72 # ------------------------------------------------------------
73 # 5 - Run the DE algorithm
74 # ------------------------------------------------------------
75 #   Noiseless Monte Carlo runs
76 np.random.seed(123)
77 rmse_nf  = np.zeros(nMC)
78 for id_run in range(nMC):
79     [a,_] = de(cost_zero, pop_size, maxIters, pc, lb, ub,
        step_size)
80     rmse_nf[id_run] = mean_squared_error(x_star,a)
81 # ------------------------------------------------------------
82 #   Monte Carlo runs with moderate noise
83 np.random.seed(123)
84 rmse_mod  = np.zeros(nMC)
85 for id_run in range(nMC):
86     [a, _] = de(cost_mod, pop_size, maxIters, pc, lb, ub,
        step_size)
87     rmse_mod[id_run] = mean_squared_error(x_star,a)
88
89 # ------------------------------------------------------------
90 #   Monte Carlo runs with high noise
91 np.random.seed(123)
92 rmse_high  = np.zeros(nMC)
93 for id_run in range(nMC):
94     [a, _] = de(cost_high, pop_size, maxIters, pc, lb, ub,
        step_size)
95     rmse_high[id_run] = mean_squared_error(x_star,a)
96
97 # ------------------------------------------------------------
98 # 6 - BoxPlots
99 # ------------------------------------------------------------
100 data_to_plot = [ rmse_nf , rmse_mod , rmse_high ]
101 xticklables = ['0','0.01 ','0.05 ']
102 title = 'Effect of Noise on the Optimization Process of DE '
103 xlabel = 'Noise Levels for Griewank '
104 ylabel = 'RMSE '
105
106 import matplotlib.pyplot as plt
107 bp = plt.boxplot(data_to_plot, notch=0, sym='+', vert=1, whis=1.5)
108 ticks = np.arange(1,len(xticklables)+1)
109 plt.xticks(ticks,labels=xticklables)
110 plt.ylabel(ylabel)
111 plt.xlabel(xlabel)
112 plt.yscale('log')
113 plt.grid(True, linestyle='-', which='major', color='lightgrey',
        alpha=0.5)
114 plt.title(title)
115 plt.show()
116
117 # change color and linewidth of the medians
118 for median in bp['medians']:
119     median.set(color='k', linewidth=2)
```

Listing 10.7: DE solving a noisy Griewank without explicit averaging.

Explicit Averaging

Explicit averaging [37] uses Monte Carlo integration to approximately calculate Equation (10.17) and thus reduce the noise-induced uncertainty in the estimation of $f_o(\cdot)$. The method involves performing a number of evaluations of $f_n(\mathbf{x})$, obtaining

$$\bar{f}_n(\mathbf{x}) = \frac{1}{m} \sum_1^m f_n(\mathbf{x}) \tag{10.19}$$

where m is the number of evaluations, also known as *sample size*. Then, the value of $f_o(\mathbf{x})$ is given by $f_o(\mathbf{x}) \approx \bar{f}_n(\mathbf{x})$.

Assuming that the samples of the noise are independent, explicit averaging reduces the standard error of $\bar{f}_n(\mathbf{x})$ by a factor of $\sqrt{m}$. If the noise samples are correlated, though, the reduction may not be that high. Things get even more complicated when the noise is a function of the solution that is being evaluated.

In any case, as a general rule, the bigger the value of m, the smaller the standard error. Increasing m though reduces the budget of evaluations of the objective function available to continue the optimization process. The value of m thus must be chosen for the problem at hand.

Example 18 *The results shown in Figures 10.6 and 10.7 were obtained without resorting to explicit averaging, that means that implicit averaging was automatically used. The effects of explicit averaging can be seen on Figures 10.8 and 10.9. In both cases, as expected, there is a direct correlation between the number of repetitions and the quality of the results obtained by both algorithms.*

The code for Figure 10.9 is in Listing 10.8. The code for Figure 10.8 is almost identical.

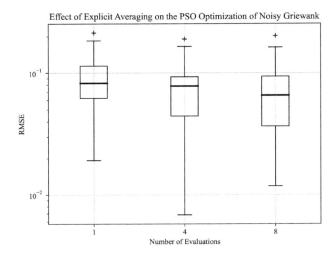

Figure 10.8: Variability of the RMSE of the solutions found by PSO with explicit averaging for the 20-d Griewank function with high noise level.

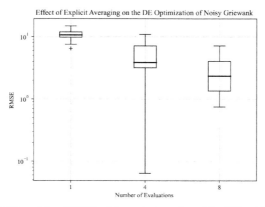

Figure 10.9: Variability of the RMSE of the solutions found by DE with explicit averaging for the 20-d Griewank function with high noise level.

```
 1 # ------------------------------------------------------------
 2 #         DE Algorithm Minimizing a Noisy Griewank
 3 #                 Explicit Averaging
 4 # ------------------------------------------------------------
 5 # file: fig_de_averaging_noisy_griewank.py
 6 #
 7 # Import the necessary libraries and functions
 8 import numpy as np
 9 from de_rep.algs.de import de
10 from test_functions_rep.so.griewank import griewank
11 from sklearn.metrics import mean_squared_error
12 # ------------------------------------------------------------
13 # 1 - Define the upper and lower bounds of the search
14 #     space
15 # ------------------------------------------------------------
16 ndim = 20               # Number of dimensions of the problem
17 lb = -5*np.ones(ndim)   # Bounds of the search space
18 ub = 5*np.ones(ndim)
19
20 # ------------------------------------------------------------
21 # 2 - Define the parameters for the optimization
22 # ------------------------------------------------------------
23 nMC = 20
24 maxIters = 300  # Number of optimization iterations
25
26 # ------------------------------------------------------------
27 # 3 - Parameters for the DE
28 # ------------------------------------------------------------
29 pop_size = 20
30 step_size=0.8
31 pc = 0.9
32
33 # ------------------------------------------------------------
34 # 4 - Define the cost function
35 # ------------------------------------------------------------
36 # the global minimum of Griewank is
37 # f(xstar) = 0.0 at xstar = [0,0,...,0]
```

```python
38 cost_fun = griewank
39 x_star = np.zeros(ndim)
40
41 def noisy_cost(xx, beta):
42     # noise-free value
43     y = cost_fun(xx)
44     # incorporate noise
45     y = y*np.exp(beta*np.random.randn())
46     # return the noisy measurement
47     return y
48
49 # ------------------------------------------------------
50 # function for performing repeated sampling
51 # ------------------------------------------------------
52 def repeated_sampling(x, fcost, noise_level, n_repeats):
53     fitness = np.zeros(n_repeats)
54     # repeated sampling
55     for id in range(n_repeats):
56         fitness[id] = fcost(x,noise_level)
57     # calculate the mean value of the samples
58     mean_fit = np.mean(fitness)
59     # return the mean value
60     return mean_fit
61
62 # ------------------------------------------------------
63 # Cost function for 1 evaluation
64 # ------------------------------------------------------
65 def cost_1(x):
66     n_repeats = 1
67     noise_level = 0.05
68     fit = repeated_sampling(x, noisy_cost, noise_level,
69                             n_repeats)
70     return fit
71
72 # ------------------------------------------------------
73 # Cost function for 4 evaluations
74 # ------------------------------------------------------
75 def cost_4(x):
76     n_repeats = 4
77     noise_level = 0.05
78     fit = repeated_sampling(x, noisy_cost, noise_level,
79                             n_repeats)
80     return fit
81
82 # ------------------------------------------------------
83 # Cost function for 8 evaluations
84 # ------------------------------------------------------
85 def cost_8(x):
86     n_repeats = 8
87     noise_level = 0.05
88     fit = repeated_sampling(x, noisy_cost, noise_level,
89                             n_repeats)
90     return fit
91
92 # ------------------------------------------------------
93 # 5 - Run the DE algorithm
94 # ------------------------------------------------------
```

```
95 # ----------------------------------------------------
96 # 1 evaluation
97 # ----------------------------------------------------
98 np.random.seed(123)
99 rmse_1_reps  = np.zeros(nMC)
100 for id_run in range(nMC):
101     [a, _] = de(cost_1, pop_size, maxIters, pc, lb, ub,
102                 step_size)
103     rmse_1_reps[id_run] = mean_squared_error(x_star,a)
104
105 # ----------------------------------------------------
106 # 4 evaluations
107 # ----------------------------------------------------
108 np.random.seed(123)
109 rmse_4_reps  = np.zeros(nMC)
110 for id_run in range(nMC):
111     [a, _] = de(cost_4, pop_size, maxIters, pc, lb, ub,
112                 step_size)
113     rmse_4_reps[id_run] = mean_squared_error(x_star,a)
114
115 # ----------------------------------------------------
116 # 8 evaluations
117 # ----------------------------------------------------
118 np.random.seed(123)
119 rmse_8_reps  = np.zeros(nMC)
120 for id_run in range(nMC):
121     [a, _] = de(cost_8, pop_size, maxIters, pc, lb, ub,
122                 step_size)
123     rmse_8_reps[id_run] = mean_squared_error(x_star,a)
124
125 # ----------------------------------------------------
126 # 6 - Boxplot
127 # ----------------------------------------------------
128 data_to_plot = [ rmse_1_reps , rmse_4_reps , rmse_8_reps ]
129 xticklables = ['1','4','8']
130 title = 'Effect of Explicit Averaging on the DE Optimization of
131        Noisy Griewank '
131 xlabel = 'Number of Evaluations '
132 ylabel = 'RMSE '
133
134 import matplotlib.pyplot as plt
135 bp = plt.boxplot(data_to_plot, notch=0, sym='+', vert=1, whis=1.5)
136 ticks = np.arange(1,len(xticklables)+1)
137 plt.xticks(ticks,labels=xticklables)
138 plt.ylabel(ylabel)
139 plt.xlabel(xlabel)
140 plt.yscale('log')
141 plt.grid(True, linestyle='-', which='major', color='lightgrey',
142        alpha=0.5)
142 plt.title(title)
143 plt.show()
144
145 # change color and linewidth of the medians
146 for median in bp['medians']:
147     median.set(color='k', linewidth=2)
```

Listing 10.8: DE solving a noisy Griewank with explicit averaging.

10.5 Evolutionary Multi-Objective Optimization

It was seen in Section 2.8 that due to the fact that the different optimization goals that comprise a MOP tend to be in conflict with each other, finding a solution to a MOP is not a trivial task. As the optimization goals are conflicting, there is no single solution that is simultaneously optimal for all goals.

Scalarization

A common approach to solving a MOP is by scalarization [60]. Scalarization means to aggregate the scalar objective functions of the MOP in a new scalar objective function, and then using the resulting function in conjunction with a single-objective evolutionary algorithm to obtain a single point in the Pareto set.

One regularly used method to convert a vectorial objective function $\mathbf{f}_o = [f_{o1}, \ldots, f_{om}]$ into a scalar objective function f_s is to use the weighted Chebyshev distance between the vectorial objective function computed at a given candidate solution and a reference point located in the objective space, as in [31] and [57]:

$$f_s(\mathbf{x}) = \max_{i \in \{1, \ldots, m\}} \lambda_i |f_{oi}(\mathbf{x}) - z_i^\star| \qquad (10.20)$$

where $\mathbf{z}^\star \in \mathbb{R}^m$ is the reference point, m is the number of goals of the multi-objective cost function .

The resulting single-objective optimization problem, also called Chebychev Scalarization Problem (CSP), is

$$\begin{aligned} \underset{x}{\text{minimize}} \quad & f_s(\mathbf{x}) \\ \text{subject to} \quad & x \in \mathcal{X}, \end{aligned} \qquad (10.21)$$

where $\lambda = [\lambda_1, \lambda_2, \ldots, \lambda_m]$ is a vector of real-valued non-negative weights, such that $\forall i \; \lambda_i \in \mathbb{R}_{\geq 0}$ and at for least one i, $\lambda_i > 0$.

It is theoretically guaranteed that for each point $\mathbf{z}_k$ in the Pareto front there is a weight vector λ that makes $\mathbf{z}_k$ a minimizer of (10.21), as long as the reference point $\mathbf{z}^\star$ is properly chosen. In other words, the CSP approach is valid because it is possible to find all solutions in the Pareto set by appropriately changing the weight vector λ [31].

Example 19 *Let us illustrate the scalarization method using the PSO algorithm to solve the ZDT1 problem. The first step is to program a fitness function that receives a candidate solution* $\mathbf{x}$ *and the ideal point* $\mathbf{z}^\star$ *as inputs and then returns the negative of the weighted Chebyshev distance between* $\mathbf{z} = \mathbf{f}_o(\mathbf{x})$ *and* $\mathbf{z}^\star$. *The negative signal is due to the fact that PSO was written as a maximization algorithm and we want it to minimize ZDT1.*

Once the fitness function is defined, define the parameters needed by PSO and run the algorithm. A Python script that performs the optimization is given in Listing 10.9.

```
1 # -----------------------------------------------------------
2 #      Scalarization Method Using the PSO Algorithm
3 #          to Minimize the ZDT1 Function
```

```
 4 # -----------------------------------------------------
 5 # file: fig_pso_scalarization_ZDT1.py
 6 # -----------------------------------------------------
 7 import numpy as np
 8 from pso_rep.pso import pso
 9 from test_functions_rep.mo.zdt1 import zdt1
10
11 # 1 - Define the upper and lower bounds of the search
12 #     space
13 lb = np.array([0, 0])
14 ub = np.array([1, 1])
15
16 # 2 - Define the parameters for the optimization
17 noP = 30          # number of particles
18 maxIters = 50     # number of optimization iterations
19 ndim = 2          # number of dimensions of the problem
20 z_star = np.array([0.5, 0.25]) # ideal point
21
22 # 3 - Parameters for the PSO algorithm
23 c1 = np.ones(ndim)   # cognitive scaling parameter
24 c2 = np.ones(ndim)   # social scaling parameter
25 w_min = 0.2*np.ones(ndim) # maximum inertia
26 w_max = 0.9*np.ones(ndim) # minimum inertia
27
28
29 # 4 - Define the fitness function
30 # arbitrary non-negativeweights
31 lambd = np.ones(ndim)
32 # fitness function returns the negative of
33 # the weighted Chebyshev distance
34 def ffit(x):
35     # Calculate the value of zdt1 at x
36     z = zdt1(x)
37     # Calculate the weighted Chebyshev distance.
38     # The minus sign is due to PSO be
39     # a maximization algorithm
40     dist = -np.max(lambd * np.abs(z - z_star))
41     return dist
42
43
44 # 5 - Run the PSO algorithm
45 xbest, _, _ = pso(ffit, maxIters, lb, ub, noP,
46                   c1, c2, w_min, w_max)
47
48 # Obtaining the point in the
49 # objective space that
50 # corresponds to xbest
51 fbest = zdt1(xbest)
52
53 # print the results
54 print('xbest: {}'.format(xbest))
55 print('fbest: {}'.format(fbest))
```

Listing 10.9: Scalarization method with the PSO algorithm to minimize ZDT1.

The result of the optimization process is depicted in Figure 10.10, where it is shown that PSO algorithm found a point of the true Pareto front where the weighted Chebyshev distance from the ideal point is minimal.

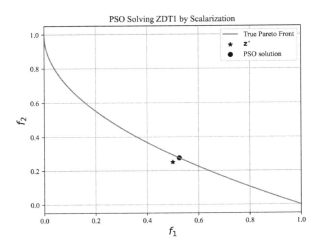

Figure 10.10: Minimization of ZDT1 with scalarization and PSO.

Limitations of the Scalarization Approach

There are other scalarization approaches besides turning the MOP into a CSP. All of them though can only find a single solution at a time. That would not be a problem if the practitioner knew where to search and, for instance, defined a z^* in Equation (10.21) in a region of interest of the search space where he/she knew there were Pareto points.

Nonetheless, as the Pareto front can have a huge number of points, it is certainly interesting for the practitioner to have access to the full Pareto front, so the most interesting solution can be chosen. That is why evolutionary multi-objective optimization algorithms, such as NSGA-II, are important.

Using Multi-Objective Evolutionary Algorithms

In this approach there is no converting the multi-objective problem into a single-objective one. The central idea is to find the best approximation of the Pareto set and hand it over to a decision maker, who will then pick the solutions he/she finds more interesting. The mathematical formulation of this approach is

$$\underset{\mathbf{x}}{\text{minimize}} \quad f_{o1}(\mathbf{x}), f_{o2}(\mathbf{x}), \ldots, f_{om}(\mathbf{x})$$
$$\text{subject to} \quad \mathbf{x} \in \mathcal{X} \tag{10.22}$$

where $m \geq 2$ is the number of individual objective functions, and $\mathcal{X}$ is the set of feasible solutions.

The two main goals of this approach are finding a set of solutions that are as diverse as possible (ideally uniformly covering the Pareto front) and are also as close as possible to the true Pareto front (accurate convergence).

Example 20 *Let us illustrate the approach using the NSGA-II algorithm (see Chapter 8) to solve the ZDT1 problem. As NSGA-II is written as a minimization algorithm, the cost function simply calculates the value of ZDT1 for the candidate solution it receives.*

Once the cost function is defined, define the parameters needed by NSGA-II, define the parameters that control the optimization and run the algorithm, which returns the solutions found. The solutions found would be given to a decision maker. A Python script that performs the optimization is given in Listing 10.10.

```
 1 # -----------------------------------------------------
 2 # Multi-Objective Optimization Using NSGA-II Algorithm
 3 #            to Minimize the ZDT1 Function
 4 # -----------------------------------------------------
 5 # file: fig_ZDT1_nsga2.py
 6 # -----------------------------------------------------
 7 import numpy as np
 8 from auxiliary.init_rv import init_rv
 9 from nsga_rep.algs.nsga2 import nsga2
10 from test_functions_rep.mo.zdt1 import zdt1
11 from operators_rep.crossover.crossover_rv_sbx import sbx_crossover
12 from operators_rep.mutation.mutation_gaussian_rv import
      mutation_gaussian_rv
13
14 # -- Problem Setting
15 fname = "ZDT1"
16 n_dim = 30
17
18 # -- Configuring the optimization
19 max_iterations = 300 # number of optimization iterations
20 pop_size = 100       # number of individuals in the population
21
22 # -- Configure NSGA-II
23 pc = 0.9             # crossover probability
24 pm = 0.1             # mutation probability
25
26 f_init  = init_rv                 # initiates a random population
27 f_cross = sbx_crossover           # performs crossover
28 f_mut   = mutation_gaussian_rv    # performs mutation
29
30 # --- Optimization
31 # the ZDT1 problem
32 f_cost = zdt1
33 n_goals = 2
34 lb = 0*np.ones(n_dim)
35 ub = 1*np.ones(n_dim)
36 # perform the optimization
37 F_cost, F_chrom = nsga2(pop_size, max_iterations, pc,
38                         pm, f_init, f_cost, f_cross,
39                         f_mut, lb, ub, n_dim, n_goals)
40
41
```

```
42 # --- PLOT
43 # plot the approximate Pareto front
44 import matplotlib.pyplot as plt
45 plt.xlabel('$f_1$', fontsize=15)
46 plt.ylabel('$f_2$', fontsize=15)
47 plt.scatter(F_cost[:, 0], F_cost[:, 1], marker=".", color='k',
        label='NSGA2')
48 ll = fname + ' - ' + str(n_dim) + ' dimensions'
49 plt.title(ll)
50 plt.legend()
51 plt.xlim(0,1)
52 plt.show()
```

Listing 10.10: Multi-objective optimization method using the NSGA-II algorithm to minimize ZDT1.

The optimization process is depicted in Figure 10.11, with the algorithm finding solutions that provide a good coverage of the true Pareto front.

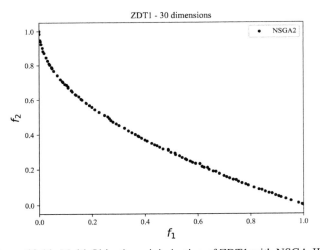

Figure 10.11: Multi-Objective minimization of ZDT1 with NSGA-II.

10.6 Some Auxiliary Functions

This section describes auxiliary functions used in the examples in this chapter. It can be skipped without loss of continuity.

Create a Random Population

Function *init_rv* creates a random population of N n-dimensional continuous vectors in the hypercube limited by $[l_b, u_b]$, where l_b and u_b are n-dimensional lower bound and upper bound vectors.

```
1 import numpy as np
2 def init_rv(M, N, lb, ub):
```

```
 3   # -----------------------------------------------------
 4   # Initiates a real-valued population of M individuals
 5   # and N decision variables in the interval [lb,ub]
 6   # ---------------------------------------------------
 7   pop_chrom = np.random.uniform(lb, ub, (M, N))
 8   pop_chrom[0] = lb
 9   pop_chrom[-1] = ub
10   return pop_chrom
```

Listing 10.11: *init_rv* and *init_bin* functions.

Selection Using Linear Ranking

Function *selection_linear_ranking_sus* selects two parents for mating, according to their ranks and using SUS. See Chapter 3 for a review of linear ranking and SUS. The Python code for linear ranking is in Listing 3.11, and the Python code for SUS is in Listing 3.14.

```
 1 # -----------------------------------------------------
 2 # Selection by Linear Ranking and Stochastic Universal Sampling
 3 # -----------------------------------------------------
 4 # pop_chrom     - population
 5 # pop_fit       - fitness values of the population
 6 # -----------------------------------------------------
 7 # file: selection_linear_ranking_sus.py
 8 # -----------------------------------------------------
 9 from operators_rep.selection.fitness_linear_ranking import
       fitness_linear_ranking
10 from operators_rep.selection.sampling_sus import sampling_sus
11 # -----------------------------------------------------
12 def selection_linear_ranking_sus(pop_chrom, pop_fit):
13     # Fitness linear ranking
14     pop_chrom, pop_fit = fitness_linear_ranking(pop_chrom,
       pop_fit)
15     # Stochastic universal sampling
16     p1_chrom, p2_chrom = sampling_sus(pop_chrom, pop_fit)
17     return p1_chrom, p2_chrom
```

Listing 10.12: *selection_linear_ranking_sus* function.

Blending Crossover

Function *blending_crossover* has been described in Section 3.6.2. Its code is in Listing 3.21.

Gaussian Mutation

Gaussian mutation has been described in Section 3.7.2 and its code is in Listing 3.26.

Elitism

Function *elitism* has been described in Section 3.8 and its code is in Listing 3.29.

Chapter 11

Assessing the Performance of Evolutionary Algorithms

Assessing the performance of an evolutionary algorithm on a given optimization problem is no trivial task. Evolutionary algorithms are stochastic, which means that different runs of the same algorithm, under the same conditions, will almost certainly yield different results. This chapter shows how to use Statistical Inference [20] tools, more specifically confidence intervals, to assess the performance of an evolutionary algorithm in a mathematically sound way.

11.1 A Cautionary Note

A commonly used method to assess the performance of a stochastic algorithm is to run Monte Carlo [86] numerical simulations on test suites of functions designed to emulate characteristics of real-world problems. Though this is a scientifically proven strategy, it does not make room for broad claims about the performance of an algorithm.

This is due to the fact that the performance of stochastic algorithms can vary a lot even for small changes in the setting of their parameters. Moreover, the simulation results obtained on a given set of test functions are hardly generalizable to test functions that represent different classes of problems, as stated by the No Free Lunch (NFL) theorems, developed in [90]. In essence, the NFL theorems state that no algorithm can perform well on all kinds of problems. The numerical results obtained on a given class of problems are thus valid for that class of problems.

11.2 Performance Metric

The performance of the algorithm can be assessed by computing the estimation error produced by the algorithm on a given optimization problem. The estimation error is the difference between the approximate solution given by the algorithm and the true solution of the problem. If we run the algorithm on the same problem N times, we end up with a random vector $X = \{X_1, X_2, \ldots, X_N\}$, where X_i is the estimation error of the ith run.

If we assume that X is a random sample of the population of all estimation errors of the algorithm on the problem at hand, we can use the concept of *confidence interval* to estimate a range of highly likely values for the true mean estimation error and use this information as a performance metric of the algorithm.

11.3 Confidence Intervals

Let us say we are interested in estimating the mean value μ of an unknown population, based solely on a random sample $X = \{X_1, X_2, \ldots, X_N\}$ of the population. The question is how to approximately compute μ, based on the information provided by random vector X.

A statistical tool that provides a range of likely values of an unknown parameter of a population is the confidence interval. This range of likely values is based on

■ a point estimate of the unknown parameter,

■ the standard error of the point estimate,

■ a desired level of confidence.

To compute a 95% confidence interval for the unknown population mean μ, we need a point estimate of μ, which we call *sample mean*. As was assumed that vector X is a random sample of the population, the sample mean, μ_X, will be given by the mean value of X

$$\mu_X = \bar{X}. \tag{11.1}$$

If we assume that the values in X are approximately Gaussian, then the standard error σ_X of the point estimate (11.1) is

$$\sigma_X = \sigma/\sqrt{N}, \tag{11.2}$$

where σ is the standard deviation of the values in X. At this point, the 95% confidence interval for the unknown mean μ can be written as

$$P(\mu_X - \sigma_X < \mu < \mu_X + \sigma_X) = 0.95, \tag{11.3}$$

which means that if we repeat the experiment over and over, 95% of the confidence intervals $[\mu_X - \sigma_X, \mu < \mu_X + \sigma_X]$ created will contain the true population mean μ.

Gaussian Samples with Known Variance

The easiest situation to compute a confidence interval for the estimate of the true mean value μ of a population is when it is known that the samples X come from a Gaussian distribution $\mathcal{N}(\mu, \sigma^2)$ with known variance but unknown mean. The true mean of the population is thus the mean of the Gaussian distribution that originates X.

If X is distributed according to $\mathcal{N}(\mu, \sigma^2)$, then the mean value $\bar{X} = \frac{1}{N}\sum_{i=1}^{N} X_i$ is distributed according to $\mathcal{N}(\mu, \sigma^2/N)$, and the random variable

$$Z = \frac{\bar{X} - \mu}{\frac{\sigma}{\sqrt{N}}} \tag{11.4}$$

has a standard normal distribution $\mathcal{N}(0, 1)$. With this information, we are going to compute the interval $[c_l, c_u]$ that covers the samples of Z with probability γ

$$P(c_l < Z < c_u) = \gamma. \tag{11.5}$$

To completely define Equation (11.5), it is necessary to first define a value for γ. If, for instance, $\gamma = 0.95$, then Equation (11.5) means that there is a 95% probability that the values of Z will fall in the interval $[c_l, c_u]$. The probability that a value of Z falls outside interval $[c_l, c_u]$ is $P(Z \geq c_u)$ or $P(Z \leq c_l)$. The sum of the probabilities of all possible values of Z is 1, thus

$$
\begin{align}
P(c_l < Z < c_u) + P(Z \geq c_u) + P(Z \leq c_l) &= 1 \tag{11.6} \\
\gamma + P(Z \geq c_u) + P(Z \leq c_l) &= 1 \tag{11.7} \\
P(Z \geq c_u) + P(Z \leq c_l) &= 1 - \gamma. \tag{11.8}
\end{align}
$$

As the standard normal distribution is symmetric around zero, we can say that

$$
\begin{align}
P(Z \geq c_u) &= (1 - \gamma)/2 \tag{11.9} \\
P(Z \leq c_l) &= (1 - \gamma)/2, \tag{11.10}
\end{align}
$$

if $\gamma = 0.95$, then $P(Z \geq c_u) = P(Z \leq c_l) = (1 - 0.95)/2 = 0.025$.

Probabilities $P(Z \geq c_u)$ and $P(Z \leq c_l)$ are called *tail probabilities*, and values c_l and c_u are called *critical values*. To find the critical values corresponding to $\gamma = 0.95$, call the script shown in Listing 11.1 with $\gamma = 0.95$ to obtain $c_l = -1.96$ and $c_u = 1.96$.

```
1 # ------------------------------------------------------------
2 # Compute and print the critical values of a standard normal
3 # ------------------------------------------------------------
4 # gamma - confidence level
5 # ------------------------------------------------------------
6 # file: compute_critical_values_standard_normal.py
7 # ------------------------------------------------------------
8 from scipy.stats import norm as rv
9 # ------------------------------------------------------------
10 def critical_values_standard_normal(gamma):
11     # 1 - Define the tail probability
```

```
12    p = (1 - gamma)/2.0
13
14    # 2 - Compute the lower critical value, cl, such that P(Z <=
      cl) = pl
15    # Compute the probability pl for using with the ppf function
16    pl = p
17    # Compute the value of the lower critical point using the
18    # percent point function (inverse of cdf)
19    cl = rv.ppf(pl, loc =0, scale = 1)
20    # Print
21    print('cl = {}'.format(cl))
22
23    # 3 - Compute the upper critical value, cu, such that P(Z >=
      cu) = pu
24    # Compute the probability pu for using with the ppf function
25    pu = 1 - p
26    # Compute the value of the lower critical point using the
27    # percent point function (inverse of cdf)
28    cu = rv.ppf(pu, loc =0, scale = 1)
29    print('cu = {}'.format(cu))
30
31    return cl, cu
```

Listing 11.1: Computing the critical values of the standard normal distribution.

To fully understand the script, let us recall the definition of *quantile* of a probability distribution. The number q such that $P(Z \leq q) = p$, is the pth quantile of the distribution of Z. The lower critical value, c_l, is thus the pth quantile of the standard normal distribution, where $p = (1 - \gamma)/2$, and the upper critical value, c_u, is the $(1 - p)$th quantile of the standard normal distribution.

In the script, function *ppf*, provided by SciPy library, is used to compute the quantiles. This function receives a tail probability as a parameter and gives the quantile corresponding to that tail probability. Thus, to compute the lower critical value, the parameter to the *ppf* function is the tail probability $p = (1 - \gamma)/2$, while to compute the upper critical value, the parameter is $1 - p$.

Figure 11.1 shows the areas of the standard normal distribution that correspond to the probabilities $P(Z \geq c_u)$ and $P(Z \leq c_l)$, for $\gamma = 0.95$.

Now that the values c_l and c_u are known, it is possible to finally obtain the 95% confidence interval for μ. To this end, we substitute Equation (11.4) in Equation (11.5) and perform algebraic transformations to obtain

$$P\left(\bar{X} - c_u \frac{\sigma}{\sqrt{N}} < \mu < \bar{X} - c_l \frac{\sigma}{\sqrt{N}}\right) = \gamma, \qquad (11.11)$$

therefore the interval that covers μ with probability $\gamma = 0.95$ is

$$\left(\bar{X} - 1.96 \frac{\sigma}{\sqrt{N}}, \bar{X} + 1.96 \frac{\sigma}{\sqrt{N}}\right). \qquad (11.12)$$

Example 21 *In this example, a 95% confidence interval for the true mean of random samples from a Gaussian distribution is computed. The variance of the generating*

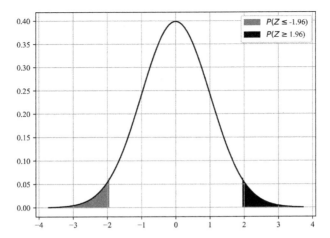

Figure 11.1: Critical values of the standard normal distribution for $\gamma = 0.95$.

distribution is assumed to be known. The confidence interval is computed using $N = 10$ samples from $\mathcal{N}(5, 0.1)$. The samples are shown in Table 11.1

Table 11.1: Random samples from $\mathcal{N}(5, 0.1)$.

X
4.89143694
5.09973454
5.02829785
4.84937053
4.94213997
5.16514365
4.75733208
4.95710874
5.12659363
4.91332596

The intermediate calculations are:

■ *the mean value of the samples is $\bar{X} = 4.973048388967366$,*

■ *the lower critical value is $c_l = -1.959963984540054$,*

■ *the upper critical value is $c_u = 1.959963984540054$.*

Now, using Equation 11.11, the resulting confidence interval is

$$[4.91106888573691, 5.035027892197823].$$

The example is implemented in Listing 11.2.

```
1 # -----------------------------------------------------------------
2 # Compute a 95% confidence interval for the mean value of
3 # normally distributed data with known variance
4 # -----------------------------------------------------------------
5 # file: example_95CI_normal_data_known_var.py
6 # -----------------------------------------------------------------
7 import numpy as np
8 from performance_rep.compute_critical_values_standard_normal \
9     import critical_values_standard_normal
10 # -----------------------------------------------------------------
11 # 1 - Define the confidence level
12 gamma = 0.95
13
14 # 2 - Compute the critical levels
15 [cl, cu] = critical_values_standard_normal(gamma)
16
17 # 3 - Generate normally distributed samples
18 delta = 0.1
19 N     = 10
20 np.random.seed(123)                  # for repeatability
21 X = np.random.normal(5,delta,N)      # generate N samples
22 print('X is {}'.format(X))
23
24 # 5 - Confidence Interval
25 Xbar = np.mean(X)                    # mean of the samples
26 print('Xbar = {}'.format(Xbar))
27 lb = Xbar - cu*(delta/np.sqrt(N))    # lower bound of the CI
28 ub = Xbar - cl*(delta/np.sqrt(N))    # upper bound of the CI
29
30 print('the {}% CI is [{},{}]'.format(gamma*100,lb,ub))
```

Listing 11.2: Computing a 95% confidence interval for normal data with known variance.

Gaussian Samples with Unknown Variance

When both the mean and the variance of the distribution that generated the samples are unknown, Equation (11.4) becomes

$$Z = \frac{\bar{X} - \mu}{\frac{S}{\sqrt{N}}} \tag{11.13}$$

where S is the sample standard deviation of the sample X.

As a result, Z now has a Student's t distribution with $N-1$ degrees of freedom, and is now called the *studentized* mean of $X = \{X_1, X_2, \ldots, X_N\}$. The t distribution resembles a Gaussian distribution, but with heavier tails. As N increases, the t distribution becomes increasingly like the Gaussian distribution. The critical values of the t distribution can be computed with the script in Listing 11.3.

```
1 # -----------------------------------------------------------------
2 # Compute the critical values of the Student's t distribution
3 # -----------------------------------------------------------------
4 # N     - number of samples
```

```
 5 # gamma  -  confidence level
 6 # ----------------------------------------------------------------
 7 # file:  compute_critical_values_student_t.py
 8 # ----------------------------------------------------------------
 9 from scipy.stats import t as t_dist
10 # ----------------------------------------------------------------
11 def critical_values_t(N, gamma):
12     # 1 -  Number of degrees of freedom and probability p
13     p      = (1 - gamma) / 2.0     # tail probability
14     nDof   = N - 1                 # degrees of freedom
15
16     # 2 -  Compute the lower critical value, cl, # such that
17     #         P(Z <= cl) = pl
18     # Compute the probability pl for using with the ppf function
19     pl = p
20     # Compute the value of the lower critical point using the
21     # percent point function (inverse of cdf)
22     cl = t_dist.ppf(pl, nDof)
23     # Print
24     print('cl = {}'.format(cl))
25
26     # 4 -  Compute the upper critical value, cu, such that
27     #         P(Z >= cu) = pu
28     # Compute the probability pu for using with the ppf function
29     pu = 1 - p
30     # Compute the value of the lower critical point using the
31     # percent point function (inverse of cdf)
32     cu = t_dist.ppf(pu, nDof)
33     print('cu = {}'.format(cu))
34
35     return cl, cu
```

Listing 11.3: Computing the critical values of the t distribution.

Figure 11.2 shows the areas of the t distribution that correspond to the probabilities $P(Z \geq c_u)$ and $P(Z \leq c_l)$, for $\gamma = 0.95$.

To compute the confidence interval, it is necessary to first compute the sample standard deviation S. This is done according to

$$S = \sqrt{\frac{1}{N-1}\sum_{i=1}^{N}(X_i - \bar{X})^2}. \tag{11.14}$$

After computing the critical values and the sample standard deviation, the confidence interval is written as

$$P\left(\bar{X} - c_u\frac{S}{\sqrt{N}} < \mu < \bar{X} - c_l\frac{S}{\sqrt{N}}\right) = \gamma. \tag{11.15}$$

Example 22 *In this example, a 95% confidence interval for the true mean of random samples from a Gaussian distribution is computed, but now the variance of the generating distribution, σ^2, is assumed to be unknown. The confidence interval is*

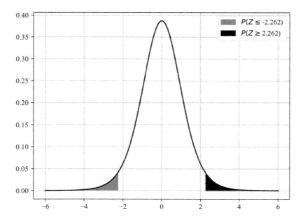

Figure 11.2: Critical values of the Student's t distribution with 9 degrees of freedom for $\gamma = 0.95$.

computed using the same $N = 10$ samples from $\mathcal{N}(5, 0.1)$ as the previous example. The samples are shown in Table 11.1. The intermediate calculations now are:

- *the mean value of the samples is $\bar{X} = 4.973048388967366$,*

- *the standard deviation of the samples is $S = 0.1303179684979754$*

- *the lower critical value is $c_l = -2.2621571627409915$,*

- *the upper critical value is $c_u = 2.2621571627409915$.*

Now, using Equation 11.15, the resulting confidence interval is

$$[4.8798245302326295, 5.066272247702103].$$

The example is implemented in Listing 11.4. The confidence interval is wider than the confidence interval in example 21. This is a result of the larger uncertainty that results from the fact that now the variance of the distribution that generates the samples is unknown and needs to be estimated.

```
1 # ------------------------------------------------------------
2 # Compute a 95% confidence interval for the mean value of
3 # normally distributed data with UNknown variance
4 # ------------------------------------------------------------
5 import numpy as np
6 from scipy.stats import t as t_dist
7 # ------------------------------------------------------------
8
9 # 1 - Define the confidence level and the number of samples
10 sigma = 0.95          # confidence level
11 N = 10                # number of samples
12
13 # 2 - Number of degrees of freedom and probability p
14 p = (1 - sigma)/2.0 # probability p
```

```
15 nDof = N -1              # degrees of freedom
16
17 # 3 - Compute the lower critical value, cl, such that P(Z <= cl) =
      pl
18 # Compute the probability pl for using with the ppf function
19 pl = p
20 # Compute the value of the lower critical point using the
21 # percent point function (inverse of cdf)
22 cl = t_dist.ppf(pl, nDof)
23 # Print
24 print('cl = {}'.format(cl))
25
26 # 4 - Compute the upper critical value, cu, such that P(Z >= cu) =
      pu
27 # Compute the probability pu for using with the ppf function
28 pu = 1 - p
29 # Compute the value of the lower critical point using the
30 # percent point function (inverse of cdf)
31 cu = t_dist.ppf(pu, nDof)
32 print('cu = {}'.format(cu))
33
34 # 5 - Normally distributed samples
35 delta = 0.1
36 np.random.seed(123)           # for repeatability
37 X = np.random.normal(5,delta,N)   # generate N samples
38 print('X is {}'.format(X))
39
40 # 6 - Compute the sample mean and sample standard deviation
41 Xbar = np.mean(X)              # sample mean
42 print('Xbar = {}'.format(Xbar))
43 S = np.sqrt((1/(N-1))*np.sum((X - Xbar)**2)) # sample sd
44 print('S = {}'.format(S))
45
46 # 6 - Confidence Interval
47 lb = Xbar - cu*(S/np.sqrt(N))    # lower bound of the CI
48 ub = Xbar - cl*(S/np.sqrt(N))    # upper bound of the CI
49
50 print('the {}% CI is [{},{}]'.format(sigma*100,lb,ub))
```

Listing 11.4: Computing a 95% confidence interval for normal data with unknown variance.

Non-Gaussian Samples

It is reasonable to assume that, in many situations of interest, the samples will not be normally distributed. This may not be a problem, if the true distribution of the samples does not deviate significantly from the Gaussian distribution. But if the true distribution of the samples deviates significantly from the normal distribution, the confidence interval found may not be valid. In such situations, there are two alternatives.

The first is to resort to a technique called *bootstrapping* [32], which uses the sample data to approximate the true distribution of Z. The second is to rely on the fact that, according to the central limit theorem, when the number of samples is big, say $N > 40$, equation (11.12) is valid. For smaller samples, the central limit theorem does not hold and equation (11.15) must be used.

11.4 Assessing the Performance of Single-Objective Evolutionary Algorithms

As the results given by an evolutionary algorithm on a given optimization problem can vary, it is not possible to assess the performance of the algorithm on a given optimization problem based on a single run. We thus perform N optimization runs and collect the solutions $\{\theta_1, \theta_2 \ldots, \theta_N\}$ produced by the algorithm, where θ_i is the solution produced in the ith run. For each solution, we calculate the estimation error

$$e(\theta, \theta^\star) = |f(\theta) - f(\theta^\star)| \tag{11.16}$$

where f is the cost function being minimized, θ is the solution returned by the algorithm, and $\theta^\star$ is the location of the global minimum of f. This procedure yields a vector of estimation errors $X = \{X_1, X_2, \ldots, X_N\}$, where $X_i = e(\theta_i, \theta^\star)$.

It will be assumed that X is generated from a Gaussian distribution with unknown mean and unknown variance. A 95% confidence interval for the unknown mean estimation error, μ_e, in then computed. It is desirable that μ_e is as close to zero as possible. A pseudocode for the whole performance assessment procedure is shown in Algorithm 11.1.

Algorithm 11.1. Assess the Performance of an Evolutionary Algorithm

---

1: **procedure** PERF
2:     $N \leftarrow$ sample size
3:     $\gamma \leftarrow$ confidence level for the confidence interval
4:     $[c_l, c_u] \leftarrow$ critical values of the t distribution according to γ and N
5:     $(F, \theta^\star) \leftarrow$ test problem and its optimal solution
6:     **procedure** MONTE CARLO RUNS
7:         $\Theta = \{\theta_1, \ldots, \theta_N\} \leftarrow$ solutions produced by the EA on F
8:     **end procedure**
9:     $X \leftarrow \{e(\theta_1), \ldots, e(\theta_N)\}$ ▷ Equation (11.16)
10:    $(\bar{X}, S) \leftarrow$ sample mean and sample standard deviation of X.
11:    **procedure** CONFIDENCE INTERVAL
12:         $\theta_l \leftarrow \bar{X} - c_u \frac{S}{\sqrt{N}}$ ▷ Equation (11.15)
13:         $\theta_u \leftarrow \bar{X} - c_l \frac{S}{\sqrt{N}}$ ▷ Equation (11.15)
14:    **end procedure**
15: **end procedure**

Example 23 *Assessing the performance of a genetic algorithm on the Griewank function. The experiment is performed without noise in the fitness function. $N = 40$ Monte Carlo runs of the minimization process are performed, yielding the vector of*

estimated solutions $\Theta = \{\theta_1, \theta_2, \ldots, \theta_{40}\}$. *Those solutions are then used to compute the estimation errors* $X = \{e(\theta_1), e(\theta_2), \ldots, e(\theta_{40})\}$, *then a 95% confidence interval for the mean estimation error in computed. The script that implements the assessment procedure is given in Listing 11.5.*

```python
1  # ----------------------------------------------------------------
2  # Performance assessment on the minimization of a noiseless
3  # function. The samples are assumed to be Gaussian with unknown
4  # variance.
5  # ----------------------------------------------------------------
6  # file: assessment_performance_GAc_noiseless.py
7  # ----------------------------------------------------------------
8  import numpy as np
9  from performance_rep.compute_critical_values_student_t import \
10     critical_values_t
11 from performance_rep.so_monte_carlo_runs import \
12     perform_MC_runs
13 from fitnessf_max.fitnessf_griewank_rv import \
14     fitness_griewank_rv, griewank
15 # ----------------------------------------------------------------
16 # 1 - Define the confidence level and the number of samples
17 sigma    = 0.95     # confidence level
18 N        = 40       # number of samples
19
20 # 2 - Compute the critical values of the t distribution
21 [cl, cu] = critical_values_t(N, sigma)
22
23 # 3 - Define the test problem and its optimal solution
24 # Define the upper and lower bounds of the search space
25 n_dim    = 2   # Number of dimensions of the problem
26 ubc      = 5
27 lbc      = -5
28 lb       = lbc * np.ones(n_dim)   # Lower bound for the
29                                   # search space
30 ub       = ubc * np.ones(n_dim)   # Upper bound for the
31                                   # search space
32 x_star   = np.zeros(n_dim)        # optimal solution
33 # Define the fitness function
34 fitness_f = fitness_griewank_rv # fitness function
35 test_f    = griewank            # test function
36
37
38 # 3 - Perform the Monte Carlo runs
39 est_solutions = perform_MC_runs(fitness_f,
40                                 n_dim, lb,
41                                 ub, N)
42
43 # Compute the best scores produced by the GA
44 best_scores = np.zeros(N)
45 for i in range(N):
46     best_scores[i] = test_f(est_solutions[i])
47
48 # 4 - Compute the estimation errors
49 X = np.abs(best_scores - test_f(x_star))
50
51 # 5 - Compute the sample mean and sample standard
```

```
52 #         deviation
53 Xbar = np.mean(X)      # sample mean
54 print('Xbar = {}'.format(Xbar))
55 S = np.std(X)          # sample sd
56 print('S = {}'.format(S))
57
58 # 6 - Compute the confidence Interval
59 lb = Xbar - cu * (S / np.sqrt(N))   # lower bound of
60                                     # the CI
61 ub = Xbar - cl * (S / np.sqrt(N))   # upper bound of
62                                     # the CI
63 print('the {}% CI is [{},{}]'.format(sigma * 100, lb, ub))
```

Listing 11.5: Assessing the performance of a GA. Main Program.

The collecting of samples θ_i, $i = 1, 2, \ldots, N$, *is shown in Listing 11.6. Here is the place where the Monte Carlo runs are performed.*

```
1 # ----------------------------------------------------------
2 #                  so_perform_MC_runs
3 #  Monte Carlo runs of a minimization process using a GA
4 # ----------------------------------------------------------
5 # file: so_monte_carlo_runs.py
6 # ----------------------------------------------------------
7 # fitness_f - function to be maximized
8 # n_dim     - dimensionality of the search space
9 # lb        - lower bound of the search space
10 # ub        - upper bound bound of the search space
11 # nMC       - number of simulations to be performed
12 # ----------------------------------------------------------
13 import numpy as np
14 from auxiliary.init_rv import init_rv
15 from operators_rep.selection.selection_linear_ranking_sus \
16     import selection_linear_ranking_sus
17 from operators_rep.crossover.crossover_uniform \
18     import crossover_uniform
19 from operators_rep.mutation.mutation_uniform_rv \
20     import mutation_uniform_rv
21 from operators_rep.elitism.elitism import elitism
22 from ga_rep.algs.gac import gac
23 # ----------------------------------------------------------
24 def perform_MC_runs(fitness_f, n_dim, lb, ub, nMC):
25     # 1 - Define the parameters of the optimization
26     npop = 20              # Number of individuals in the population
27     maxIterations = 300    # Maximum number of iterations
28
29     # 2 - Parameters for the algorithm
30     pc          = 0.9      # Crossover probability
31     pm          = 0.5      # Mutation probability
32     er          = 0.1      # Elitism rate
33     init_f      = init_rv            # Creates the initial
34     population
35     crossover_f = crossover_uniform  # Implements crossover
36     mutation_f  = mutation_uniform_rv # Implements mutation
37     elitism_f   = elitism            # Implements elitism
38     selection_f = \
```

```
38      selection_linear_ranking_sus     # Implements selection
39
40   # 3 - Run the GAc algorithm
41   best_thetas  = np.zeros((nMC, n_dim)) # Store the best
     solutions
42   np.random.seed(123)                   # For repeatability
43   for id_MC in range(nMC):              # Monte Carlo runs
44       a, _ = gac(npop, maxIterations, pc, pm,
45                  er, fitness_f, selection_f, crossover_f,
46                  mutation_f,  lb, ub)
47       best_thetas[id_MC] = a
48   # Return the solutions found
49   return best_thetas
```

Listing 11.6: Monte Carlo runs of a GA minimizing Griewank.

The results of this experiment are shown in Table 11.2. As the algorithms are stochastic, the results obtained will vary.

Table 11.2: Results after 40 Monte Carlo runs.

Mean Value of the Estimation Error		
$\bar{E}(\theta)$	0.0011968103677915398	
Confidence Interval for the Estimation Error		
95% CI	0.0004394828666802851	0.0019541378689027947

11.5 Assessing the Performance of Multi-Objective Evolutionary Algorithms

It has been seen in Section 2.8 that the two main goals of Evolutionary Multi-Objective Optimization (EMO) are 1) to find a finite set of non-dominated points that are as close as possible to the true Pareto front (convergence) and 2) that those non-dominated points are uniformly distributed along the true Pareto front (coverage). The fact that these are conflicting goals [55] makes the task of assessing the performance of MOEAs more difficult. Fortunately there are widely used performance metrics that help the practitioner accomplish this otherwise daunting task.

The two most used performance metrics for multi-objective optimization are the IGD [74] and the R2 indicator [27]. Given the approximated Pareto front $\hat{P}$ obtained by the MOEA and the true Pareto front $P^\star$ of the problem at hand, they measure both the convergence of $\hat{P}$ to $P^\star$ as well as the extent to which the points in $\hat{P}$ cover $P^\star$. Both metrics convey the same information, but the IGD is easier to grasp and to implement in a computer program.

Inverted Generational Distance

The IGD metric works by calculating the average Euclidean distance for all members in $P^\star$ to their nearest solutions in $\hat{P}$. It is calculated according to

$$\text{IGD}(\hat{P}, P^\star) = \frac{\sum_{\mathbf{x}^\star \in P^\star} \text{dist}(\mathbf{x}^\star, \hat{P})}{|P^\star|} \tag{11.17}$$

where $\text{dist}(\mathbf{x}^\star, \hat{P})$ is the Euclidean distance between point $\mathbf{x}^\star \in P^\star$ and its nearest neighbor in the approximate Pareto front $\hat{P}$, and $|P^\star|$ is the number of solutions in $P^\star$.

Figure 11.3 displays the distances between two points in the true Pareto front and their nearest neighbors in an approximate Pareto front with "good" coverage and convergence, while Figure 11.4 displays the same situation but with a worse approximate Pareto front. In the first figure, the distances between the points on the true Pareto set and their nearest neighbors on the approximate Pareto set are smaller than their counterparts shown in the second figure. According to Equation (11.17), the IGD value for the situation depicted in the first figure will be smaller than the IGD value of the situation shown in the second figure. The lower the value of IGD, the better the approximate $\hat{P}$ is [74].

Assessing the Performance

As there is no single optimal solution in multi-objective optimization problems, it is not possible to use Equation (11.16) to assess the performance of a MOEA. Instead, the IGD is used. The better the performance of a MOEA, the closer is the IGD to zero. IGD thus works similarly to the error metric in Equation (11.16).

The performance assessment procedure will compute a confidence interval for the IGD values obtained with N Monte Carlo runs of the minimization of a test function, as described in Algorithm 11.2.

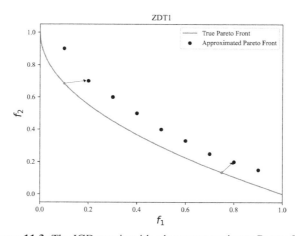

Figure 11.3: The IGD metric with a better approximate Pareto front.

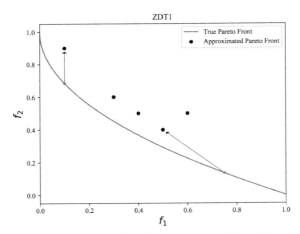

Figure 11.4: The IGD metric with a worse approximate Pareto front.

Algorithm 11.2. Assess the Performance of a MOEA

1: **procedure** PERF
2:      $N \leftarrow$ sample size
3:      $\gamma \leftarrow$ confidence level for the confidence interval
4:      $[c_l, c_u] \leftarrow$ critical values of the t distribution according to γ and N
5:      $(F, P^\star) \leftarrow$ test problem and its optimal Pareto front.
6:      **procedure** MONTE CARLO RUNS
7:          $\mathcal{P} = \{P_1, \ldots, P_N\} \leftarrow$ solutions produced by the EA on F
8:      **end procedure**
9:      $X \leftarrow \{IGD(P_1, P^\star), \ldots, IGD(P_N, P^\star)\}$
10:      $(\bar{X}, S) \leftarrow$ sample mean and sample standard deviation of X
11:      **procedure** CONFIDENCE INTERVAL
12:          $\theta_l \leftarrow \bar{X} - c_u \dfrac{S}{\sqrt{N}}$ ▷ Equation (11.15)
13:          $\theta_u \leftarrow \bar{X} - c_l \dfrac{S}{\sqrt{N}}$ ▷ Equation (11.15)
14:      **end procedure**
15: **end procedure**

Example 24 *This example assesses the performance of algorithm NSGA-II on the minimization of the ZDT1 function, according to the procedure described in Algorithm 11.2. 40 Monte Carlo runs are performed and a 95% confidence for the IGD metric is computed. This example is implemented in Listing 11.7.*

```
1 # ------------------------------------------------------------
2 # Performance assessment on the minimization of a noiseless
3 # function. The samples are assumed to be Gaussian with unknown
4 # variance.
5 #
6 # file: assessment_performance_NSGA2_noiseless.py
7 # ------------------------------------------------------------
```

```
 8 import numpy as np
 9 from nsga_rep.algs.nsga2 import nsga2
10 from auxiliary.init_rv import init_rv
11 from test_functions_rep.mo.zdt1 import zdt1
12 from performance_rep.compute_critical_values_student_t import \
13     critical_values_t
14 from operators_rep.crossover.crossover_rv_sbx import \
15     sbx_crossover
16 from operators_rep.mutation.mutation_polynomial_rv import \
17     mutation_polynomial_rv
18 # ------------------------------------------------------------
19 # Compute the IDG metric
20 # ------------------------------------------------------------
21 def calc_IDG_metric(true_pf, approx_PF):
22     from scipy.spatial.distance import euclidean
23     normZ = len(true_pf)
24     normA = len(approx_PF)
25
26     # IGD
27     dist = np.zeros((normZ, normA))
28     for idz in range(normZ):
29         for ida in range(normA):
30             dist[idz, ida] = euclidean(true_pf[idz], approx_PF[ida
])
31     idg = 0
32     for idz in range(normZ):
33         idg = idg + np.min(dist[idz])
34     idg = (1 / normZ) * idg
35     return idg
36 # ------------------------------------------------------------
37 # Generate the true PF of ZDT1
38 # ------------------------------------------------------------
39 def generate_zdt1_pf():
40     # define the number of points to be generated
41     n_samples = 1000
42     # by definition, we have f1 = x_1
43     x1 = np.linspace(0, 1, n_samples)
44     f1 = x1
45     # at the front, we have g(x_2, ..., x_n) = 1,
46     # thus f2 = 1 - np.sqrt(f1)
47     f2 = 1 - np.sqrt(f1)
48     pareto_front = np.array([f1, f2]).T
49     return pareto_front
50 # ------------------------------------------------------------
51 # MC runs
52 # ------------------------------------------------------------
53 def perform_MC_runs(cost_f, true_pf, n_dim, n_goals, lb, ub, nMC):
54     # 1 - Define the parameters of the optimization
55     npop = 200              # Number of individuals in the
population
56     maxIterations = 500     # Maximum number of iterations
57
58     # 2 - Parameters for the algorithm
59     pc          = 0.9       # Crossover probability
60     pm          = 1/n_dim       # Mutation probability
61
```

```
62    init_f       = init_rv                      # Creates the initial
      population
63    crossover_f = sbx_crossover                 # Implements crossover
64    mutation_f  = mutation_polynomial_rv        # Implements mutation
65
66    # 3 - Run the NSGA2 algorithm
67    IGD          = np.zeros(nMC) # Store IGD values
68    np.random.seed(123)                          # For repeatability
69    for id_MC in range(nMC):                     # Monte Carlo runs
70        approx_PF, _ = nsga2(npop, maxIterations, pc, pm,
71                       init_f,
72                       cost_f,
73                       crossover_f,
74                       mutation_f,
75                       lb, ub, n_dim, n_goals)
76
77        IGD[id_MC] = calc_IDG_metric(true_pf, approx_PF)
78    # Return the solutions found
79    return IGD
80 # ------------------------------------------------------------------
81 # Assessing the performance
82 # ------------------------------------------------------------------
83 # 1 - Define the confidence level and the number of samples
84 sigma    = 0.95     # confidence level
85 N        = 40       # number of samples
86
87 # 2 - Compute the critical values of the t distribution
88 [cl,cu] = critical_values_t(N,sigma)
89
90 # 3 - Define the test problem and its optimal solution
91 f_name = 'ZDT1'
92 n_dim = 30
93 f_cost = zdt1
94 n_goals = 2
95 ubc = 1
96 lbc = 0
97 lb = lbc * np.ones(n_dim)  # Lower bound for the
98 # search space
99 ub = ubc * np.ones(n_dim)  # Upper bound for the
100 # search space
101 true_PF = generate_zdt1_pf()
102
103 # 4 - Perform the Monte Carlo runs
104 X = perform_MC_runs(f_cost,
105                       true_PF,
106                       n_dim,
107                       n_goals,
108                       lb,
109                       ub,
110                       N)
111
112 # 5 - Compute the sample mean and sample standard
113 #       deviation
114 Xbar = np.mean(X)   # sample mean
115 print('Xbar = {}'.format(Xbar))
116 S = np.std(X)       # sample sd
117 print('S = {}'.format(S))
```

```
118
119 # 6 - Compute the confidence Interval
120 lb = Xbar - cu * (S / np.sqrt(N))   # lower bound of
121                                      # the CI
122 ub = Xbar - cl * (S / np.sqrt(N))   # upper bound of
123                                      # the CI
124 print('the {}% CI is [{},{}]'.format(sigma * 100, lb, ub))
```

Listing 11.7: Assessing the performance NSGA2.

The results of this experiment are shown in Table 11.3.

Table 11.3: Results after 40 Monte Carlo runs.

Mean Value of the IGD Index	
$\overline{IGD}$	0.002657835665596562
Confidence Interval for the IGD Index	
95% CI	0.00261820611867771	0.002697465212515414

11.6   Benchmark Functions

Benchmark problems are mathematical test functions conceived to confront optimization algorithms with one or more characteristics of real-world optimization problems. To illustrate the concept of benchmark functions, this sections shows some functions of a widely used suite of multi-objective test functions, proposed in [94]. The test functions implement characteristics of real-world optimization problems such as convexity, non-convexity, discreteness, multi-modality, and biased search spaces. The true Pareto fronts of all test functions are known, allowing assessing the performance of an optimization algorithm on the class of problems that the test function represents.

ZDT1

ZDT1 is a two-objective n-dimensional unconstrained optimization problem with a convex Pareto-optimal front, written as

$$g(\mathbf{x}) \;=\; 1 + \frac{9}{n-1} \sum_{j=2}^{n} x_j \tag{11.18}$$

$$f_1(\mathbf{x}) \;=\; x_1 \tag{11.19}$$

$$f_2(\mathbf{x}) \;=\; g(x)\left(1 - \sqrt{\frac{x_1}{g(x)}}\right) \tag{11.20}$$

$x_j \in [0,1]$. The Pareto optimal front is formed with $g(\mathbf{x}) = 1$.

ZDT2

ZDT2 is a two-objective n-dimensional unconstrained optimization problem with a non-convex Pareto-optimal front, written as

$$g(\mathbf{x}) \quad = \quad 1 + \frac{9}{n-1} \sum_{j=2}^{n} x_j \tag{11.21}$$

$$f_1(\mathbf{x}) \quad = \quad x_1 \tag{11.22}$$

$$f_2(\mathbf{x}) \quad = \quad g(x)\left[1 - \left(\frac{x_1}{g(x)}\right)^2\right] \tag{11.23}$$

$x_j \in [0,1]$. The Pareto optimal front is formed with $g(\mathbf{x}) = 1$.

ZDT3

ZDT3 is a two-objective n-dimensional unconstrained optimization problem which represents the discreteness feature, with its Pareto front consisting of noncontiguous convex parts. There is no discontinuity in the parameter space. The function is written as

$$g(\mathbf{x}) \quad = \quad 1 + \frac{9}{n-1} \sum_{j=2}^{n} x_j \tag{11.24}$$

$$f_1(\mathbf{x}) \quad = \quad x_1 \tag{11.25}$$

$$f_2(\mathbf{x}) \quad = \quad g(x)\left[1 - \sqrt{\frac{x_1}{g(x)}} - \left(\frac{x_1}{g(x)}\right)\sin(10\pi x_1)\right] \tag{11.26}$$

$x_j \in [0,1]$. The Pareto optimal front is formed with $g(\mathbf{x}) = 1$.

ZDT4

ZDT4 is a two-objective n-dimensional unconstrained optimization problem which represents multi-modality. The function is written as

$$g(\mathbf{x}) \quad = \quad 1 + 10(n-1) + \sum_{j=2}^{n}(x_j^2 - 10\cos(4\pi x_j)) \tag{11.27}$$

$$f_1(\mathbf{x}) \quad = \quad x_1 \tag{11.28}$$

$$f_2(\mathbf{x}) \quad = \quad g(x)\left[1 - \sqrt{\frac{x_1}{g(x)}}\right] \tag{11.29}$$

$x_1 \in [0,1]$ and $x_2,\ldots,x_n \in [-5,5]$. The Pareto optimal front is formed with $g(\mathbf{x}) = 1$, while the best local Pareto-optimal front is formed with $g(\mathbf{x})=1.25$. Local Pareto-optimal sets are distinguishable in the objective space.

Some Results

Figures 11.5,11.6, 11.7 and 11.8 display the results obtained by the NSGA-II algorithm on the minimization of ZDT1, ZDT2, ZDT3 and ZDT4.

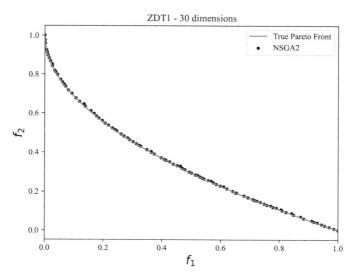

Figure 11.5: NSGA-II solving ZDT1.

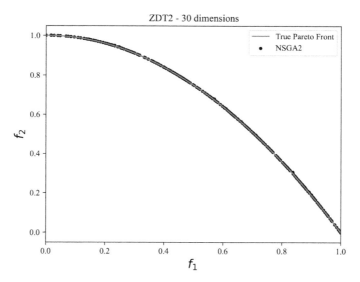

Figure 11.6: NSGA-II solving ZDT2.

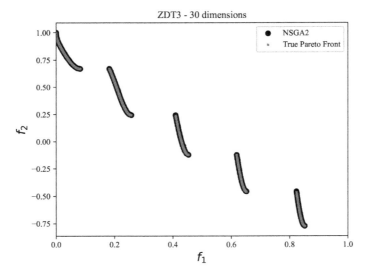

Figure 11.7: NSGA-II solving ZDT3.

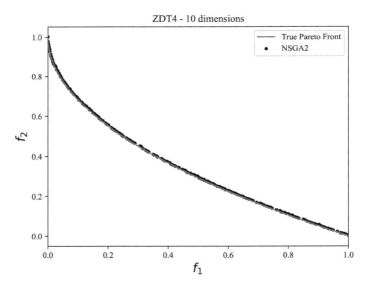

Figure 11.8: NSGA-II solving ZDT4.

Chapter 12

Case Study: Optimal Design of a Gear Train System

The design of a double reduction gear train problem has been used on performance comparisons between different evolutionary algorithms [58]. The problem, first proposed in [73], displays low density of solutions in some areas of the Pareto optimal front, a characteristic that makes it harder for metaheuristics to solve it. The problem was chosen as a case study for the reasons below:

1. it is a multi-objective optimization problem, a usual characteristic of real-world problems;

2. it features a discrete search space with integer-only variables, a characteristic of many real-world problems;

3. it features a constrained search space, also a usual characteristic of real-world problems.

The problem consists in designing a double-reduction gear train with four gears, named D, B, A and F, as seen in Figure 12.1. The design variables, n_D, n_B, n_A and n_F are the number of teeth in each gear. To simplify the notation we will respectively denominate them x_1, x_2, x_3 and x_4. The design variables are integer numbers constrained to the interval $[12, 60]$.

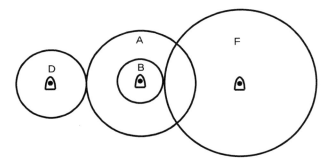

Figure 12.1: Double reduction gear train.

The optimization goal is to obtain values for x_1, x_2, x_3 and x_4 so that the double-reduction gear train transmission ratio, $\frac{x_1 x_2}{x_3 x_4}$, is as close as possible to $\frac{1}{6.931}$ and no constraint is violated. This single-objective optimization problem is written as

$$\underset{x_1, x_2, x_3, x_4}{\text{minimize}} \quad \left(\frac{1}{6.931} - \frac{x_1 x_2}{x_3 x_4} \right)^2 \tag{12.1}$$
$$\text{subject to} \quad 12 \le x_i \le 60, \quad i = 1, 2, 3, 4.$$

Problem (12.1) becomes a multi-objective optimization problem when the number of teeth in each gear is also to be minimized, as proposed in [46]. The multi-objective formulation of the problem is

$$\underset{x_1, x_2, x_3, x_4}{\text{minimize}} \quad [f_1(x_1, x_2, x_3, x_4), f_2(x_1, x_2, x_3, x_4)] \tag{12.2}$$
$$\text{subject to} \quad 12 \le x_i \le 60, \quad i = 1, 2, 3, 4.$$

where $f_1(x_1, x_2, x_3, x_4) = \left(\frac{1}{6.931} - \frac{x_1 x_2}{x_3 x_4} \right)^2$ and $f_2(x_1, x_2, x_3, x_4) = max(x_1, x_2, x_3, x_4)$.

Solution by Enumeration

The search space of the multi-objective problem (12.2) is comprised of 4 dimensions, with each dimension comprised by the 49 discrete numbers $\{12, 13, 14, \ldots, 58, 59, 60\}$. The search space is thus comprised of $49^4 = 5764801$ 4-dimensional points, but many different solutions yield the same values of the objective function It is thus possible to explicitly enumerate all solutions and find the Pareto front.

Figure 12.2 displays the Pareto front of (12.2) together with all feasible solutions to the problem. The figure shows that the density of solutions near the Pareto front with low values of $f_1(\mathbf{x})$ is poor. It is this low density that makes it harder to find good solutions in this area of the search space [58]. The x axis of the figure is in logarithmic scale for better visualization of the Pareto front.

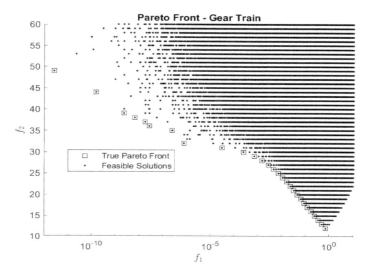

Figure 12.2: Pareto optimal front and feasible solutions of the multi-objective optimization problem given in (12.2).

Solving the Problem

To illustrate the application of a multi-objective evolutionary algorithm, the gear problem will be solved with the MOEA/D algorithm. To this end, the algorithm described in Chapter 9 has to be slightly modified to be able to cope with the integer nature of the decision variables of the problem. Uniform crossover (see Section 3.6.1) and random resetting (see Section 3.7.3) were adopted because they can deal with integer representations.

Objective function. The objective function is obtained by simply implementing Equation 12.2.

Optimization. The optimization process performed 4000 iterations of the algorithm with a population of 50 individuals. The probability of crossover was $p_c = 1$ and the probability of mutation was $p_m = 0.6$.

Integer version of MOEA/D. The pseudocode for the integer version of MOEA/D used in this case study is shown in Algorithm 12.1. The Python code is shown in Listing 12.5.

Algorithm 12.1. MOEA/D for Integer Representation

1: $N \leftarrow$ population size
2: $N_e \leftarrow$ maximum size of the external population
3: $M \leftarrow$ maximum number of iterations
4: $T \leftarrow$ number of neighbors
5: $F \leftarrow$ multi-objective goal function
6: $lb \leftarrow$ lower limits of the search space
7: $ub \leftarrow$ upper limits of the search space
8: $nGoals \leftarrow$ number of optimization goals of F
9: $p_c \leftarrow$ crossover probability
10: $p_m \leftarrow$ mutation probability
11: $v \leftarrow$ vector of permissible values for the genes
12: **procedure** MOEA/D
13:      EP $\leftarrow$ empty external population
14:      $\lambda \leftarrow$ initialize N evenly spread weight vectors
15:      $B_i \leftarrow$ compute the T nearest neighbors of weight vector λ_i, $i \in \{1,\ldots,N\}$
16:      $P \leftarrow$ initialize the population with N individuals
17:      $F_P \leftarrow$ compute the multi-objective cost of the individuals in P
18:      $\mathbf{z} \leftarrow$ create the reference point according to F_P
19:      **for** $id\_i \in \{1,\ldots M\}$ **do**
20:          **for** $id\_p \in \{1,\ldots,N\}$ **do**
21:              $\mathbf{p}_1,\mathbf{p}_2 \leftarrow$ with probability p_c, randomly select two individuals from B_{id_p} or from P
22:              $\mathbf{y} = \text{crossover}(\mathbf{p}_1,\mathbf{p}_2)$ ▷ produce a child by recombing $\mathbf{p}_1$ and $\mathbf{p}_2$
23:              $\mathbf{y} = \text{mutation}(\mathbf{y}, p_m)$ ▷ with probability p_m mutate the child
24:              $\mathbf{y}' = \text{repair}(\mathbf{y})$ ▷ Repair and/or improve $\mathbf{y}$
25:              $\mathbf{z} = \text{update}(\mathbf{z}, F(\mathbf{y}'))$ ▷ Update $\mathbf{z}$
26:              $P, F_P = \text{update\_neighborhood}(id\_p, B_{id\_p}, P, F_P, \mathbf{z}, \mathbf{y}', F(\mathbf{y}'))$ ▷ update neighbors of P_{id_p}
27:              $EP = \text{update\_EP}(EP, \mathbf{y}', F(\mathbf{y}'), N_e)$ ▷ Update the external population
28:          **end for**
29:      **end for** return EP
30: **end procedure**

Results

The code that performs the experiment is shown in Listing 12.1.

```
1 # ------------------------------------------------------------
2 #          MOEA/D Optimization for the Gear Train System
3 # ------------------------------------------------------------
4 # file: run_moead_gear.py
5 # ------------------------------------------------------------
6 import numpy as np
7 import matplotlib.pyplot as plt
8 from case_study_gear.f_goal_gear import f_Gear
9 from moead_rep.algs.moead_int import moead_int
10 from case_study_gear.gear_true_PF import true_PF
11 # ------------------------------------------------------------
12
```

```
13 # Define the optimization problem
14 f_goal = f_Gear                      # goal function
15 n_dim = 4                            # 4 decision variables
16 n_goals = 2                          # number of individual goals
17 ubc = 60                             # upper and lower bounds
18 lbc = 12
19 lb = lbc*np.ones(n_dim,dtype=int)
20 ub = ubc*np.ones(n_dim,dtype=int)
21
22 pc = 1.0                             # crossover probability
23 pm = 0.6                             # mutation probability
24
25
26 # Optimization process
27 M    = 4000                          # number of optimization iterations
28 Ne = 500                             # maximum number of individuals in
29                                      # the external population
30 # Set MOEAD hyperparameters
31 N    = 50
32 T = np.maximum(np.ceil(0.15 * N), 2)    # number of neighbors
33 T = np.minimum(np.maximum(T,2),15)
34 T = np.int(T)
35
36 v = np.arange(lbc,ubc+1)             # list of valid gene values
37
38 # Call the optimization algorithm
39 F_cost, F_chrom = moead_int(N, Ne, M, T, f_goal, lb, ub,
40                             n_goals, pc, pm, v)
41 # Save the optimization results
42 f_fit_file = 'moead_f_cost.npy'
43 f_chrom_file = 'moead_f_chrom.npy'
44 np.save(f_fit_file, F_cost)
45 np.save(f_chrom_file, F_chrom)
46
47
48 # Plot the scores per iteration
49 str = "Gear Train System"
50 plt.scatter(F_cost[:,0], F_cost[:,1], label='MOEA/D', marker='.',
       c='k'),
51 plt.scatter(true_PF[:,0], true_PF[:,1], label='true PF', marker='
       +', c='k')
52 plt.title(str)
53 plt.ylabel('$f_{1}$')
54 plt.xlabel('$f_{0}$')
55 plt.legend()
56 plt.show()
```

Listing 12.1: Objective function for the multi-objective gear train.

Figure 12.3 shows the results of one run of the optimization process. It is possible to see that the algorithm was able to find all but 2 points of the true Pareto front. The missed points of the true Pareto front are located exactly in the area of the search space with very low density of feasible solutions.

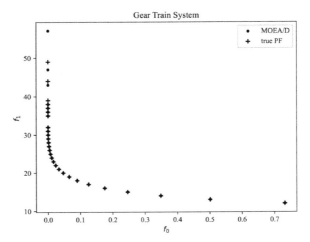

Figure 12.3: MOEA/D solving the multi-objective optimization problem given in (12.2).

The results are influenced by the following factors:

■ *hyperparameter settings* - the values of the hyperparameters greatly influence the results. Sometimes small changes to them can lead to dramatic changes in the results obtained.

■ *number of optimization iterations* - in principle, the more iterations the better will be the results obtained.

■ *initial population* - both the size and the spread of the initial population have impacts on the results obtained. If the initial population has individuals close to the Pareto solutions the final results tend to be better.

Listings

All python codes used to implement this case study are given in this section. The

■ Objective function - Implemented in Listing 12.2.

■ Scalarized cost function - implemented in Listing 9.2.

■ Computed weight vectors and their neighborhoods - implemented in Listing 9.3.

■ Initialize the population - implemented in Listing 12.3.

■ Produce offspring by crossover - implemented in Listing 3.20.

■ Mutate offspring - implemented in Listing 3.28.

■ Repair offspring - implemented in Listing 9.6.

- Updating **z** - implemented in Listing 9.7.

- Updating neighboring solutions - implemented in Listing 9.8.

- Check domination - implemented in Listing 9.9.

- Updating external population - implemented in Listing 9.10.

```
# ------------------------------------------------------
# Objective Function for the Multi-Objective  Gear
# Train Problem
# ------------------------------------------------------
# file: f_goal_gear.py
# ------------------------------------------------------
import numpy as np
# ------------------------------------------------------
def f_Gear(x):
    f1 = (1 / 6.931 - (x[0] * x[1]) / (x[2] * x[3]))** 2
    f2 = np.max(x)
    f = np.array([f1, f2])
    return f
```

Listing 12.2: Objective function for the multi-objective gear train.

```
import numpy as np
def init_int(M,N,lb, ub):
    # ------------------------------------------------------
    # Initiates an integer coded population of
    # M individuals
    # ------------------------------------------------------
    pop_chrom = np.random.randint(lb,ub,size=(M,N))
    return pop_chrom
```

Listing 12.3: Initialization of a population of integer vectors.

```
# ----------------------------------------------------------------
#                Random Resetting Mutation
# ----------------------------------------------------------------
# Inputs:
#     x      - n-dimensional individual to be mutated
#     v      - vector of permissible values for the genes
#     pm     - probability that a gene will undergo mutation
# Outputs:
#     mutated_x - mutated individual
# ----------------------------------------------------------------
# file: mutation_rand_reset_int.py
# ----------------------------------------------------------------
import numpy as np
# ----------------------------------------------------------------
def mutation_rand_reset(x,v, pm):
    # No mutation is performed
    if pm == 0:
        return x
    # Create the mutated individual
    mutated_x = np.copy(x)
```

```
21    # Dimensionality
22    numVar = len(x)
23    # Random changes
24    for ll in range(numVar):
25        if np.random.rand() < pm:
26            mutated_x[ll] = np.random.choice(v)
27    # return the mutated individual
28    return mutated_x
```

Listing 12.4: Mutating the offspring.

```
1  # ----------------------------------------------------------
2  # MOEA/D - Implemented for integer minimization
3  # ----------------------------------------------------------
4  # Inputs
5  #   N    - population size
6  #   Ne - maximum size of the external population
7  #   M  - maximum number of iterations
8  #   T        - number of the weight vectors in a
9  #                  neighborhood
10 #                  of each weight vector
11 #   F        - multi-objective cost function
12 #   lb       - lower limit of the search space
13 #   ub       - upper limit of the search space
14 #   nGoals   - number of goals of F
15 #   pc       - crossover probability
16 #   pm       - mutation probability
17 #   v        - vector of permissible values for the
18 #                genes
19 # Outputs:
20 #   EP_f     - Approximate Pareto front
21 #   EP_x     - Approximate Pareto set
22 # ----------------------------------------------------------
23 # file: moead_int.py
24 # ----------------------------------------------------------
25 import numpy as np
26 from auxiliary.init_int import init_int
27 from moead_rep.utils.z_update import z_update
28 from moead_rep.utils.update_EP import update_EP
29 from moead_rep.utils.repair_child import f_repair
30 from moead_rep.utils.update_neighborhood import
       update_solutions_in_B
31 from moead_rep.utils.initialize_L_B import
       initialize_lambda_neighbors
32 from operators_rep.crossover.crossover_uniform import
       crossover_uniform as f_cross
33 from operators_rep.mutation.mutation_random_reset_int import
       mutation_rand_reset
34 # ----------------------------------------------------------
35 def moead_int(N, Ne, M, T, F, lb, ub, nGoals, pc, pm, v):
36     ## 1 - Initialization
37     numVar = np.shape(lb)[0]   # problem dimension
38     # initialize neighborhoods and weight vectors
39     lambd, B = initialize_lambda_neighbors(N, T, nGoals)
40     # Randomly generate a population respecting upper
41     # and lower bounds
42     pop_chrom = init_int(N, numVar, lb, ub)
```

```
43    # create the reference point
44    z = np.infty*np.ones(nGoals)
45    # Calculate the multi-objective cost values of the
46    # population and update the reference point
47    pop_cost = np.zeros((N, nGoals))
48    for i in range(N):
49        pop_cost[i] = F(pop_chrom[i])
50        # update the reference point
51        z = z_update(z,pop_cost[i])
52    # Indicate if the external population has been created
53    EP_created = False
54    ## Optimization loop
55    for id_i in range(M):
56        for id_p in range(N):
57            # Reproduction ------------------------------
58            if np.random.rand() < pc:
59                # Randomly select two parents from the
60                # neighborhood of sub-problem id_p
61                ids_n = B[id_p]
62                id_parents = np.random.choice(ids_n, 2,
63                                              replace=False)
64                p1_chrom = pop_chrom[id_parents[0]]
65                p2_chrom = pop_chrom[id_parents[1]]
66            else:
67                # Randomly select two parents from the
68                # entire population
69                id_parents = np.random.choice(range(N),
70                                              2,
71                                              replace=False)
72                p1_chrom = pop_chrom[id_parents[0]]
73                p2_chrom = pop_chrom[id_parents[1]]
74            # produce a child by crossover
75            y_prime_chrom, _ = f_cross(p1_chrom, p2_chrom, pc)
76            # mutate the child
77            y_prime_chrom = mutation_rand_reset(y_prime_chrom,
78                                                v,pm)
79            # Improvement and/or repair ------------------
80            y_prime_chrom = f_repair(y_prime_chrom,lb,ub)
81            # child's cost
82            y_prime_cost = F(y_prime_chrom)
83            # Update z ---
84            z = z_update(z,y_prime_cost)
85            # Update of neighboring solutions ------------
86            pop_chrom, pop_cost = update_solutions_in_B(id_p,
87                                                        B,
88                                                        pop_chrom,
89                                                        pop_cost,
90                                                        y_prime_chrom,
91                                                        y_prime_cost,
92                                                        z,lambd)
93            # Updating EP --------------------------------
94            if EP_created == False:
95                EP_created = True
96                # create external population
97                EP_x = np.array([y_prime_chrom])
98                EP_f = np.array([y_prime_cost])
99            else:
```

```
100        # update external population
101        EP_x, EP_f = update_EP(y_prime_chrom,
102                               y_prime_cost,
103                               EP_x,
104                               EP_f)
105    # Limit the size of the EP. This is just to
106    # prevent the EP from growing too much and
107    # thus demanding too much memory
108    if len(EP_f)>Ne:
109        # random selection of the survivors
110        ids = np.random.choice(len(EP_f),
111                               Ne,
112                               replace=False)
113        # keep just the selected survivors
114        EP_f = EP_f[ids]
115        EP_x = EP_x[ids]
116
117    return EP_f, EP_x
```

Listing 12.5: MOEA/D for integer representation.

Chapter 13

Case Study: Teaching a Legged Robot How to Walk

One challenging task in the field of robotics is to develop walking behaviors for humanoid and animal-like legged robots. The walking behavior of the robot is produced by a computer-based controller that is constantly analyzing inputs provided by a number of sensors and issuing appropriate commands for the actuators that control the robot. Solving this problem with traditional control engineering strategies, such as Optimal Control ([11], [50]), usually requires formulating a mathematical description of the process to be controlled. As technology evolves and robots get increasingly complex, developing mathematical models that describe the motion dynamics of legged robots is by itself a daunting task. One widely adopted alternative to traditional control techniques is to resort to model-free approaches, such as evolutionary algorithms ([72], [84]).

Since evolutionary algorithms are based on the idea that the dynamic system being optimized is a black-box, many researchers have investigated the application of evolutionary algorithms to control problems in robotics. In fact, there is a whole research field dedicated to researching the application of evolutionary algorithms to problems in robotics, called Evolutionary Robotics [63]. In general, evolutionary robotics researchers are interested in the development of controllers that allow the robot to perform a given task.

When trying to develop a controller using evolutionary algorithms, the practitioner is usually faced with a number of difficulties. The first difficulty is related to noise. A robot has many sources of noise, such as magnetic fields and a plethora of mechanical imprecisions of all sorts and levels. As a result, the fitness function used by the evolutionary algorithm will be noisy. The second difficulty is related to the complexity inherent to the field of robotics. The fitness function will inevitably be complex and costly to evaluate, because performing an experiment with a real robot takes time, spends resources and is not free of risks, such as potential damage to the robot. The complexity of the robot dynamics also makes it hard or even impossible to develop precise mathematical models of their subsystems. The third difficulty is related to constraints. A robot has physical limitations that, if not respected, can lead to accidents, property damage and even risk to human operators. The objective function is thus heavily constrained. A fourth difficulty is related to the inherent multi-objective nature of problems in the field of robotics, with goals being normally in conflict. For instance, one must wish to develop a controller that makes the robot traverse a given path in the shortest possible time, while also minimizing the amount of energy spent. Given all these characteristics, it is safe to conclude that developing a controller for a robot using evolutionary algorithms is not an easy task.

Teaching Legged Robots to Walk

To illustrate the application of evolutionary algorithms to the development of controllers in the field of robotics, the following experiment develops a controller that makes a simulated bipedal robot walk.

The Simulated Robot

The legged robot used in this example is a simulated environment that is part of OpenAI Gym [10], which is a set of free simulated environments widely used by the Artificial Intelligence (AI) community as benchmark problems for comparing new algorithms and approaches. Those interested in reproducing this experiment can find the simulator and all necessary documentation on the web site of OpenAI Gym (https://gym.openai.com/).

The environment is called Bipedal Walker. It simulates a two dimensional bipedal robot with no arms that must learn to walk and move forward, based only on its sensors. To complete its task, the robot must travel a certain distance within a given amount of time. The terrain is slightly uneven and changes from one episode to the next, thus preventing the controller from only memorizing a sequence of control actions. Changing the terrain amounts to injecting noise in the optimization process, since each time an episode is run (with the same controller) a different result is obtained. The time limit is relatively short, forcing the robot to increase its speed, but the robot must also minimize the amount of energy its spends. This is thus a two-objective problem with conflicting goals.

The state vector (the variables of the dynamic system that describe everything that is important for the purposes of control) is comprised of 24 variables, with 22 being continuous variables and 2 being binary. The control signal is comprised of 4 continuous variables, which control the torques of its 4 motors.

Scoring

The environment works like a game that has a time limit. An episode of the game begins with the robot starting in the upright position, motionless, placed at the beginning of the path that it must traverse. Then the controller computes control actions that are applied to the robot. For each control action applied to the robot, the simulator returns the resulting state of the robot and a partial score. An episode is finished in two situations: after the time limit, regardless of the position of the robot, or whenever the robot falls. The total score of the episode is the summation of all partial scores. The higher the score, the better the controller performed. The pseudocode for an episode is seen in Algorithm 13.1.

Algorithm 13.1. Simulator Episode

```
 1: procedure EPISODE(w)
 2:     env ← instantiate a robot simulator
 3:     NN ← instantiate a controller
 4:     NN.weights(w) ← make w the NN weights
 5:     s = env.reset() ← initial state of the robot
 6:     while simulation not finished do
 7:         u = NN.control(s) ← compute the control vector
 8:         s, r = env.step(u) ← apply the control vector to the simulator
 9:         R = R + r ← update the total score
10:     end while
11:     return R
12: end procedure
```

The scoring function of the simulator manages to convert a two-objective problem to a single-objective problem by aggregating the two objectives. The first objective is that starting at horizontal position $x(0) = 0$, the agent reaches $x(t) > 90$ as fast as it can. There is thus a positive score for speeding, computed by

$$r_1(t) = \alpha(x(t) - x(t-1)),\qquad(13.1)$$

where α is a constant scalar weight. The bigger the difference between two consecutive positions, the better.

The second goal is minimizing the amount of energy spent, which can be computed as minimizing the sum of the absolute values of the 4 control variables. The scoring related to this goal is computed by

$$r_1 = -\beta \sum_{i=0}^{3} |u_i|,\qquad(13.2)$$

where β is a constant scalar weight. The lower the absolute values of the control components the better.

The aggregated score at a given discrete time instant t is computed as

$$r(t) = r_1(t) + r_2(t) - 100 I_{fall}, \qquad (13.3)$$

where I_{fall} is a boolean variable that is True when the robot falls and False otherwise.

The total score of an episode is $R = \sum_{i=0}^{i=T-1} r(t)$, where T is the final time step of the episode. A controller that manages to achieve a mean total reward of 300 or more over 100 test episodes is considered to be a fully functional controller.

The Controller

The controller is implemented as a Feed-Forward Neural Network (FFNN)[71], with one hidden layer. The controller receives the state variables of the simulated robot as inputs and then outputs a control action that is intended to make the robot behave as desired, as shown in Figure 13.1.

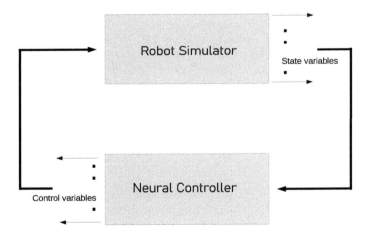

Figure 13.1: Neural controller.

As there are 24 state variables, the NN that implements the controller has $D = 24$ neurons in the input layer. Likewise, as there are four control variables, the output layer has $K = 4$ neurons. There is a single hidden layer with $M = 32$ neurons. The activation function of the hidden layer is the hyperbolic activation function. The number of hidden layers and the number of neurons in each hidden layer are not directly defined by the characteristics of the dynamic system. More neurons and hidden layers give the NN more learning power, but the increase in the number of neurons and hidden layers also makes the optimization problem harder, due to problems related to dimensionality, such as overfitting. In essence, a higher number of neurons implies that the evolutionary algorithm would face a higher dimensional problem, something which is not desirable.

The number of neurons in each layer of the NN is as computed as follows. The number of weights connecting the input neurons to the neurons of the hidden layer is $D \times M$. The number of weights connecting the hidden layer to the output layer is $M \times K$. There are also M bias weights for the neurons of the hidden layer and K for the neurons of the output layer. The total number N_w of weights of the NN is thus

$$N_w = (D \times M) + M + (M \times K) + K \tag{13.4}$$
$$N_w = (24 \times 32) + 32 + (32 \times 4) + 4 \tag{13.5}$$
$$N_w = 932. \tag{13.6}$$

The weights of the NN can be represented by a single real-valued vector with 932 dimensions.

Obtaining the Controller

Obtaining the controller means finding the weights of the NN that make the dynamic system work as intended. Developing the controller is thus an optimization process, where the candidate solutions are real-valued vectors that act as the weights of the NN. The search space thus has 932 dimensions. The NN acts as the controller that must make the robot walk as fast as possible to its final destination while spending as few energy as possible.

As any evolutionary optimization process, it is necessary to define a fitness function. The fitness function receives a candidate solution $\mathbf{w}$ as input, converts it into the weights of the NN and then tests the neural controller on the simulator by running an episode of the game. The total score R obtained by the controller on the episode is the fitness value of candidate solution $\mathbf{w}$. The pseudocode for the fitness function is shown in Algorithm 13.2.

Algorithm 13.2. Fitness Function

1: **procedure** $f(\mathbf{w})$
2:     $\mathbf{w}_{nn} \leftarrow$ convert $\mathbf{w}$ into the weights of the neural controller.
3:     $R \leftarrow$ episode($\mathbf{w}_{nn}$)   ▷ run an episode of the game
4:     return R
5: **end procedure**

The NES algorithm is used to perform the optimization. The main modification made to Algorithm 5.5 is to use Adaptive Moment Estimation (Adam)[49] to compute the update of the candidate solution, instead of using Stochastic Gradient Descent (SGD).

Adam is an adaptive learning rate optimization algorithm designed initially for training deep neural networks. While SGD maintains a single learning rate for all weight updates, Adam maintains a different learning rate for each network weight (parameter), a very interesting feature. To this end, the algorithm computes estimates of the first and second moments of the gradient as exponential moving averages. Let us remember that the nth moment of a random variable $\mathcal{X}$ is

$$m_n = \mathrm{E}[\mathcal{X}^n], \tag{13.7}$$

as a result, the first moment of $\mathcal{X}$ is its mean, and the second order moment is its uncentered variance. Adam works according to Algorithm 13.3.

Algorithm 13.3. Adam for Maximization

1: $\mathbf{m}_0 = 0$	▷ first moment estimate
2: $\mathbf{v}_0 = 0$	▷ second moment estimate
3: $\mathbf{w}_0 \leftarrow$ NN weights at $t = 0$	
4: **for** t = 1,...,T **do**	
5: $\quad \mathbf{g} = \nabla F(\mathbf{w}_{t-1})$	▷ compute the gradient of the fitness function
6: $\quad \mathbf{m}_t = \beta_1 \mathbf{m}_{t-1} + (1 - \beta_1)\mathbf{g}$	▷ update the first moment estimate
7: $\quad \mathbf{v}_t = \beta_2 \mathbf{v}_{t-1} + (1 - \beta_2)\mathbf{g}^2$	▷ update the second moment estimate
8: $\quad \hat{\mathbf{m}}_t = \mathbf{m}_t / (1 - \beta_1^t)$	▷ bias correction
9: $\quad \hat{\mathbf{v}}_t = \mathbf{v}_t / (1 - \beta_2^t)$	▷ bias correction
10: $\quad \mathbf{w}_t = \mathbf{w}_{t-1} + \alpha \frac{\hat{\mathbf{m}}_t}{\sqrt{\hat{\mathbf{v}}_t} + \varepsilon}$	▷ update the weights
11: **end for**	
12: return $\mathbf{w}_t$	

The hyperparameters of Adam are:

■ α is the learning rate or step size. A typical value is $\alpha = 0.001$,

■ β_1 is the exponential decay rate for the first moment estimates. A typical value is $\beta_1 = 0.9$,

■ β_2 is the exponential decay rate for the second moment estimates. A typical value is $\beta_2 = 0.999$,

■ ε is a very small number needed to prevent division by zero. A typical value is $\varepsilon = 10^{-8}$.

Algorithm NES modified with Adam is show in Algorithm 13.4.

Algorithm 13.4. NES with Adam

1: $F \leftarrow$ fitness function
2: $pop\_size \leftarrow$ population size
3: $max\_iter \leftarrow$ number of iterations
4: $\sigma \leftarrow$ perturbation strength
5: $\mathbf{w} \leftarrow$ inital NN weights
6: **for** k = 1,...,K **do**
7:     **for** i=1,..., n **do**
8:         $\varepsilon_i \sim \sigma \mathcal{N}(\mathbf{0}, \mathbf{I})$ ▷ generate random perturbation
9:         $\mathbf{w}_p[i] = \mathbf{w} + \varepsilon_i$
10:        $\mathbf{r}_i = F(\mathbf{w}_p[i])$ ▷ compute the fitness value of $\mathbf{w}_p[i]$
11:     **end for**
12:     $R = \frac{(\mathbf{r} - \text{mean}(\mathbf{r}))}{\text{std}(\mathbf{r})}$ ▷ normalizing the scores
13:     $\mathbf{w} = \text{adam}(\mathbf{w}, k)$ ▷ update the weights vector using Adam
14: **end for**
15: return $\mathbf{w}$

The optimization process is described in Algorithm 13.5. In essence, finding the controller is accomplished by searching for the vector of weights of the NN that make the simulated robot successfully accomplish the task.

Algorithm 13.5. Finding the Controller

1: $F \leftarrow$ fitness function
2: $pop\_size \leftarrow$ population size for NES
3: $max\_iter \leftarrow$ number of iterations for NES
4: $\sigma \leftarrow$ perturbation strength for NES
5: $\mathbf{w} = \text{nes}(F, pop\_size, max\_iter, \sigma)$ ▷ optimization process
6: return $\mathbf{w}$ ▷ best weights vector found by NES

Results

The hyperparameters of the optimization process were set as follows:

- $pop\_size = 100$

- $max\_iter = 6000$

- $\sigma = 0.1$

At each iteration of the optimization process, the average of the scores obtained by each candidate solution was computed and stored. The evolution of the average score is shown in Figure 13.2. There is a clear ascending pattern, indicating that the optimization process was working.

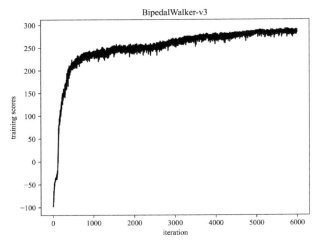

Figure 13.2: Evolution of the population mean score during the optimization of the bipedal robot gait.

The weights vector obtained by the optimization process was then used to test the controller in a sequence of 100 episodes. It is important to stress that the test episode does not involve any form of optimization. A test episode simply follows the steps shown in Algorithm 13.1.

The individual scores of each test episode are shown in Figure 13.3. Also shown are the mean of all test scores and the 95% confidence interval for the true score value. The results clearly show that the optimization process was able to find a controller that solved the problem.

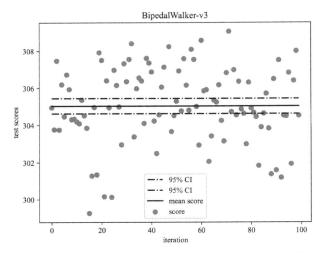

Figure 13.3: Results of 100 episodes using the trained neural controller of the bipedal robot.

Relation to Real-World Problems

This case study has four important characteristics of real world optimization problems discussed in Section 1.1. These characteristics are listed bellow.

High dimensionality - The development of the controller demands finding good values for 932 real-valued variables.

Conflicting goals - The objective function involves two conflicting goals, which are maximizing the robot speed and minimizing its energy consumption.

Lack of knowledge about the problem structure - The dynamics of the simulated robot are unknown to the evolutionary algorithm.

Nonlinear dynamics - The equations that govern the simulation are nonlinear.

Noise - As the terrain is constantly changing, a given controller will obtain a different result each time an episode is run.

Listings

All python codes used to implement this case study are given in this section.

- Configurations - Implemented in Listing 13.1.

- Adam - Implemented in Listing 13.2.

- Fitness function - Implemented in Listing 13.3.

- NES - Implemented in Listing 13.4.

- NN - Implemented in Listing 13.5.

- Optimization process - Implemented in Listing 13.6.

```
1 #--------------------------------------------------------
2 # Configuration File for the Bipedal Walker Problem
3 #--------------------------------------------------------
4 # file: config.py
5 #--------------------------------------------------------
6 from case_study_bipedal.mlp import ANN
7 #--------------------------------------------------------
8 # Simulator
9 env_name = 'BipedalWalker-v3' # simulator name
10 n_fevals = 1                  # if n_fevals >1 then we are using
11                               # resampling
12 #--------------------------------------------------------
13 # Settings for the NN hidden layer
14 n_hidden = 32       # number of neurons
15 activ_f = 'tanh'    # activation function
16
17 # Get the initial weights and the dimensionality of the weights
18 # vector
```

```
19 model = ANN(env_name, n_hidden, activ_f)
20 nVar = model.n_params
21 initial_w = model.get_weights()
22 # delete this NN
23 del model
24 # -----------------------------------------------------------------
25 # Select the optimizer for NES
26 # optimizer = 'SGD_momentum'
27 # optimizer = 'SGD'
28 optimizer = 'Adam'
29 # -----------------------------------------------------------------
30 # Test episodes
31 n_reps_test    = 100    # number of test episodes
32 save_interval  = 500    # periodically save the NN weights
33 # -----------------------------------------------------------------
34 # Folders and files
35 training_folder = "./box2d_training/" + env_name + "/nes/"+
       optimizer+"/"
36 weights_file   = training_folder + 'weights.npy'
37 rewards_file   = training_folder + 'rewards.npy'
```

Listing 13.1: Configurations for the bipedal walker problem.

```
1 # -----------------------------------------------------------------
2 # Adam optimizer for maximization
3 # -----------------------------------------------------------------
4 # t          - discrete time
5 # m_adam     - past mean estimate
6 # v_adam     - past variance estimate
7 # w          - weights vector (candidate solution)
8 # grad       - gradient of F(w)
9 # -----------------------------------------------------------------
10 # file: adam.py
11 # -----------------------------------------------------------------
12 import numpy as np
13 # -----------------------------------------------------------------
14 def adam_gd(t, m_adam, v_adam, w, grad):
15     beta_1 = 0.9
16     beta_2 = 0.999
17     epsilon = 1e-08
18     lr = 0.01
19     g = grad
20     t = t + 1  # because t starts with zero
21     m_adam = beta_1 * m_adam + (1 - beta_1) * g
22     v_adam = beta_2 * v_adam + (1 - beta_2) * np.power(g, 2)
23     m_hat = m_adam / (1 - np.power(beta_1, t))
24     v_hat = v_adam / (1 - np.power(beta_2, t))
25     w = w + lr * m_hat / (np.sqrt(v_hat) + epsilon)
26     return w, m_adam, v_adam
```

Listing 13.2: Adam for maximization.

```
 1 # -----------------------------------------------------------------
 2 #  Fitness function and episode function for the Bipedal Problem
 3 # -----------------------------------------------------------------
 4 # file: fitness_openai.py
 5 # -----------------------------------------------------------------
 6 import gym
 7 import numpy as np
 8 from case_study_bipedal.config import *
 9 # -----------------------------------------------------------------
10 # run an episode
11 # -----------------------------------------------------------------
12 # env            -  simulator instance
13 # controller     -  NN controller
14 # -----------------------------------------------------------------
15 def run_episode(env,model):
16     # run one episode and return the total reward
17     episode_reward = 0
18     done = False
19     state = env.reset()
20     while not done:
21         # get the action
22         action = model.sample_action(state)
23         # perform the action
24         state, reward, done, _ = env.step(action)
25         # update total reward
26         episode_reward += reward
27     return episode_reward
28 # -----------------------------------------------------------------
29 #  fitness function
30 # -----------------------------------------------------------------
31 # w  - weights vector (candidate solution)
32 # -----------------------------------------------------------------
33 def fitness(w):
34     # instantiate neural controller with weights w
35     controller = ANN(env_name, n_hidden, 'tanh')
36     controller.set_weights(w)
37     episode_reward = np.zeros(n_fevals)
38     # instantiate the simulator
39     env = gym.make(env_name)
40     # perform n_fevals episodes
41     for id in range(n_fevals):
42         episode_reward[id] = run_episode(env,controller)
43     # return the fitness value of w
44     return np.mean(episode_reward)
```

Listing 13.3: Fitness function and episode function for the bipedal walker.

```
 1 # -----------------------------------------------------------------
 2 import os
 3 import numpy as np
 4 import multiprocessing
 5 from multiprocessing import Pool
 6 from datetime import datetime
 7 from case_study_bipedal.adam import adam_gd
 8 from case_study_bipedal.config import nVar, initial_w
 9 from case_study_bipedal.config import training_folder, \
```

```
10      save_interval
11 # ------------------------------------------------------------
12 # Natural Evolution Strategies with Adam
13 # ------------------------------------------------------------
14 # Implemented as a maximization algorithm
15 # ------------------------------------------------------------
16 # f        - function to be maximized
17 # pop_size - number of candidate solutions
18 # sigma    - standard deviation of the isotropic mutation
19 # maxIters - maximum number of optimization iterations
20 # ------------------------------------------------------------
21 # file: nes.py
22 # ------------------------------------------------------------
23 def nes(f,
24      pop_size,
25      sigma,
26      max_iters):
27     # initial weights of the neural controller (comes from
28     # config.py)
29     w = initial_w
30     # storage for the mean score of the population
31     mean_score = np.zeros(max_iters)
32     # multiprocessing - to speed up processing
33     n_procs = multiprocessing.cpu_count()-1
34     p = Pool(n_procs)
35     # optimization process
36     for id_iter in range(max_iters):
37         # starting time of this iteration
38         t0 = datetime.now()
39         # perturbations and population scores
40         N = np.random.randn(pop_size, nVar)
41         # parallel fitness evaluation (multiprocessing)
42         W_try = w + sigma*N # jitter w using gaussian noise
43         R = p.map(f, [ww for ww in W_try]) # fitness values
44         R = np.array(R) # convert to numpy array
45         # standardize the rewards to have a zero-mean gaussian
46         # distribution
47         m = R.mean()
48         s = R.std()
49         # can't proceed if std = 0
50         if s == 0:
51             print("Skipping")
52             continue
53         # store the mean population score of this iteration
54         mean_score[id_iter] = m
55         # normalization
56         A = (R - m) / s
57         # perform the parameter update. The matrix multiply
58         # below is just an efficient way to sum up all the
59         # rows of the noise matrix N, where each row N[j]
60         # is weighted by A[j]
61         grad = (1 / (pop_size * sigma)) * np.dot(N.T, A)
62         # Weight vector update with Adam
63         if id_iter == 0:
64             m_adam = 0
65             v_adam = 0
66         w,m_adam,v_adam = adam_gd(id_iter, m_adam, v_adam,
```

```
67                                          w, grad)
68          # Periodically save the weights
69          if id_iter % save_interval== 0:
70              folder = training_folder + np.str(id_iter)
71              file_name = folder + '/weights.npy'
72              if not os.path.exists(folder):
73                  os.makedirs(folder)
74              np.save(file_name,w)
75          # Print
76          print("Iter:", id_iter, "avg fit: %.3f" % np.mean(R),
77                  "best fit: %.3f" % R.max(),
78                  "Duration:", (datetime.now() - t0))
79      # close the pool of processes
80      p.close()
81      # return values
82      return w, mean_score
```

Listing 13.4: NES for the bipedal walker.

```
1  # -------------------------------------------------------------
2  #                  MLP with one hidden layer
3  # -------------------------------------------------------------
4  # env_name       - name of the simulation environment
5  # n_hidden       - number of neurons in the hidden layer
6  # activ_f        - activation function
7  # -------------------------------------------------------------
8  # file: mlp.py
9  # -------------------------------------------------------------
10 import os
11 import gym
12 import numpy as np
13 # -------------------------------------------------------------
14 # ReLU
15 def relu(x):
16     return x * (x > 0)
17 # Sigmoid
18 def sigmoid(x):
19     return 1.0 / (1.0 + np.exp(-x))
20 # tanh
21 def tanh(x):
22     return np.tanh(x)
23 # -------------------------------------------------------------
24 class ANN:
25     def __init__(self, env_name, n_hidden, activ_f = 'tanh'):
26         # Create OpenAI environment to obtain the number of input
27         # and output neurons
28         env = gym.make(env_name)
29         self.D = len(env.reset())    # D - number input neurons
30         self.M = n_hidden            # M - number hidden neurons
31         self.K = env.action_space.shape[0] # K - number output
32                                      # neurons
33         # Set the activation function
34         if activ_f == 'tanh':
35             self.activ_f = tanh
36         elif activ_f == 'relu':
37             self.activ_f = relu
```

```
38      else:
39          print('Activation %s not implemented' % (activ_f))
40          exit()
41      # Obtain the maximum value of the output variables
42      # It is assumed that the maximum and minimum values
43      # have the same absolute value
44      self.action_max = env.action_space.high[0]
45      self.n_params = self.D * self.M + self.M + \
46                      self.M * self.K + self.K
47      del env # don't need it anymore
48      # Random initialization of the weights
49      self.W1 = \
50          np.random.randn(self.D, self.M) / np.sqrt(self.D)
51      self.b1 = \
52          np.zeros(self.M)
53      self.W2 = \
54          np.random.randn(self.M, self.K) / np.sqrt(self.M)
55      self.b2 = \
56          np.zeros(self.K)
57  # Compute the forward pass
58  def forward(self, X):
59      Z = self.activ_f(X.dot(self.W1) + self.b1)
60      return np.tanh(Z.dot(self.W2) + self.b2) * \
61          self.action_max
62  # Compute a control action
63  def sample_action(self, x):
64      X = np.atleast_2d(x)
65      Y = self.forward(X)
66      return Y[0]  # the first row
67  # Returns the weights a single vector
68  def get_weights(self):
69      return np.concatenate([self.W1.flatten(),
70                      self.b1, self.W2.flatten(),
71                      self.b2])
72  # Receives a weights vector and converts it into the NN
73  # weights
74  def set_weights(self, params):
75      # params is a flat list
76      # unflatten into individual weights
77      self.W1 = \
78          params[:self.D * self.M].reshape(self.D, self.M)
79      self.b1 = \
80          params[self.D * self.M:self.D * self.M + self.M]
81      self.W2 = \
82          params[self.D * self.M + self.M:self.D * self.M
83          + self.M + self.M * self.K].reshape(self.M,
84                                              self.K)
85      self.b2 = \
86          params[-self.K:]
87  # Saves the NN weights as a single vector in a file
88  def save_weights(self, foldername):
89      arqname = foldername + '/weights.npy'
90      # Creates the folder
91      if not os.path.exists(foldername):
92          os.makedirs(foldername)
93      w = self.get_weights()
94      try:
```

```
95          np.save(arqname,w)
96      except:
97          print("FAILED saving weights to %s " % (arqname))
98          exit()
99  # Load the NN weights from a file
100 def load_weights(self, foldername):
101     try:
102         fname = foldername+'weights.npy'
103         w0 = np.load(fname)
104         self.set_weights(w0)
105         return w0
106     except:
107         print("FAILED loading weights from " % (fname))
108         exit()
```

Listing 13.5: NN for the bipedal walker.

```
1  # ----------------------------------------------------------------
2  #           Optimization for the Bipedal Walker
3  # ----------------------------------------------------------------
4  # file: run_nes_bipedal.py
5  # ----------------------------------------------------------------
6  import os
7  import numpy as np
8  from case_study_bipedal.nes import nes
9  import matplotlib.pyplot as plt
10 from case_study_bipedal.config import *
11 from case_study_bipedal.fitness_openai import fitness
12 # ----------------------------------------------------------------
13 # Create folder to store training files
14 if not os.path.exists(training_folder):
15     os.makedirs(training_folder)
16 # Set NES hyperparameters
17 f          = fitness
18 pop_size   = 100
19 sigma      = 0.1
20 max_iters  = 6000
21 if __name__ == '__main__':
22     # perform optimization
23     w, scores = nes(f,
24                     pop_size,
25                     sigma,
26                     max_iters)
27     # save the solution
28     try:
29         np.save(weights_file, w)
30     except:
31         print("save_weights -> error trying to save %s "
32             % (weights_file))
33         exit()
34     # save the scores vector
35     try:
36         np.save(rewards_file, scores)
37     except:
38         print("save_weights -> error trying to save %s "
39             % (rewards_file))
```

```
40        exit()
41 # plot the scores per iteration
42 str = env_name
43 plt.plot(scores)
44 plt.title(str)
45 plt.ylabel('mean population score')
46 plt.xlabel('iteration')
47 plt.show()
```

Listing 13.6: Optimization for the bipedal walker.

References

[1] Richard Allmendinger, Michael Emmerich, Jussi Hakanen, Yaochu Jin and Enrico Rigoni. 2017. Surrogate-assisted multicriteria optimization: Complexities, prospective solutions, and business case. Journal of Multi-Criteria Decision Analysis 24(1-2).

[2] D.V. Arnold and H. Beyer. 2002. Local performance of the $(1 + 1)$-es in a noisy environment. IEEE Transactions on Evolutionary Computation 6(1): 30–41.

[3] D.V. Arnold and H. Beyer. 2006. A general noise model and its effects on evolution strategy performance. IEEE Transactions on Evolutionary Computation 10(4): 380–391.

[4] Thomas Bäck. 1996. Evolutionary Algorithms in Theory and Practice: Evolution Strategies, Evolutionary Programming, Genetic Algorithms. Oxford University Press, Inc., New York, NY, USA.

[5] James E. Baker. 1985. Adaptive selection methods for genetic algorithms. pp. 101–111. *In*: Lawrence Earlbaum (ed.). Proceedings of an International Conference on Genetic Algorithms.

[6] James E. Baker. 1987. Reducing bias and inefficiency in the selection algorithm. pp. 14–21. *In*: Proceedings of the Second International Conference on Genetic Algorithms.

[7] Richard Bellman. 1957. Dynamic Programming. Princeton University Press, Princeton, NJ, USA, 1 Edition.

[8] Hans-Georg Beyer and Hans-Paul Schwefel. 2002. Evolution strategies—a comprehensive introduction. Natural Computing 1: 3–52.

[9] Mohammad Reza Bonyadi, Zbigniew Michalewicz, Frank Neumann and Markus Wagner. 2016. Evolutionary computation for multicomponent problems: opportunities and future directions. CoRR, abs/1606.06818.

[10] Greg Brockman, Vicki Cheung, Ludwig Pettersson, Jonas Schneider, John Schulman, Jie Tang and Wojciech Zaremba. 2016. Openai gym.

[11] A.E. Bryson. June, 1996. Optimal control-1950 to 1985. IEEE Control Systems Magazine 16(3): 26–33.

[12] D. Buche, P. Stoll, R. Dornberger and P. Koumoutsakos. 2002. Multiobjective evolutionary algorithm for the optimization of noisy combustion processes. IEEE Transactions on Systems, Man, and Cybernetics, Part C (Applications and Reviews) 32(4): 460–473.

[13] Gary B. Lamont Carlos Coello Coello and David A. van Veldhuizen. Evolutionary Algorithms for Solving Multi-Objective Problems. Genetic and Evolutionary Computation. Springer US, 2007.

[14] R.A. Caruana and J.D. Schaffer. 1988. Representation and hidden bias: Gray vs binary coding. In 6th International Conference in Machine Learning, pp. 153–161.

[15] Shelvin Chand and Markus Wagner. 2015. Evolutionary many-objective optimization: A quick-start guide. Surveys in Operations Research and Management Science 20(2): 35–42.

[16] Raymond Chiong, Thomas Weise and Zbigniew Michalewicz. 2011. Variants of Evolutionary Algorithms for Real-World Applications. Springer Publishing Company, Incorporated.

[17] Christian Blum, Raymond Chiong, Maurice Clerc, Kenneth De Jong, Zbigniew Michalewicz, Ferrante Neri and Thomas Weise. 2011. Evolutionary optimization. pp. 1–29. *In*: Thomas Weise Raymond Chiong and Zbigniew Michalewicz (eds.). Variants of Evolutionary Algorithms for Real-World Applications, Springer.

[18] Carlos A. Coello Coello. July 2016. Constraint-handling techniques used with evolutionary algorithms. *In*: GECCO'16 Companion: Proceedings of the 2016 on Genetic and Evolutionary Computation Conference Companion, pp. 563–587.

[19] Dorigo M. Colorni and A. Maniezzo. 1991. Distributed optimization by ant colonies. pp. 134–142. *In*: European Conference on Artificial Life, Paris, Prance.

[20] D.R. Cox. 2006. Principles of Statistical Inference. Cambridge University Press.

[21] Tobias Glasmachers, Yi Sun, Jan Peters, Daan Wierstra, Tom Schaul and Jürgen Schmidhuber. 2014. Natural evolution strategies. Journal of Machine Learning Research 15(1): 949–980.

[22] Dipankar Dasgupta and Zbigniew Michalewicz. 1997. Evolutionary Algorithms—An Overview. Springer Berlin Heidelberg, Berlin, Heidelberg, pp. 3–28.

[23] K. Deb, A. Pratap, S. Agarwal and T. Meyarivan. April, 2002. A fast and elitist multiobjective genetic algorithm: Nsga-ii. IEEE Transactions on Evolutionary Computation 6(2): 182–197.

[24] Kalyanmoy Deb. 2011. Multi-objective optimization using evolutionary algorithms: An introduction. pp. 3–34. *In*: Lihui Wang, Amos H.C. Ng and Kalyanmoy Deb (eds.). Multi-objective Evolutionary Optimisation for Product Design and Manufacturing, Springer Publishing Company, Incorporated.

[25] Kalyanmoy Deb and Samir Agrawal. 1999. Artificial Neural Nets and Genetic Algorithms. Niched-Penalty Approach for Constraint Handling in Genetic Algorithms. Springer, Vienna.

[26] Kalyanmoy Deb and Debayan Deb. February, 2014. Analysing mutation schemes for real parameter genetic algorithms. International Journal of Artificial Intelligence and Soft Computing 4(1): 1–28.

[27] Tobias Wagner, Dimo Brockhoff and Heike Trautmann. July, 2012. On the properties of the r2 indicator. pp. 465–472. *In*: Proceedings of the 14th Annual Conference on Genetic and Evolutionary Computation (GECCO'2012), Philadelphia, United States, ACM.

[28] Robert W. Doran. 2007. The gray code. J. UCS 13: 1573–1597.

[29] M. Dorigo. 1992. Optimization, Learning and Natural Algorithms. Ph.D. Thesis, Dipartimento di Elettronica, Politecnico di Milano, Milan.

[30] D. Doufene, S. Bouazabia and A. Haddad. 2020. Shape and electric performance improvement of an insulator string using particles swarm algorithm. IET Science, Measurement Technology 14(2): 198–205.

[31] Michael T.M. Emmerich and André H. Deutz. September, 2018. A tutorial on multiobjective optimization: fundamentals and evolutionary methods. Natural Computing 17(3): 585–609.

[32] H.P. Lopuhaä, F.M. Dekking, C. Kraaikamp and L.E. Meester. 2005. A modern introduction to probability and statistics. Springer Texts in Statistics. Springer-Verlag London, 1 Edition.

[33] A.I.J. Forrester, A.J. Keane and N.W. Bressloff. October, 2006 Design and analysis of 'noisy' computer experiments. AIAA Journal 44(10): 2331–2339.

[34] Alexander I.J. Forrester, Andras Sobester and Andy J. Keane. 2008. Engineering Design via Surrogate Modelling—A Practical Guide. Wiley.

[35] T.V. Geetha G. Pavai. 2016. A survey on crossover operators. ACM Computing Surveys (CSUR) 49(4): 1–43.

[36] David E. Goldberg. January, 1989. Genetic Algorithms in Search, Optimization, and Machine Learning. Addison-Wesley Professional, Boston, MA, USA, 1 Edition.

[37] Gayathri Gopalakrishnan, Barbara Minsker and David E. Goldberg. December 2004. Optimal sampling in a noisy genetic algorithm for risk-based remediation design.

[38] Peter J.B. Hancock. 1994. An empirical comparison of selection methods in evolutionary algorithms. *In*: T.C. Fogarty (eds.). Evolutionary Computing. AISB EC 1994. Lecture Notes in Computer Science, volume 865. Berlin, Heidelberg.

[39] N. Hansen. 2006. The CMA evolution strategy: a comparing review. pp. 75–102. *In*: J.A. Lozano, P. Larranaga, I. Inza and E. Bengoetxea (eds.). Towards a New Evolutionary Computation. Advances on Estimation of Distribution Algorithms, Springer.

[40] N. Hansen and A. Ostermeier. May, 1996. Adapting arbitrary normal mutation distributions in evolution strategies: the covariance matrix adaptation. pp. 312–317. *In*: Proceedings of IEEE International Conference on Evolutionary Computation.

[41] Nikolaus Hansen. 2016. The CMA evolution strategy: A tutorial. CoRR,abs/1604.00772.

[42] Nikolaus Hansen and Andreas Ostermeier. June, 2001. Completely derandomized self-adaptation in evolution strategies. Evol. Comput. 9(2): 159–195.

[43] Hisao Ishibuchi, Noritaka Tsukamoto and Yusuke Nojima. 2008. Evolutionary many-objective optimization: A short review. In 2008 IEEE Congress on Evolutionary Computation (IEEE World Congress on Computational Intelligence), pp. 2419–2426.

[44] John H. Holland. 1975. Adaptation in Natural and Artificial Systems: An Introductory Analysis with Applications to Biology, Control and Artificial Intelligence. University of Michigan Press, Ann Arbor, MI.

[45] M.K. Hussein and M.H. Mousa. 2020. Efficient task offloading for iot-based applications in fog computing using ant colony optimization. IEEE Access, pp. 1–1. Doi: 10.1109/ACCESS.2020.2975741.

[46] Amrit Pratap Kalyanmoy Deb and Subrajyoti Moitra. 2020. Mechanical component design for multiple objectives using elitist non-dominated sorting ga. *In*: M. Schoenauer (ed.). Parallel Problem Solving from Nature PPSN VI (Lecture Notes in Computer Science), volume 1917, Springer, Berlin, Germany.

[47] Karthik Sindhya Kalyanmoy Deb and Tatsuya Okabe. July, 2007. Self-adaptive simulated binary crossover for real-parameter optimization. *In*: Proceedings of the 9th Annual Conference on Genetic and Evolutionary Computation, pp. 1187–1194.

[48] J. Kennedy and R. Eberhart. December, 1995. Particle swarm optimzation. *In*: Proceedings of the IEEE International Conference on Neural Networks 4: 1942–1948.

[49] Diederik P. Kingma and Jimmy Ba. 2014. Adam: A method for stochastic optimization.

[50] D.E. Kirk. 2004. Optimal Control Theory: An Introduction. Dover Books on Electrical Engineering Series. Dover Publications.

[51] S. Koziel and Z. Michalewicz. March, 1999. Evolutionary algorithms, homomorphous mappings, and constrained parameter optimization. Evolutionary Computation 7(1): 19–44.

[52] H. Kuribayashi, M. Souza, D. Gomes, K. Silva, M. Silva, J. Costa and C. Francês. 2020. Particle swarm-based cell range expansion for heterogeneous mobile networks. IEEE Access, pp. 1–1. Doi: 10.1109/ACCESS.2020.2975981.

[53] A.J. Owens, L.J. Fogel and M.J. Walsh. 2014. From chaos to order: How ants optimize food search. https://www.pik-potsdam.de/news/pressreleases/archive/2014/from-chaos-to-order-how-ants-optimize-foodsearch?searchterm=from chaos to order.

[54] Larry J. Eshelman, Richard A. Caruana and J. David Schaffer. 1989. Biases in the crossover landscape. pp. 10–19. *In*: Proceedings of the 3rd International Conference on Genetic Algorithms, Morgan Kaufman.

[55] K. Li, K. Deb and X. Yao. 2018. R-metric: Evaluating the performance of preference-based evolutionary multiobjective optimization using reference points. IEEE Transactions on Evolutionary Computation 22(6): 821–835.

[56] W. Liu. 2020. Route optimization for last-mile distribution of rural e-commerce logistics based on ant colony optimization. IEEE Access 8: 12179–12187.

[57] Antonio López Jaimes and Carlos Coello. 2015. Many-Objective Problems: Challenges and Methods, pp. 1033–1046. 01.

[58] M. Méndez, D.A. Rossit, B. González and M. Frutos. 2020. Proposal and comparative study of evolutionary algorithms for optimum design of a gear system. IEEE Access 8: 3482–3497.

[59] Zbigniew Michalewicz. November, 2012. Ubiquity symposium: Evolutionary computation and the processes of life: The emperor is naked: Evolutionary algorithms for real-world applications. Ubiquity 2012(November): 3:1–3:13.

[60] Kaisa Miettinen. 1998. Nonlinear Multiobjective Optimization, volume 12 of International Series in Operations Research & Management Science. Springer US.

[61] M. Mitchell. 1999. An Introduction to Genetic Algorithms. The MIT Press, Cambridge, MA.

[62] H. Mühlenbein and D. Schlierkamp-Voosen. 1993. Predictive models for the breeder genetic algorithm. Evolutionary Computation 1(1): 25–49.

[63] Andrew Nelson. 2019. Evolutionay Robotics (accessed November 10, 2019).

[64] Dirk Arnold, Nikolaus Hansen and Anne Auger. 2015. Evolution strategies. *In*: Janusz Kacprzyk and Witold Pedrycz (eds.). Handbook of Computational Intelligence.

[65] Michael A. Osborne, Roman Garnett and Stephen J. Roberts. 2009. Gaussian processes for global optimization. 3rd International Conference on Learning and Intelligent Optimization (LION3), pp. 1–15.

[66] Victor Picheny, Tobias Wagner and David Ginsbourger. 2013. A benchmark of kriging-based infill criteria for noisy optimization. Structural and Multidisciplinary Optimization 48(3): 607–626.

[67] Kenneth Price and Rainer Storn. 2020. Differential evolution (de) for continuous function optimization (an algorithm by kenneth price and rainer storn). retrieved April 04, 2020, from https://www1.icsi.berkeley.edu/~storn/code.html.

[68] N. Radcliff. 1991. Forma analysis and random respectful recombination. *In*: Morgan Kauffman (ed.). Proc. 4th Int. Conf. on Genetic Algorithms. San Mateo, CA.

[69] Pratyusha Rakshit, Amit Konar and Swagatam Das. 2017. Noisy evolutionary optimization algorithms—a comprehensive survey. Swarm and Evolutionary Computation 33: 18–45.

[70] I. Rechenberg. 1973. Evolutions strategie: Optimierung technischer Systeme nach Prinzipien der biologischen Evolution. Number 15 in Problemata. Frommann-Holzboog, Stuttgart-Bad Cannstatt.

[71] David E. Rumelhart and James L. McClelland. 1987. Parallel Distributed Processing: Explorations in the Microstructure of Cognition: Foundations, volume 1. MIT Press.

[72] Tim Salimans, Jonathan Ho, Xi Chen and Ilya Sutskever. 2017. Evolution strategies as a scalable alternative to reinforcement learning. CoRR, abs/1703.03864.

[73] E. Sandgren. 1990. Nonlinear integer and discrete programming in mechanical design optimization. Journal of Mechanical Design 112(2): 223–229.

[74] H. Sato, H.E. Aguirre and K. Tanaka. 2004. Local dominance using polar coordinates to enhance multiobjective evolutionary algorithms. *In*: Proceedings of the 2004 Congress on Evolutionary Computation (IEEE Cat. No.04TH8753) 1: 188–195.

[75] Hans Paul Schwefel. 1977. Numerische Optimierung von Computer-Modellen mittels der Evolution-sstrategie. Birkhäuser.

[76] Y. Shi and R. Eberhart. May, 1998. A modified particle swarm optimizer. In 1998 IEEE International Conference on Evolutionary Computation Proceedings. IEEE World Congress on Computational Intelligence (Cat. No.98TH8360), pp. 69–73.

[77] Dan Simon. 2013. Evolutionary Optimization Algorithms. Wiley.

[78] A. Song, W. Chen, X. Luo, Z. Zhan and J. Zhang. 2020. Scheduling workflows with composite tasks: A nested particle swarm optimization approach. IEEE Transactions on Services Computing, pp. 1–1. Doi: 10.1109/TSC.2020.2975774.

[79] N. Srinivas and K. Deb. 1994. Muiltiobjective optimization using nondominated sorting in genetic algorithms. Evolutionary Computation 2(3): 221–248.

[80] Rainer Storn. 1996. Differential evolution design of an iir-filter. *In*: IEEE Conference on Evolutionary Computation, Nagoya, Japan, pp. 268–273.

[81] Rainer Storn. 1996. On the usage of differential evolution for function optimization. *In*: Conference of the North American Fuzzy Information Processing Society, Berkley, California, pp. 519–523.

[82] Rainer Storn and Ken Price. 1996. Minimizing the real functions of the icec'96 contest by differential evolution. *In*: IEEE Conference on Evolutionary Computation, Nagoya, Japan, pp. 842–844.

[83] Rainer Storn and Ken Price. 1997. Differential evolution—a simple and efficient heuristic for global optimization over continuous spaces. Journal of Global Optimization 4(11): 341–359.

[84] Felipe Petroski Such, Vashisht Madhavan, Edoardo Conti, Joel Lehman, Kenneth O. Stanley and Jeff Clune. 2017. Deep neuroevolution: Genetic algorithms are a competitive alternative for training deep neural networks for reinforcement learning. CoRR, abs/1712.06567.

[85] Oleg Sudakov, Dmitri Koroteev, Boris Belozerov and Evgeny Burnaev. 2019. Artificial neural network surrogate modeling of oil reservoir: A case study. pp. 232–241. *In*: Huchuan Lu, Huajin Tang and Zhanshan Wang (eds.). Advances in Neural Networks—ISNN 2019, Cham. Springer International Publishing.

[86] Nick T. Thomopoulos. 2013. Essentials of Monte Carlo Simulation. Springer-Verlag New York, 1 Edition.

[87] Rohit K. Tripathy and Ilias Bilionis. 2018. Deep uq: Learning deep neural network surrogate models for high dimensional uncertainty quantification. Journal of Computational Physics 375: 565–588.

[88] Chen Wang, Qingyun Duan,Wei Gong, Aizhong Ye, Zhenhua Di and Chiyuan Miao. 2014. An evaluation of adaptive surrogate modeling based optimization with two benchmark problems. Environmental Modelling and Software 60(0): 167–179.

[89] D. Wierstra, T. Schaul, J. Peters and J. Schmidhuber. June, 2008. Natural evolution strategies. In 2008 IEEE Congress on Evolutionary Computation (IEEE World Congress on Computational Intelligence), pp. 3381–3387.

[90] D.H. Wolpert and W.G. Macready. April, 1997. No free lunch theorems for optimization. IEEE Transactions on Evolutionary Computation 1(1): 67–82.

[91] A.H. Wright. 1991. Genetic algorithms for real parameter optimization. pp. 205–218. *In*: J.E. Rawlins (ed.). Foundations of Genetic Algorithms, Morgan Kaufmann.

[92] Q. Zhang and H. Li. 2007. Moea/d: A multiobjective evolutionary algorithm based on decomposition. IEEE Transactions on Evolutionary Computation 11(6): 712–731.

[93] R. Zhang, S. Song and C. Wu. April, 2020. Robust scheduling of hot rolling production by local search enhanced ant colony optimization algorithm. IEEE Transactions on Industrial Informatics 16(4): 2809–2819.

[94] Eckart Zitzler, Kalyanmoy Deb and Lothar Thiele. 2000. Comparison of multiobjective evolutionary algorithms: Empirical results. Evolutionary Computation 8: 173–195.

Index